Death Throes of a Dynasty

Charles Edward Ewing and Bessie Smith Ewing in 1904.

Death Throes of a Dynasty

*Letters and Diaries
of Charles and Bessie Ewing,
Missionaries to China*

Edited by
E. G. Ruoff

THE KENT STATE UNIVERSITY PRESS
Kent, Ohio, and London, England

© 1990 by The Kent State University Press, Kent, Ohio 44242
All rights reserved
Library of Congress Catalog Card Number 90–35339
ISBN 0–87338–414–8
Manufactured in the United States of America

Library of Congress Cataloging-in-Publication Data

Ewing, Charles, d. 1927.
    Death throes of a dynasty : letters and diaries of Charles and
Bessie Ewing, missionaries to China / edited by E. G. Ruoff.
        p.   cm.
    ISBN 0–87338–414–8 (alk. paper) ∞
    1. Ewing, Charles, d. 1927. 2. Ewing, Bessie, d. 1966.
3. Missionaries—China—Correspondence. 4. Missionaries—China—
Diaries. 5. Missionaries—United States—Correspondence.
6. Missionaries—United States—Diaries. 7. China—
History—1861–1912—Sources. 8. China—History—1912–1928—
Sources. 9. China—Church history—19th century—Sources.
10. China—Church history—20th century—Sources. I. Ewing,
Bessie, d. 1966. II. Ruoff, E. G., 1926–   . III. Title.
BV3427.E89A4   1990
266′.00951′09041—dc20   90–35339
                                                              CIP

British Library Cataloging-in-Publication data are available.

To Andrew Goodyear Ewing
1902–1989

Contents

Preface

MY interest in China began in November 1945, when as a nineteen-year-old marine I departed Sasebo, Japan, and landed several days later in Tientsin, China. Never in my young life had I seen anything quite like what I was to see in China. My first residence there was in a vacated Japanese girls' school located less than a mile from where Charles and Bessie Ewing had lived during their first year in China. Little did I know at that time how well I would get to know Tientsin and its environs through the Ewing correspondence.

The short historical summaries of Chinese events that I have written are aimed at providing background for the Ewings' writings. In addition, the use of footnotes may make some of the baffling events that took place during a twenty-year period in China more readily understood. My editing of the Ewing papers was designed to eliminate duplication, reduce the routine clerical aspects of missionary correspondence to the minimum, and remove personal material that had no effect on life in China.

Since I do not read or write Chinese, I have had to rely upon English and French written material to help with the explanations. All Chinese names and places are shown in a slightly modified Wade-Giles system of transliteration. Since Wade-Giles was the most common Chinese-to-English system in use at the time the Ewings were in China, I have employed it rather than the Pinyin system currently in use. Therefore it is Tientsin and Peking rather than Tianjin and Beijing.

The Ewing correspondence came from two sources: first, the personal letters and diaries of the Ewing family, which were held in the possession of Andrew Goodyear Ewing of Hudson, Ohio, until his death in 1989; and second, the official records of the American Board of Commissioners for Foreign Missions, now located at the Houghton Library of Harvard University.

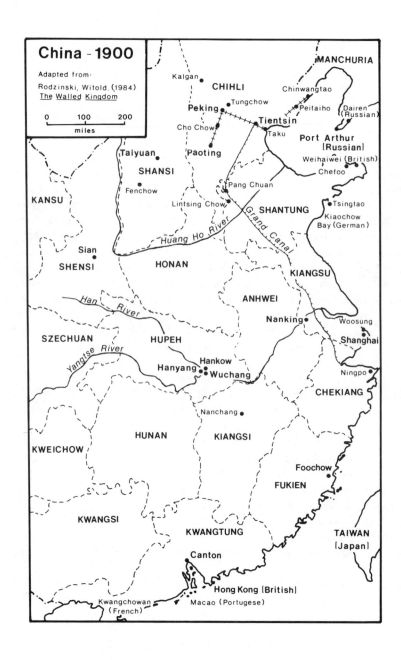

China - 1900

Adapted from:

Rodzinski, Witold. (1984)
The Walled Kingdom

0   100   200
miles

MANCHURIA

Kalgan

CHIHLI

Chinwangtao

Peking
Tungchow
Peitaiho
Dairen
(Russian)

Cho Chow
Tientsin
Taku
Port Arthur
(Russian)

Paoting

Weihaiwei (British)

Taiyuan

Chefoo

SHANSI

Fenchow

Pang Chuan

Tsingtao

Lintsing Chow

SHANTUNG
Kiaochow
Bay (German)

KANSU

Huang Ho River

Grand Canal

Sian

HONAN

KIANGSU

SHENSI

Han River

ANHWEI

SZECHUAN

HUPEH

Nanking

Woosung

Hankow

Shanghai

Yangtse River

Hanyang
Wuchang

Ningpo

CHEKIANG

Nanchang

HUNAN

KIANGSI

KWEICHOW

Foochow

FUKIEN

KWANGSI

TAIWAN
(Japan)

KWANGTUNG

Canton

Hong Kong (British)

Kwangchowan
(French)
Macao (Portugese)

Introduction

THIS is the story of the work of American missionaries Charles Edward and Bessie Smith Ewing in China between 1894 and 1913 and the events, a number of which they were eyewitnesses to, that were then shaking that ancient land to its very foundations. It was a time of turmoil, of change, of fighting and revolution. Yet it was also a time when foreigners, men and women, could preach a new doctrine in the cities and villages of China that had been little changed in centuries. The Ewings would first go to China as newlyweds to teach that doctrine and to do "God's work." They would establish their permanent home in North China, first in Peking and later in Tientsin. Their first two children, daughters Marion and Ellen, were born in China. Edward and Andrew, although born in the United States, would, along with their older sisters, spend their early years living in the missionary compounds of their parents.

Charles Ewing claimed that from about the age of ten he wanted to be a missionary in China. It was in 1879 that he first heard an American missionary from that distant country speak at his father's church in Enfield, Massachusetts. Both he and his brother, Henry Ewing, made up their minds to devote their lives to preaching the gospel to the Chinese. What caused this son of a New England Congregationalist minister to attend divinity school and then to go so far afield to spend much of his adult life in a land so different and distant from his own? Part of the answer certainly lay in the dreams of a ten-year-old boy, but there was a larger picture as well.

Following the end of the American Civil War, there was a strong surge of Protestant revivalist activities in the northern part of the United States, and particularly in New England and the Midwest. By the later half of the 1880s this movement had led to the formation of Bible study groups, student volunteer activities, and foreign mission conferences at colleges as geographically separated as Yale and Oberlin. Among the better-known organizers of such activities were Dwight Moody and Ira Sankey. At Oberlin College in Ohio a professor of church history, Judson Smith, encouraged his students to go into missionary work. Later he would become secretary of the China division of the American Board of Commissioners for Foreign Missions and a part of the Ewings' life. The revivalist movement resulted in the organization of the Student Volunteer Movement and the Yale Volunteer Band. In addition, the Young Men's Christian Association witnessed an upsurge of interest in and subsequent recruitment into foreign service. The young people—there were both men and women in the movement—were not only the well educated but also pious, reared in the church and with a strong sense of moral duty. They were drawn primarily from America's burgeoning small-town white middle class. These "crusaders" tended to believe that the ills of Old World societies could be cured if the proper combination of the gospel message and modernization could be applied. They were therefore both idealistic and imperialistic.

With the realization that the western frontier was fading into history, the urge to provide peoples in far-off lands with the blessings of America proved stronger and stronger. The proselytizing of the non-Christian population of China was also far more romantically appealing than addressing the needs of the teeming crowds in the industrial cities of America with their recently arrived European migrants of predominantly Roman Catholic, Greek Orthodox, and Jewish faiths. An equally less attractive alternative was the needs of the recently freed blacks of the American South. Although essentially an enlightened and charitable activity, the missionary movement was viewed by both American and British industrialists as a furtherance of their plans to open new markets for their products.

Another feature of the American social scene was to have an impact upon the Ewings' decision to become missionaries in the Orient. That was the role of women in American society. By the end of the Civil War that role had made a dramatic turn. Women were no longer devoting themselves exclusively to homemaking but were also teaching, nursing, and working in factories. Some were approaching the male bastion of the medical doctor. The foreign mission field allowed American women the opportunity of working in professional fields and exercising power with their husbands or, if unmarried, then as equals with men. It was a measure of equality not always available in America and offered respectable careers that allowed women to focus their energies upon mainstream work and not auxiliary service. By the first decade of the twentieth century half of the American missionaries in China were women. The majority of those women were supported by their own women's organizations in America. As Jane Hunter wrote in *The Gospel of Gentility*, "They [women] believed that Christianity was responsible for the elevated status of Western women; in preaching the Gospel they were only sharing what they had received in such bounty."[1]

How, then, did it come about that the idealistic young American clergy and other professionals who were caught up in spreading the gospel and in

---

[1] Jane Hunter, *The Gospel of Gentility* (New Haven: Yale University Press, 1984), 51.

providing education, health benefits, and other assistance to the uninitiated came to make China their primary target? Certainly Americans had been interested in China and things Chinese since the China-clipper days. This was particularly true of New England, where most of the ships of that era had originated. Since the opening of China to the West following the Opium Wars of the early 1840s, the European imperial powers had demonstrated their military superiority over the Chinese. That superiority came to be viewed by some as a cultural superiority as well, one which included modernization and Christianity. British missions were quick to introduce evangelizing Protestantism into that vast Chinese sea of oriental mysteries: Confucianism, Taoism, and Buddhism. The Americans were to follow with fervor. China appeared to the evangelist ready and indeed willing to accept a new way, a rebirth, a remaking. With the advent of the steamship as well as the safe havens in the European concessions after 1860, the movement into China became not only possible but a calling. China, that strange, mysterious, and ominous world, became the place to go and undertake missionary work since there was so much to be done there.

Like most young missionary couples, Charles and Bessie Ewing were both well educated. Charles had degrees from Amherst and Yale, and Bessie had training at a New Haven, Connecticut, normal school and had worked as a schoolteacher. In addition, Bessie had received a year of training in household management from her maternal aunt and foster mother, Myra McQueen (Mrs. Andrew Goodyear) Smith. Such training was not only to help Bessie manage her home in China but also to prepare her to teach Chinese women how to perform modern homemaking tasks.

In the Ewing correspondence that follows each introductory background section, it is possible to see the Ewings' changing appreciation of China. They clearly spelled out those problems associated with missionary life during a twenty-year period: the relationship of the foreign missionary and the Chinese convert, the lack of a national Chinese church, the materialism of the Chinese, the Boxer Uprising and the siege of Peking, the rise of Chinese nationalism, the opium addiction of many Chinese, the lengthy separations necessitated by missionary life, the harsh realities of famine and insurrection, the difficulties of travel, and the peculiar features of the extraterritorial city of Tientsin with its foreign concessions, sporting events, soldiers, and gunboats. During the two decades covered in the following pages, event piled upon event in China. It was a time of enormous change, and China was like a kaleidoscope as it presented a series of colorful patterns, slightly out of control and with no turn ever to be repeated.

1

The Encroachment
1892–1898

THE war between the aggressive and recently modernized Japanese military and the mistake-prone and traditional Chinese armed forces began on August 1, 1894. The conflict, which was to cost China dearly, was primarily fought over the issue of which of the two countries would dominate Korea. The fighting on land took place in China's eastern provinces of Manchuria, the homeland of the reigning dynasty, the Manchu or Ching. By early 1895 Japan had occupied Korea, the Manchurian port cities of Dairen and Port Arthur, Weihaiwei on the Shantung peninsula, and the islands of Formosa (Taiwan) and the Pescadores (Peng-hu). What these humiliating occupations had fully revealed was the weakness of China at a time when the powers of Europe were in the throes of their most aggressive imperialism.

Since China had been defeated, it was the empire's chief modernizer, Viceroy Li Hung-chang, whom the throne called upon to negotiate the humbling settlement. Viceroy Li, who had his viceregal headquarters at Tientsin, had been ordered to Japan by the emperor, a twenty-three-year-old Manchu who ruled under the reign name of Kuang Hsu. He had come of age under the tutelage and domination of his aunt, the Dowager Empress Tzu Hsi. Kuang Hsu was neither politically astute nor, because of his upbringing largely at the hands of the eunuchs of Peking's Forbidden City, did he have any understanding of international affairs. Furthermore, he lacked physical strength and emotional maturity.

Although the Dowager Empress had officially ended her regency in 1889, when Kuang Hsu reached maturity, she had in fact never completely given up control of the throne. In 1895 she was in her sixty-first year; she had first learned to enjoy the exercise of power thirty-four years earlier during the infancy of her son, the Emperor Tung Chih. Tzu Hsi had maintained her influence not only through such appointments as Prince Jung Lu, her cousin and longtime "special friend," but through her contact with and use of the palace eunuchs. The eunuchs had originally been placed into the Imperial Court more than 2,000 years before as a staff of servants and as neutralized protectors of the women of the court. Over a period of many

years, though, these Chinese men had become the controllers of court intrigue and a power unto themselves. It was Tzu Hsi who had learned to
manipulate the eunuchs and who used their power as her own. They not
only provided her with information about the empire's administration and
court intrigue but arranged substantial loans and became executioners when
called upon.

At the Peking level, the Manchu dynasty employed the Grand Council
and Grand Secretariat to supervise a massive bureaucracy. Below that were
such powerful viceroys as Li Hung-chang in North China, Chang Chih-tung
in Central China, and the eighteen provincial governors. Below them were
hundreds of district officers and thousands of lower-level officials, all appointed from Peking. This vast bureaucratic machine was designed primarily to keep the peace, collect the taxes, and maintain such public works
as canals, roads, and dikes.

Following the peace settlement of 1895, Russia, France, and Germany
intervened by forcing Japan to give up the Manchurian territory it had won
in battle. Japan continued its protectorate over Korea and retained Formosa
and the Pescadores outright. Extraterritorial privileges and a huge indemnity
of $185 million were to be given to Japan by China. Although other foreign
powers were encroaching on China, Great Britain remained the paramount
foreign power in the last decade of the nineteenth century. British businesses reigned supreme in the field of China's foreign commerce. British
interests dominated most of the treaty ports. Those ports were primarily
protected by British gunboats. Through Sir Robert Hart and the Imperial
Maritime Customs, the British dominated China's treaty port tax collection.
Hart, an Irish-born Englishman, had been Inspector General of customs
since 1867. British banks such as the Hong Kong and Shanghai were foremost in the field of trade and loans. Altogether some 360 British banks and
business firms had offices in China, although Britain's position was threatened by China's defeat in 1895.

By the mid-1890s the primary concern of the Western powers' commercial
penetration of China was railway construction and mining enterprises. The
treaty port of Tientsin was not only the primary entry point for such European activities in North China but the gateway to Peking. By the treaty of
Tientsin in 1860, China had granted Great Britain, France, and other foreign nations the right to utilize small portions of land bordering the Pei Ho
River. It did not take long for the foreign powers to establish extraterritorial
privileges on those enclaves. In time the Tientsin "concessions" became
small bits of Europe in China, with restaurants, churches, hotels, clubs,
schools, and even a racetrack. In 1895 it became possible to entrain at
Tientsin and travel the 85 miles northwest to Peking's Machiapu Station, or
the more than 200 miles northeast to Shanhaikwan in southern Manchuria.

In addition to commerce, another kind of Western penetration was making deep inroads into China. The Christian missionary movement was beginning to have an impact upon the Chinese way of life. Two very distinct and mutually antagonistic Christian communities, the Roman Catholic and the Protestant, existed in China. The Roman Catholic was dominated by the French but also had significant German and Italian elements. Catholic missionaries, who numbered over 750, had made about 500,000 converts by 1897. The man who ministered to the Catholic flock, at least in North China, was Monsignor Alphonse Favier, a French Lazarist priest who was vicar apostolic of Peking. Father Favier spoke fluent Chinese, had assumed Chinese dress, wore his hair in a queue, was a friend of Prince Jung Lu, and was considered by many to be the best informed European on Chinese affairs.

The second group of Christian missionaries in China, the Protestants, were dominated by British and American congregations. A substantial increase in the number of Protestant missionaries took place during the last decade of the nineteenth century. Although the exact number is difficult to determine, one student of Western activities in China has estimated that 2,800 Protestant missionaries were in China toward the end of the century.[1] More than half of these were of British or British Empire nationality. About one thousand were Americans. Among the most active of the congregations or societies were the American Board of Commissioners for Foreign Missions, American Presbyterian (North) Society, China Inland Mission, Christian and Missionary Alliance, Church Missionary Society, English Baptist Missionary Society, London Missionary Society, Methodist Episcopal Missionary Society, and the Church of England's Society for the Propagation of the Gospel.

The reason for the great increase of Protestant missionaries in China and the subsequent upsurge of evangelistic activity, was the previously explained belief in America and Great Britain that a great opportunity, indeed heavenly call, for the expansion of Christianity was at hand. The missionaries and their supporters "back home" believed that spiritual salvation of the "heathen" Chinese was essential to the modernization and revitalization of China. In the belief that the Chinese people were doomed to perdition and damnation unless the word of God reached them, missionaries journeyed deep into China's interior, preachers went from village to village, street chapels were established, and tracts and Bibles were distributed. Another kind of response came from the missionaries when late in the nineteenth century China experienced a series of catastrophic natural disasters.

[1] Edmund S. Wehrle, *Britain, China, and the Antimissionary Riots, 1891–1900* (Minneapolis: University of Minnesota Press, 1966), 12.

At that time many missionary societies organized to undertake widespread programs of health, education, and social assistance to the blind, deaf, addicted, orphaned, and to women (destitute widows and girls or women who might be helped by anti-foot-binding campaigns were of particular concern). However, many missionaries continued to feel that such activities took away from their "true calling" of simply spreading the gospel message.

All of the above activities, including evangelism, were organized and carried out from mission stations or compounds. Although there were some variations, most of the mission compounds throughout China consisted of a chapel, a hall, a school, a clinic or dispensary, a warehouse or godown, and the residences of the missionaries. The compound was usually surrounded by a high, solidly built wall. These centers became a kind of small *tache d'huile*, or oil spot, from which the Christian message was spread into the vast sea of Chinese tradition and customs. They also were enclaves of "foreign territory," protected by the extraterritorial clauses of the various treaties imposed upon China. Even though the government of China had reservations about the extraterritorial privileges assumed by the missionaries, the Western diplomats in the treaty ports did not, and the Westerners acted accordingly.

Although the issue concerning the extraterritorial privileges granted many mission compounds was a bone of contention between the Manchu dynasty and the Westerners, it proved to be less important than the question of the protection of Chinese Christian converts by the foreigners. As conversions increased in number and converts began to appear in the interior, serious incidents occurred in which the missionaries and their flocks were pitted against Chinese who were determined to retain their traditional ways and religious customs. In time, the Chinese gentry and provincial administrations were involved in the quarrels, which often had to do with the purchase of property by the missionaries for chapels and schools; injuries done to converts by zealots who guarded the traditions; the payment of taxes to support festivals and quasi-religious activities that the Christians found, or were encouraged to find, objectionable; and the problems associated with acquiring and caring for Chinese orphans.

The Chinese gentry class was particularly threatened by the missionary activities away from the treaty ports. The gentry, around whom societal customs revolved, were pitted against literate foreigners who, among other things, questioned the divinity of the emperor and the customs accorded him. The missionaries went so far as to argue that only God was divine. To the gentry and local officialdom it appeared that in many instances the poorest and least-educated elements in a village had become Christian converts in order to obtain material benefits or escape punishment. The gentry viewed these so-called rice Christians with contempt and considered those who had converted them a dangerous threat to the time-tested Chinese ways. Because of their education and position, the Chinese gentry had a strong social class snobbery. Both their position and their attitude directly affected converts and missionaries.

Many missionaries considered the gentry and officialdom directly responsible for the antiforeign outbreaks that had periodically occurred. Since corruption was rampant in Chinese officialdom, the missionaries viewed, from a Christian and Victorian perspective, the entire class as beyond redemption. Reform seemed possible only from converted Christians or by outside force. Many of the conflicts between gentry and officialdom on one side and Christian converts and missionaries on the other were sent to consulates and legations for resolution. Such conflicts were often legalistic and subject to a variety of interpretations, realities that made them difficult to resolve. A number of missionaries realized that certain converts took advantage of their church affiliation and pressed for legal support that should not have been requested. A number of more farsighted missionaries believed with conviction that they should never have been granted or assumed the legal right of defending the convert.

By the late 1890s the American legation at Peking and its consulates in the treaty ports estimated that fully half of their time was spent on conflicts between the Chinese government and the converts of the missionaries. Diplomats were more and more of the view that they had been drawn into an area outside their traditional field of work. As it has been aptly put, "The encounter of missionary and diplomat pitted men of burning ardor against men of slow deliberation. It was a contest of enthusiasm against sophistication, of dedication against detachment."[2]

It was not until 1898 that the impact of the Japanese victory over the Chinese in 1895 fully hit China. In that year the European powers grabbed for additional concessions of land at an unprecedented rate. What set the land grab in motion was a minor incident involving the death of two German priests in Shantung in November 1897. The incident provided the pretext for Germany to seize the port of Tsingtao on Kiaochow Bay. On the following March 6, China conceded to Germany all of Kiaochow Bay, encompassing some 200 square miles. In a separate agreement China gave to Germany the right to build railways and work mines in Shantung province.

Not wishing to miss an opportunity to stake out some desirable Chinese territory, the Russians soon followed Germany's move. The czar's government demanded Port Arthur and by the end of March 1898, the Chinese had agreed to lease it and the surrounding territory. Russia now had the ice-free port that it had "saved" for China from Japan only three years

[2]Wehrle, *Antimissionary Riots*, 46.

earlier. All that had to be done was to connect it by rail with the Trans-Manchurian Railway to form a link with European Russia.

Fearing that the Russian fleet at Port Arthur would control the strategic Gulf of Chihli and therefore the entrance to Tientsin and Peking, British diplomats were hurriedly instructed by Queen Victoria's government in London to have the Manchu court cede the port of Weihaiwei in Shantung to Britain. In addition, the British demanded, and were eventually able to obtain, additional territory at Kowloon in order to expand the Hong Kong colony. Not to be outdone by Germany, Russia, and Great Britain, the French moved naval units into the Bay of Kwangchowan in southern China. By April 1898, the Manchu dynasty had granted a long-term lease for the bay in Kwantung province for use by the French navy as a coaling station.

The defeat of China by Japan and the subsequent payment of an indemnity and loss of territory to the Europeans were blows that the Manchu dynasty never fully recovered from. With the granting of the concessions to the Europeans, the emperor had lost confidence in the traditionalists administering the government. In June of 1898 he turned to a young reform-minded scholar, Kang Yu-wei, for inspiration and a new direction. Kang, a classical scholar, believed that it was possible to adapt Confucian teaching to the reformation of Chinese institutions. Kang wrote that the dynasty could lead the country to modernization through a reform movement. It was to be reform from the top down.

From June 11 to September 16 the reformers led by Kang drafted, and the emperor issued, more than forty reform edicts. The edicts did not overturn the dynasty nor establish a parliament; they were more evolutionary than revolutionary. Although the edicts had been issued, few of the reforms were put into practice. The vast bureaucracy waited to see what the Empress Tzu Hsi would do. Would she accept the reforms, or would she follow the suggestions of the concerned traditionalists and put an end to the reformist lark?

On September 21, Tzu Hsi struck. Her palace coup d'etat was swift and simple. She claimed that her life was in danger and therefore had Emperor Kuang Hsu arrested and exiled to a palace within the Forbidden City. Some reformers fled into exile; most were killed or imprisoned.

Ewing Papers,
December 1892 to November 1898

Charles Ewing (hereafter Charles) to Reverend Judson Smith,[1] December 8, 1892, New Haven, Connecticut

Dear Sir:

This morning's mail brought to my brother [Henry] and myself the gratifying announcement of our appointments to the North China Mission. This is the field to which I especially desired to go. It has been brought to my attention repeatedly of late and in a variety of ways. . . . You speak [write] of my preparation [to go to China] as being deficient in one respect. I am so fully conscious of this fact that I should consider it a mistake for me to go to China unmarried; but I have put myself at the service of the Board, and that if wanted before I have found my companion I will go. But I have a few words to write to you in a confidential way in this matter. The young lady whom I should hope to ask to accompany me is a Freshman in college, and is only twenty years of age. She [Bessie Smith] is very anxious to go as a missionary, and I am sure she will do so if possible, in spite of the objections of her parents. Moreover she prefers the North China Mission. It is a question with me whether I ought to ask her to put her work of preparation off now. I should like to ask your advice as to this. If it is wiser for me to wait for her, then it would raise the further question as to how I could make the best use of the time between now and our going. It is possible that the young lady herself may have a very decided answer to any question I may put to her, but she has received me very kindly thus far.

[1]Judson Smith was the secretary general of the American Board of Commissioners for Foreign Missions in Boston, Massachusetts. This was Charles Ewing's first letter to the Reverend Dr. Smith. His last letter was sent on May 12, 1906. All or part of fifty letters from Charles to Dr. Smith are contained in this book.

Edward C. Ewing (Charles's father) to Judson Smith, May 10, 1893, Dawes, Connecticut

Dear Brother Smith:

It is reported to us that the position at Tungchow [location of the American Board's school in North China] which our Henry was expecting to occupy has been assigned to another. I know not who. If this is so, it is disappointing to us, as Henry seems best fitted for educational work, and we cannot judge to what position he will now be assigned. If however the result be that the two brothers [Charles and Henry] go together to Peking, that arrangement would offer alleviations. Can you say what is likely to come from this changed condition?

Another matter interests me not a little, and I wish to consult you about it. Charles is suggesting the propriety of postponing his going abroad for another year, [and that it] be spent in additional study and in the hope that then he may take a companion [wife] with him. . . . I do not myself know what is best in this case, and I shall advise Charles to confer with you respecting it if he has not already done so.

Charles to Judson Smith, April 3, 1894, New Haven, Connecticut

Dear Dr. Smith:

I write to ask concerning the best time and route for going to China. Miss [Bessie] Smith and I had thought that it would be very pleasant for us if we could go in company with Mr. Merritt,[1] whom I have met. . . . You thought we should sail about the middle of August [1894]. I wish to ask also concerning the route to be taken. We are informed that the boat [*sic*] of the Canadian line is superior to those that sail from San Francisco. On the other hand it would be exceedingly pleasant for us to see the Western part of our own country, and also to visit friends in California. However, Dr. Merritt writes that he thinks the Board prefers the Canadian route, as being the cheaper. And in the present financial condition of the Board, such fact would have special weight.

Letters from my brother [Henry] send word of his pleasant location in Peking, and his enjoyment of the Chinese language.

[1] Dr. C. A. W. Merritt was also an American Board missionary bound for China.

Charles to his grandfather, George Clinton Ewing, October 18, 1894, Tientsin, China

Dear Grandpa:

The foreign houses [non-Chinese] are built of brick, but the bricks are dried in such a way that instead of coming out red they are gray. Many of the houses are only one story in height, but some, including this in which I am, are of two stories. . . . The roof is, in most cases laid with heavy tiles. . . . In this compound, there are four houses, one building for the office of the mission treasurer, one godown (which is the universal term for storehouses in all the foreign settlements in Asia), one chapel, two

Charles and Bessie on their wedding day, July 12, 1894, New Haven, Connecticut.

buildings for the boys' school, one building for the girls' school, and also a little room by the gate of the compound for the gatekeeper. This compound, . . . must be at least 250 feet wide and 500 [feet] in length, giving a space of about three acres. . . . Around the compound there is a brick wall, well, seven or eight feet in height.[1]

[1]The newly married Charles and Bessie Ewing, aged twenty-five and twenty-four respectively, had reached Shanghai on September 27, 1894, and Tientsin one week later. Although Charles has described the American Board's compound at Tientsin, which also contained a school play yard and tennis court, in most ways it is typical of extraterritorial missionary compounds of the late nineteenth century in China. The high wall surrounding the compound is particularly so.

Charles to Frank Goodyear Smith, cousin of Bessie, October 31, 1894, Tientsin

Dear Cousin Frank:

In the river [the Pei Ho at Tientsin] there are several foreign gunboats for our protection in case of necessity the United States, Great Britain, France, Germany, and Russia are thus represented. . . . The paving [in the Chinese city] is of great blocks of flat stone, over the joints of which the jinrikisha jolts along, giving the passenger vigorous shaking. Or if you prefer to walk, you have to keep dodging out of the way of jinrikishas, wheelbarrows, sedan chairs, mules, and other pedestrians, and as the stones are not only worn smooth and rounded at the edges, but are also covered with wet, the path is a slippery one. . . . Tientsin is not as bad as Peking anyway, partly because the streets there are so broad that there is room for refuse of all the residents, partly because here the river affords a place for some such things. . . . As one looks out to the plains about the city, he can see a vast number of mounds of various sizes. These are built over graves. The interference with such graves, you will remember, is one cause of Chinese opposition to the introduction of railroads. . . . You may be interested to know a little about the Chinese army. I am told that when they go into battle, every tenth man carries a standard of some kind, almost all have fans, and some have umbrellas also. Of course they make a formidable array, but you can easily understand how the Japanese, being finely drilled and carrying about the best arms in the world, can expect to win in every battle. In addition to this, the Japs have ambition and patriotism: and the Chinese lack both. . . . They [the Chinese] very much dislike to have their heads get wet. . . . The best way to drive a Chinaman away is to turn the hose on him. It is generally supposed among the foreigners that a Chinese mob could be easily repelled by the free use of water. . . . If we can scare them they will run; and it is easy to scare them. Ten men with rifles could probably stop a mob coming up the street toward the [foreign] settlement, more by scaring than by shooting. . . . Armed resistance on the part of civilians, however interesting and exciting it might be, will hardly be called for, while we have the gunboats at hand.[1] Why, the very presence of those armed creatures is enough to terrify the natives. . . . Our American vessel is the "Monocacy," built during the war [American Civil War] for use in the Southern rivers.[2]

So much has been said about the way in which the Chinese treat foreigners that one scarcely expects to find himself much favored on account of being a member of one of the "most favored nations." Indeed one rather anticipates that he must "look out for number one," if "number one" is to be looked out for at all. But, on the contrary, I find here a U.S. consul and vice-consul, ready to protect my interests, provided I am not so rash as to provoke native opposition continually. If I am insulted all I have to do is report it to the consul, and he will see to it that a proclamation is issued, or something is done, that will prevent a recurrence of the insult. Of course, outside of Tientsin, there would not be the same freedom from insult that we have here. . . . Some missionaries do not care to report such occurrences [insults and racial slurs such as being called "foreign devil"], thinking it wise to go on with their work without calling in the aid of the law, but many look on the matter as demanding vigorous handling.[3] . . . The Chinese are really, in many things, like grown-up children; and they have often to be treated like children; they cannot be reasoned with, but they may be easily amused or frightened—just like children.

If we were in Peking, there would be no consul there; but we should be under the protection of the American minister. . . . The government [of China], so far from failing to respond, has issued proclamation after proclamation, until as one of our missionaries says the Chinese are almost afraid to look at a foreigner. Now, I should like to know whether an American court would do anything in the way of making reprisal to a Chinaman who was insulted, whether by having the boys in the street holler "Heathen Chinee" or in any other way. Would an American judge punish such offenders? Or would he even issue a proclamation enjoining upon all citizens the respectful treatment of foreigners? And yet, they have as much a right to walk the streets in New Haven as I in Tientsin. . . . As far as the official action is concerned, is there not more justice done here in China? China does not insist on her rights; and America like most Americans, goes on the selfish and un-Christian principle of getting all you can and giving as little as you can. But most Americans *will* not see it so; blinded by prejudice, they care more for self preservation than for justice. . . .

Our work with the [Chinese] language is progressing. There is little doubt that, if our health keeps good and there is nothing especial to interfere, we shall easily accomplish the required work before the annual meeting [of the American Board of Commissioners for Foreign Missions] next

April. . . . Some of the missionaries never learn them [the sounds and tones] thoroughly.

[1]After only a few weeks in China, Charles is parroting a number of beliefs common in the foreign community, i.e., that the Chinese lacked ambition and patriotism and could easily be frightened. He was to learn otherwise.

[2]Tientsin had been a treaty port since 1860 and the USS *Monocacy* and the other foreign gunboats were the "guardian angels" of the foreign community. The *Monocacy* was to remain in North China and play a role in the Boxer Uprising.

[3]The treaty between China and the United States provided for protection for Americans. If American dwellings or property were "threatened or attacked by mobs, incendiaries, or other violent or lawless persons, the local [Chinese] officers, on requisition of the [American] consul shall immediately dispatch a military force to disperse the rioters, apprehend the guilty individuals and punish them with the utmost rigor of the law" (Hunter Miller, ed., *Treaties and Other International Acts of the United States of America* [Washington, D.C.: Government Printing Office, 1931], 7:905).

Bessie Smith Ewing (hereafter Bessie) to Myra Smith (Mrs. Andrew Goodyear Smith), October 13, 1894, Tientsin

Dear Aunt Myra:

Charles and I together have our Chinese teacher six hours a day. As our location [for assignment] is to be Peking, we had to secure a teacher who spoke pure Pekingese [*sic*], for the pronunciation here is different, especially the tones. . . . Our first examination is due [in April 1895].[1]

[1]Mastery of Mandarin Chinese was absolutely essential to successful mission work in North China. Charles and Bessie Ewing spent nearly a year of language study before undertaking a permanent assignment. Bessie's assignment was further modified by the birth of her first child, their daughter Marion, on May 15, 1895.

Charles to Edward Cornelius Ewing, November 10, 1894, Tientsin

Dear Father:

A few rods from us is the viceroy's hospital and medical school, at the head of which is Dr. Lin, whom we used to know when he lived in Enfield [Massachusetts]. . . . The viceroy, Li Hung Chang, promises help and Dr. Lin who is the viceroy's personal physician, will give his services [to the Red Cross society]. Speaking of the viceroy, we find that the majority of the common people look on him as a traitor. Grant [Ulysses S. Grant] probably overestimated him, altho there is no doubt of his great sagacity.[1]

[1]Li Hung-chang first came to the notice of the West during the Taiping Rebellion (1850–65). Subsequently he came to represent the most progressive elements in China and attempted to counteract the Western powers by rebuilding part of the Chinese army and navy and opening the country to railroads and mineral exploitation. During the time when Li conducted Chinese foreign relations, he met Ulysses S. Grant, who was then on his world tour. Li Hung-chang was well known for his personal ambition and love of money.

Charles to Judson Smith, January 10, 1895, Tientsin

Dear Dr. Smith:

Our journey hither was sperious [*sic*] and delightful. In San Francisco we were invited to a farewell meeting at the First Church [Congregational], where we were glad to see and converse with many of those interested in the work of the Board. . . .

The entrance into the tropics [at Honolulu] caused some malarial fever for me, emphasizing again the wisdom of a more northern location for my future work. In Yokohama we found it necessary to wait a week before there was any steamer for Shanghai. . . .

The foreign residents in Tientsin are so many that we have many social and other opportunities that we had not expected to find in China. The only thing to disappoint me is the climate, which I find to have that fickleness which I had supposed China had not, as New England has.

We [Charles and Bessie] have both applied ourselves to the [Chinese] language, and I think that we have worked about as hard as regard for continued good health would allow. Indeed, I have been compelled to "hold in" once or twice, but that was mainly due to lack of systematic exercise. I have arranged for that.[1] . . . having no other regular Sunday work, [I] have been glad to take part, together with Miss Mary Stanley,[2] in the holding of a Sunday afternoon meeting on the berth-deck of the "Monocacy." We hope that these meetings may at least have an effect of keeping Christianity before the minds and hearts of some of the men. . . . The American residents held a Thanksgiving service for which I was asked to prepare the discourse; secondly I was chosen to preach the sermon at the church[3] on Christmas day. I thought it wise and proper to take the necessary time from my studying [of Chinese] for the required preparation.

As to the country people of China. I think that my reading had given me fairly correct ideas; but I am of course finding it necessary to modify my tentative conclusions more or less.

[1]The arrangement (and antidote) was to play tennis.

[2]Mary Stanley was the daughter of Dr. Charles Stanley, Sr., and Mrs. Louise Stanley, long-time American Board missionaries in Tientsin.

[3]Charles does not say which church, but Tientsin at this time had a Union Church at which Protestant services were held in English.

Charles to Andrew Goodyear Smith, March 1895, Tientsin

My Dear Uncle Andrew:

One likes to get a fling at the English because they are so much inclined to think that they are "the People," with every one else secondary. In this, the Chinese are similar. They have thought of themselves for ages as being superior to all other nations. Foreign ambassadors have always been received and regarded as emissaries from tributary nations. It will be a bitter pill for them to swallow, when they are compelled to admit that they are beaten by a foreign nation, especially by the detested Japanese. I hope they will be made to swallow it. . . . For the best of China herself, most of the missionaries here seem to think that a thorough-going defeat will be most advantageous.[1] . . . I believe that in spite of all that is displeasing in the Chinese character, there is much also that is admirable, and that it will become more and more evident as time goes on that if any people is worth saving, these people are, for whom we hope to work.

[1]Charles and the missionaries were not alone in believing that a Chinese defeat by the Japanese would be for the good of China. Numerous Chinese of varying political persuasions were already convinced that the Manchu dynasty needed to be replaced and that the administrative machinery of the empire needed drastic modification. In addition, many foreign residents of China, including diplomats and those in business and finance, believed that both China and the European powers would benefit if China was divided into spheres of influence so that the trade, education, and culture of the West could be brought to the Chinese people. A Japanese victory could lead to the end of the Manchus, to the establishment of European dominated spheres, or to both.

Charles to Judson Smith, May 18, 1895, Tientsin

Dear Dr. Smith:

When I wrote to you on Jan. 10, I was hoping soon to take a trip to Peking, to visit our future home and field of labor. But I was not feeling very vigorous, and I hardly cared to combat the cold weather at that time, traveling in a Chinese cart and sleeping in a Chinese inn, and so I deferred the trip.[1] . . .

At Peking I was very glad to make the acquaintance of most of those with whom I hope to live and work, to meet some of the representatives of other mission boards, and to see all that I could of the field and the work. From what I have seen or heard concerning other stations, there is no place where I should be more pleased to be stationed. My first sight of the city itself was perhaps a little disappointing, but that was largely because it is impossible for a one-story city to be very attractive to one traveling on its dusty or muddy streets. The most impressive thing about the city is its immense size, as it stretches over so many square miles,[2] and its walls and gates, which are massive indeed. Our own [American Board] compound is so crowded and so bysinthine [sic] in its arrangement that my slight [annoyance] with Peking is not owing to my first impression there. Indeed it is not the first impression that has drawn me to Peking: it is rather the apparent permanence and promise of the work tinged with the pride that I feel it as being my own station.

While at Peking I had the opportunity of taking a trip into the country with Mr. [William] Ament.[3] . . . I wished to see a little of the outstation work, and I was glad to seize this opportunity. It was a novel experience for me. I had never ridden a mule before, scarcely even a horse, and here I was to travel on muleback for fifty miles and back. Only once [in seven months] had I indulged in Chinese food and now I was cutting myself off from foreign supplies for a week. When we arrived at the inland city of Cho Chow[4] on Saturday at noon a rain-storm had set in that before it ceased on Monday afternoon, had broken down at least one wall of half of the houses in every village, ruined many places even in the city, submerged many wheat fields, and so flooded the country roads that they were practically impassable for several days. . . . if I were to recount all the amusing, pathetic, and terrible things we saw, I should write too long a letter; but they all go to formulating one's opinions concerning China without Christ, as well as furnishing—in some instances—evidences of what changes Christ can work. Let me only mention two cases. One of these was the case of a little girl one or two years of age, whom her father had beaten to death. Many people were standing around while the corpse lay in a basket covered with a coarse cloth. But there was no punishment for the father, for according to Chinese custom a daughter is her father's property to be used as he may desire.

The other case is of another little girl, but this time the father was a Christian and one of our native preachers. This father has consumption, is not likely to recover, [and] his wife is dead. But the little girl, who is now about six years old, has the blessing of Christian parentage, will be cared for by Christian friends, and may perhaps become one of the strong Christian women of the next generation.

. . . on my return to Tientsin I found that the rain had beat in through the brick wall of one of the rooms, and, as it is on the north, it is not dried even yet. . . .

My progress with the [Chinese] language is not as rapid as I should like. I allowed myself to be interfered with during February and March by acceding to the request of the Union Church here [in Tientsin] . . . to preach a series of sermons on four successive Sunday evenings.

[1]Charles traveled to Tungchow and Peking between April 11 and May 10. The mode of travel is not stated.

[2]The enormous wall around Peking's Chinese and Tartar cities enclosed approximately twenty-seven square miles.

[3]William Ament was an American Board missionary then assigned to Peking. Both Ewings alternated the terms *Dr.* and *Mr.* in references to him; he held the doctorate in divinity.

[4]Cho Chow is about forty miles from Peking.

Charles to Myra Smith, July 1895, Western Hills

Dear Aunt Myra:

As the doctor said that Bessie was strong enough to travel [Bessie had a mild attack of malaria shortly after the birth of Marion on May 15] and the sooner we got out of the city the better, we hurried our moving and came here [to the Western Hills] three weeks ago. From Tientsin to Tungchow the trip was by a small houseboat which we hired for three days.[1] . . .

On the top of one of these [Western] hills are the five summer cottages built by the [American] Board for the use of the missionaries. . . . We get very little of the "bracing" style of atmosphere here, perhaps because our elevation is not very great. We are 600 feet above the plain, but the land is so level from here to the sea that we may be no more than a thousand feet above sea level.

[1]After two days in Tungchow the Ewings started for Peking, some fifteen miles away. Bessie and the baby traveled in a sedan chair, and Charles alternately walked and rode a donkey.

Charles to Edward C. Ewing, August 1895, Western Hills

Dear Father:

Cholera has begun its ravages in Peking, much earlier in the season than ordinarily. All missionaries who are in the city are constantly besieged with appeals for help and medicine. We intend to stay here at the hills until near the end of September, when the worst of the plague will be past. . . . It seems as though we were here in the midst of nature's paradise [because of the early morning clouds to the east], even though vice and degradation is all around us, and the filthiest city in the world only twelve miles away.[1]

[1]The Western Hills (Hsi Shan) were only fifteen miles' walking distance from Peking but because of their elevation served as a kind of summer hill station for the foreign community. Small bungalows with vistas of the plain below had been built, and hiking was a popular pastime.

Bessie to Myra Smith, October 11, 1895, Peking

Dear Aunt Myra:

We left the "Hills" last week, reaching here a little after five, a ride of nearly six hours in a sedan chair. Charles walked all the way. . . . It [riding in a sedan chair] is as though you sat on a very springy bed and were going up and down with a steady continuous shaking of the bed. The bamboo poles give all the spring, as there is none in the chair, but the men give a swing in their walk. . . .

The whole [American Board] compound [in Peking] was once an official [Chinese] residence and our house was an open reception hall. After the Board bought the premises, walls and windows were added and board floors put in. We are having matting laid in the rooms, as is the custom rather than carpet or rugs.[1]

[1]In October 1895 the Ewing family took up permanent residence in Peking. The American Board had been located there since 1864. The Ewing home was within the mission compound called the Teng Shih Kourh. The compound consisted of numerous buildings, several of which were 400 years old, and was located inside the Tartar City and east of the walled Imperial Palace. It was close to the Roman Catholic East Cathedral and just off the wide "boulevard," called the Great Eastern Street. That street led to the Ha Tà Gate and the Chinese City. In the Ewing correspondence both the English word "gate" and the Chinese word "men" are used to refer to the entrance gateways into Peking.

Charles to his grandfather, Christopher Columbus Alvord, October 1895, Peking

Dear Grandpa:

In spite of open sewers on all the large streets, these broad open places [streets 100 feet wide] make Peking more habitable to foreigners than most other Chinese cities. This is almost the only Chinese city where the foreigners really live inside of city walls.[1] On Sunday I go to our North Chapel,[2] about a mile and a half from here [the American Board compound]. I always walk and in spite of all you have heard of the danger to foreigners in China I do not feel that such a walk is more dangerous here in Peking than it would be in Boston.

[1]In Tientsin the Ewings had lived outside the city wall in the French Concession.
[2]The North Chapel was located within the Tartar City of Peking.

Bessie to her father, George Walstein Smith, November 1895, Peking

Dear Papa:

Mrs. Mateer[1] owns a sedan chair, which I borrowed for the trip [to Tungchow]. Marion [six months old] and I left our house a little before nine and reached Tungchow before one, only four hours instead of the usual five. . . . The chair bearers took me by the dirt road and by-paths but the cart [with the Ewing's sewing woman and a Chinese schoolgirl] had to go on the old stone road, as the rains had made the other route impassable. This stone road is the main thoroughfare and was built a thousand years ago. It is raised above the plain, as railroad beds are at home, and is about the width of Chapel Street [in New Haven, Connecticut]. The paving stones are about the size of the old State House stepping stones. When these were new and fitted closely the road might have been good, but now the edges are worn off and the stones have settled, leaving wide cracks, some stones are entirely gone and consequently there are deep holes and ruts. The earth at the side has fallen away and some stones have fallen down until in some places the road is not more than half its rightful width.[2]

[1]Mrs. John L. Mateer was an American Board missionary. She is not to be confused with Ada Haven Mateer.

[2]This was Bessie's second visit to Tungchow, where the American Board had established in 1889 its North China College and a divinity school. Tungchow had had an American Board mission since 1867. The college was headed by Dr. Develo Z. Sheffield, its founder and administrator for twenty years.

Charles to Judson Smith, April 2, 1896, Peking

Dear Dr. Smith:

The work at this station [Peking] has moved on for the most part, very smoothly, little that needed to be written. . . . The Bridgman school has had to get along without Miss [Abbie] Chapin for a considerable part of the time, partly because she is so invaluable as a nurse.[1] And now we have "lent" her to Tientsin to take Miss Stanley's work for a time. . . . Dr. Murdock[2] is ever active, and enlarging the scope of her work. She now has two dispensaries in the city, and also goes occasionally to two nearby villages to dispense medicine, taking with her one or two [Chinese] members of the church to talk and preach to the crowds that gather. And now she is reaching out with the hope of hiring a place at the town[3] that is to be the terminus of the new railroad from Tientsin. You will remember that the [Chinese] authorities refused to permit the railroad nearer to the Imperial city [Peking] than this point, eight or ten miles away. It will be a valuable centre for work, and if we do not take it some other mission will. It is on the same great road with two of our outstations. . . .

The work at Nan Meng[4] has been given a new impetus by the securing of a ten year lease of desirable chapel property and the transfer of Pastor Hung to that place. This was the work of Miss Russell[5] on her first trip, and the money for the purchase and needed repairs came from friends of Miss Russell in America. . . .

I want to keep myself under and be in readiness for any use the Lord may make of me. I believe that a man thoroughly consecrated, and living so close to God that even every obstacle is removed and he may be freely used—I believe that such a man would be a power for God in this city and this land. This field is a hard one, but would a prophet of righteousness and repentance face any harder task here than that of Jonah in Nineveh? . . . As yet my preaching [in Chinese] is rather halting and I fear not easily apprehended; but I think the people gain something from it, and I myself am much blessed and benefited by all such service that I can render. My progress in the language has not been such that I can yet converse freely, but when I stand up to preach, especially in street chapel, God seems to give me more of skill and fluency in speaking than at other times. . . .

We have all been blessed, missionaries, native-helpers, and church members, by the Conference of Christian Workers held at the Methodist Mission from Sept. 12 to Sept. 17. Mr. Mott, of the intercollegiate Y.M.C.A.

and the Student Volunteer Movement, was present; his addresses were very helpful, to both the missionaries and the Chinese who heard the talks translated.[6]

Excuse me for asking your time to mention the visit of some "globe-trotters." But, because of the unfortunate fact that most sight-seers pay little attention to missionary work, the presence of these visitors was so welcome an exception as to be deserving of mention. . . .

This past summer we spent [time] at Kalgan[7] together with my brother's family. The malarial atmosphere of Peking had already had unpleasant effects on Mrs. Ewing and myself, and we were very glad to have the experience of the tonic air of Kalgan, as well as the invigoration that resulted from frequent mountain climbing and long walks. . . .

My own work has been partly study and partly a beginning at missionary work. I have reached the point where I learn more of the language from my active intercourse with the Chinese than from my teacher. And as I do not much relish some of the study work, I fear that I am inclined to be too careless with regard to it. . . . My work at the North Chapel is rendered easy by the fact that we have an excellent native preacher there. (His name we spell Jên, but pronounce like a cross between our English words wren and run). He takes charge of most of the work, and has preached nearly every Sunday. Just now he has gone for a visit to his father at his boyhood home—where he has not been for nine years. Another helper, who has been at Cho Chow, is helping in his place, taking charge of the street chapel preaching, and he will probably preach the next two Sundays. After that, I may preach one Sunday before Mr. Jên returns. I preached my first Chinese sermon last Sunday on the text, Ye are my witnesses (Acts 1:8). Poorly as I can as yet use the language, it is a delight to find myself able to talk freely and correctly, especially if I can present heavenly things to the exceedingly earthly minds of these devil-deceived people. It is in the way of conversation, which is more necessary and I think also more important and valuable in missionary work, that I find myself particularly lacking. I can neither understand nor reply to a great deal of what is said by the Chinese. But I am improving, and expect still to advance. . . . Leading or taking part in prayer meetings has also been helpful. Prayer is what I have found as hard as anything. I am even told that one of the oldest missionaries of another mission said, "In Chinese, we pray, not for what we want, but for what we know." . . .

I met with many of the church members [in the villages near Peking] whom I shall hope to come to know more in the future. And I have now seen most of our country work. I find that I shall enjoy the touring, tolerate the wearing of an outside layer of Chinese clothing, and find some relish in eating Chinese food.

[1]Bridgman was a school operated by the American Board in Peking for Chinese girls. It was named for Reverend Mr. Elijah C. Bridgman, who was the first American missionary in China. His wife Eliza founded the school, which in 1904 became the North China Union College for Women. In 1920 it became part of Yenching University. Abbie Chapin was an American Board Missionary.

[2]Dr. Elizabeth Murdock was a medical missionary for the American Board.

[3]The town of Fengtai was six miles from the eastern wall of Peking's Chinese City.

[4]Nan Meng is approximately fifty miles south of Peking.

[5]Nellie Russell was an American Board missionary whose work was primarily concerned with Chinese women in their homes. She traveled extensively throughout Chihli province.

[6]John Raleigh Mott was a leading figure in the international Y.M.C.A. movement.

[7]Kalgan is over one hundred miles northwest of Peking and on the route to Mongolia and the Gobi Desert.

Bessie to Myra Smith, June 1896, Peking

My Dear Aunt Myra:

The end of May we all went to Tungchow to attend the annual Mission meeting. All the families try to come then from our seven stations in North China. As the college is closed we live in the dormitories, eat together and hold our meetings in the large reading room. Here in Tungchow we are out in the open country and have good air and a large compound in which the children play. This year there are seventeen children present, Marion being next to the youngest.[1]

[1]The American Board's seven missions then in North China were at Peking, Tientsin, Kalgan, Paoting, Cho Chow, Liang Hsiang Hsien, and Wen An Hsien.

Charles to Edward and Ellen Ewing, June 1896, Peking

Dear Father and Mother:

This condition [the Chinese being like children] is evidenced in the terms used for all paid workers in the church. They are always referred to as "helpers" . . . I most earnestly hope that the church of Christ in China may avoid being organized according to foreign ideas; the Chinese ought to do their own organizing and directing of church affairs. This directing by foreigners is now in large part a necessity, but it bodes evil for the future of the church unless great care is used when the time for self-direction and self-support arrives.[1]

[1]Charles expresses in this letter a concept that was much ahead of its time, advocating that the Chinese should organize and direct their own church. He was to see this happen, although it took another fifteen years.

Charles to Edward and Ellen Ewing, Summer 1896, Kalgan

Dear Father and Mother:

The main reason for servants [in China] is that there is no kind of city services or central businesses such as laundry, dairy, telephone, water supply, or delivery. . . . Again the cost of a staff of three men and one woman is about two hundred dollars a year and our food bills are just about that much less than in America. Meat is from five to ten cents a pound no matter the cut. Eggs are about twenty cents a hundred.[1]

[1]American missionaries felt the need to justify the extensive use of Chinese servants to the folks back home. At the time of the siege of Peking, the servants, most of whom were Christian converts, at first proved a dilemma for the missionary families. The dilemma was whether to send them away to almost certain death or keep them in the Legation Quarter with the Europeans. The latter course was the one taken.

Charles to Judson Smith, November 19, 1896, Nan Meng

Dear Dr. Smith:

Today a fair is being held in this market town [Nan Meng], and pastor, Mr. Hung, and myself have had the opportunity of preaching to crowds that pressed into the chapel to hear. The attitude of the people of this place and of this whole region is favorable to the Christian doctrine, and very many listen most attentively to the gospel message. When asked to express themselves concerning the Christian truth, they frequently say "Don't understand" it. Others say, "Doctrine good." Still others make their interest evident by coming frequently to hear or by asking questions, or by treating the native pastor or the missionary with marked kindness. . . .

This man, tho under forty years of age, had been chosen as head man of his village. He told me that one of the temples [probably Buddhist] in the village has been emptied of idols, that about ten of the 160 families have given up the idols in their homes, that many others do not believe any longer in their power, and that tho there are few Christians in the village, the attitude toward Christianity is favorable. . . .

Mr. Ament has allowed five tiao (about $1.50) a month for a boys' school here, provided the rest be made up by the Christians or others in Nan Meng. The result is that, as I sit here writing, I can hear from a nearby room the voices of ten or a dozen boys studying their lessons out loud according to the Chinese custom. They are studying Christian books; some are at work on a simple catechism that is studied by all children in our Christian schools. The teacher, who is well educated in the Chinese classics and has received the first scholar's degree, tho not a Christian, is an inquirer. He is quite constant in his attendance [at] our services, and seems to be a very hopeful inquirer. Some of the boys are from Christian families, but some also are the children of outsiders.

Mrs. Hung, the pastor's wife, has a school for girls. Outside of her own family, there are seven or eight in attendance, and these also are partly from Christian and partly from outside [non-Christian] families. Thus, tho slowly, the truth of Christ is making its impress on the minds of future wives and mothers.

The pastor tells me that the priest at a neighboring Buddhist temple believes in the truth of Christianity, but as his money all comes from the Buddhist religion, he is not going to renounce that and accept Christ, as he would then be without means of livelihood. However he is by no means the only priest who is persuaded of the falsity of his own religion and the truth of ours. Our criticisms of idol worship are coming to be considered as incontrovertible, however slowly they may seem to influence [others]. It is to be hoped that this will not be the casting out of one devil that seven worse may come in. Pray for China that as old religions lose their hold Christ may take control.

Charles to Judson Smith, December 28, 1896, Peking

Dear Dr. Smith:

Two of the new deacons [elected by the Chinese members of the South Chapel in Peking] are Manchus, and both of them have helped a great deal in street chapel preaching. The third [deacon] was formerly a student at Tungchow, and was a great favorite of Mr. Harlin P. Beach's,[1] but has now for some years been barber for the foreigners in Peking and has been very helpful to the church both spiritually and financially. The deacon who still holds over, the senior deacon, is a prosperous tailor, and Mr. Ament and I, as well as others, have our Chinese clothes made by him. . . .

On my return to Peking [from the village of Shun I Hsien] I found that Mr. Ament was dealing with a case of persecution.[2] You will remember that Dr. Murdock has been carrying on work at a village six miles outside of the city, being there to dispense medicine and hold meetings every ten days. This village is the home of our tailor-deacon, Mr. Kus. As a result of the work of Dr. Murdock, several inquirers have been gained there, and a few have joined the church. The leader among these is a poor man, whose business in the winter is collecting kindling, for his own use and for sale. One night his stock of kindling, worth over fifteen dollars (a large sum for a poor Chinese) was burned, and he was also warned that if he did not move out of town within ten days his house would be burned. The case was reported to Dr. Ament. He went immediately to see the proper official, and the result was that before the ten days were half gone, the two men who made the threat were in jail, and there was evidence in hand sufficient to convict one of them of the burning of the pile of kindling. The official seems disposed to push the case, and these men are not likely soon to be free, in spite of the efforts of a large number of friends.

Another favorite way of persecuting Christians is to forbid their getting water from the village well. That has been threatened in one of the villages near Shun I Hsien, but has not been carried out. . . .

In the villages near Cho Chow where there are Christians, on account of persecution, the head man of the district has posted notices forbidding such performances and declaring the Christians free from temple taxes.[3] Similar notices may soon be required in the Shun I Hsien district.

[1]Mr. Harlin P. Beach was a teacher at the North China College in Tungchow.

[2]Cases of Christian persecution, real or imagined, were often a bone of contention between Chinese authorities on one hand and foreign missionaries and their diplomatic representatives on the other.

[3]Temple taxes were paid by all villagers to support the local Buddhist temples and were considered a community obligation.

Charles to Judson Smith, January 22, 1898, Peking

Dear Dr. Smith:

The [American Board] Press is of no great advantage to members of the Mission, as they can get their work done elsewhere more satisfactorily, and more cheaply at least, so I understand. The Press has been of benefit to the Mission and to Mission work in general, but the same work that it does can be done elsewhere, at no greater expense. And all these years the Press has required the oversight of a missionary, and so has been a financial burden. In the future, if a special manager be continued, his salary can probably never be paid from Press earnings, and if a preaching missionary has charge he will lose more to the Mission by neglect of other work than he will gain by oversight of the Press. . . .

I want now to give a brief résumé of the work in [the Peking station's] . . . various parts.

Cho Chow. This is our longest established outstation. For several years its growth has been most encouraging. The list of members there at the present time will be something like a hundred. At the time of my trip there in December [1897], one very pleasant feature was the coming of whole families to the Sunday service. Early in the year, Mr. Ament baptized ten new members at Cho Chow, and in December I received five more into fellowship. . . . The helper is a man of nearly forty, a bachelor, very pleasing and winning in his manner, [who] . . . is to be married to a widow, whose father is a church member, as her first husband also was. She herself is not a church member, on the account of the objection (so I am told) of her mother-in-law (a personage whose authority in the Chinese home is almost unlimited, who often outdoes the mother-in-law of the newspaper paragraphers), but she has a good temper—a Chinese woman is a terror if she hasn't, and is a good housekeeper. The chapel property at Cho Chow is very serviceable, neither too large nor too small for the requirements of the work, and I am happy to say, the Board owns it free of debt.

Nan Meng. This is an unwalled market town. Our property there is leased for ten years, Miss Russell having secured it in 1895 for a very reasonable sum, the money being a special gift. The native helper, Mr. Hung, is the only ordained helper in connection with the Peking work. . . . it is hard for him to be so isolated from helpful fellowship, nearly sixty miles distant from Peking, and about equally distant from Tientsin and Paoting. He has a promising field of labor, there being little opposition and numerous inquirers, yet the number of additions to church membership is few.

Pai Mu Chiao.[1] This field is still further away than Nan Meng, beyond it to the south. I have not been there for more than a year, and when I was there, I considered the church to be in such a condition that effort there would be wasted, until the Spirit shall move. . . . There can be no expectation of winning "outsiders" while the "insiders" are hostile to the spirit of the humble and loving Master.

Wen An [Hsien]. This place is still to the south of Pai Mu Chiao. At neither of the two places is there a chapel or a helper, but both are under the oversight of Pastor Hung at Nan Meng. The church members in and about Wen An are few, but some of them make us happy in their faithfulness, in spite of opposition from relatives and far from Christian fellowship and counsel.

Liang Hsiang Hsien. This city is twenty-five miles south-west of Peking, half way to Cho Chow on the direct road. There are no church members in the city. . . . We have a nice chapel property, purchased and fitted up in '96, it is on the main street of the city in an excellent location. We have not as yet been able to place a good helper there; to make up for this lack, I have two men there; one is well educated in the classics, but old and not energetic enough nor well enough versed in Christian truth. The other is young, not able, and not satisfactory. Probably I can make a change there before summer, then we may hope, not merely to open the chapel, but to win a hearing for the gospel.

Pu An Tun. This is a village south-east of the city of Liang Hsiang [Hsien]. There are numerous church members, but they are most of them back-sliders. So I fear, for I have not given the place the personal attention that I should like. . . . I have the lease of a building there, with several years yet to run, and when it runs out, the place reverts to an orphan boy whom I am supporting.

Shun I Hsien. At this city twenty miles northeast of Peking church affairs are at an interesting stage. The helper who had been there for some years didn't seem to be entirely satisfactory, and so I called him in to be my personal teacher. For the summer [of 1897] I stationed there a young Manchu who has been very earnest, endured persecution, and finally asked for the opportunity of becoming a teacher. He was in the midst of the two years "short-cut" course in the seminary [at Tungchow], and so was placed at Shun I Hsien only for the summer. He did earnest work, but failing to control his temper, his success was not unmarred. He had also the idea that he did not want to receive pay from the mission money, but I found that his idea was one of reciprocity: he would work for the church for no salary, but the church was to support him. . . . On Friday, January 14, I went to Shun I Hsien, on Saturday I bought new chapel premises, on Sunday I received six new members into the church, [and] on Monday I returned home. . . . The place I have secured has cost us about two hundred dollars, which means only a bit over five years' rent. The money for this new purchase has already been given in small part by a special gift from home of twenty-five dollars. . . .

Ping Targrh. This is a village only a few miles from the eastern [Chi Hua] gate of Peking and does not really count as an out-station. One of the deacons of the south church has his home there, and Dr. Murdoch has been there regularly to dispense medicine. . . .

North Church [Chapel], Peking. The helper [Jên] who has been here for some years still continues his faithful and efficient work. He, with the help of the chapel-keeper and two or three church members, preaches daily to those who attend the street chapel. He also has charge of Sunday preaching. . . . We hope to call a council to ordain him in May. . . .

The school [at North Church] has had a new teacher since last May, a young man that graduated from college, and has done finely. . . . The school is one of the very best of its kind in the Mission. Many of the heathen boys become saturated with Christian truth, some of them join the church, and some bring their parents. . . .

After the ordination [in May] it is proposed that the North Church with the assistance of the larger South Church, shall assume the support of the pastor. . . .

South Church [Chapel], Peking. This is our home church, and it receives more care from the missionaries than any other part of the work. . . . it is the largest, grows the most rapidly, has the fullest development of Christian and Church activity, and gives the largest contributions. During the past year the native membership has contributed one thousand Peking taels, which means over fifty dollars gold. With the help of the foreigners they have supported the country pastors and a boys' day school. . . . The girls at the Bridgman school give great help and encouragement, by their constant attendance, their attentiveness and reverence, and their earnest and tuneful singing. . . . Street chapel preaching has never been kept up more faithfully, . . . [however] the additions to the Church [membership] have not been as many, but there are numerous hopeful inquirers and probationers. The day school is in charge of an elderly man, without training in any Western studies, and too easy with the boys. . . . Here at Peking, we feel our need is for workers [not just money], native and foreign, fitted for the work, and fully consecrated.

[1]Pai Mu Chiao is about sixty miles south of Peking.

Charles to Edward and Ellen Ewing, February 1898, Peking

Dear Father and Mother:

The American Bible Society has a book store next to our street chapel and a few days ago a man came to them with a written order so worded that there can be no doubt it was from the Emperor, as the messenger himself admitted. It was an order for 160 books, many of them books of Western science and learning, but 30 of them distinctly Christian. This was an unexpected order, and it strengthens the faith and makes glad the hearts of our church members, who have been praying so earnestly for the blessing of God on the Emperor. Last week the same messenger came again, saying that he wanted copies of all Christian books that have been printed. The next day we selected from our Mission book room 400 volumes of 73 different books, to fill this order so far as we are able. These books are probably not for the Emperor, but for those influential men who live in the palace, the Emperor's personal suite. At least, so I suppose, and I am further inclined to the opinion that these men, learning of the Emperor's new departure now venture for the first time to examine Christian books. Whatever it means, we take it as a cause for great thanksgiving and praise.[1]

The Russians want control of Chinese railways and Chinese customs. They have already ousted the man in charge of Korean customs, and now they want to put out Sir Robert Hart here in Peking. But Britain would have something to say, and the British minister, Sir Claude MacDonald,[2] seems to be a strong man. Some say the way to be sure of one's point with China is to bully her; whatever we may think of John Bull as a bully, he doesn't come up to the brazen assurance and overbearing demands of the young Emperor of Germany [Wilhelm II] who wants to be Almighty with a big A.

Sir Robert Hart is one of the features of Peking. He is a man of wide knowledge of men and affairs, of great practical wisdom, bright and kindly. He is interested in everyone; he gives a Christmas tree every year for the foreign children, whom he rejoices to make happy with the most overwhelming number of gifts, but he has no use for children under five years.

[1]This book purchase may have been a forerunner of the One Hundred Day period in 1898 when the Emperor Kuang Hsu was under the influence of Kang Yu-wei and other officials who wished to reform China.

[2]MacDonald has been described by Peter Fleming in *The Siege of Peking* (New York: Harper, 1959) as a "tall, thin, canny, man of forty-eight, with a Highlander's narrow head, Ouidan moustaches, and serious, faintly censorious eyes" (p. 15).

Bessie to Myra Smith, March 1898, Peking

My Dear Aunt Myra:

Henry [Charles' brother] is going to put up a summer cottage, as the Board is not providing them anymore. An association of many foreigners has been formed and a tract of land bought on the shore at Pei-chih-li. Mr. Stanley [of the American Board] is one of the charter members of this association.[1]

[1]This association resulted in the beach resort of Peitaiho, which, like the Western Hills, was a summer resort for foreigners.

Charles to Edward and Ellen Ewing, March 1898, Peking

Dear Father and Mother:

We [Charles and Mr. George D. Wilder of the American Board] had to cross some flooded land and stopped in a city [outside Peking] where the surrounding farm lands have been overflowed for twenty-five years. Because the crops were good then [1897], one of our church members had sufficient income to carry out a plan that he had cherished for some years. His plan was to put up a small building, next to his own house, that might be used by the missionary or by the native preacher on his visits in that locality. A neighbor promised to sell him the land and he purchased material. But others, when they heard that the property was to be used by the Christian church, prevented the sale and burned the wood that he had bought. At our visit we saw the district official and asked for his authority to be used to insure the purchase, as planned. Altho he promised, we found a few days later that the opposers have beaten our church member and refused to let him build in peace. Another letter from us, insisting on punishment and future protection was also ignored, so we are appealing to his superior in Peking, as such protection is guaranteed in the U.S. treaty with China.[1]

[1]According to the government of China, protection for Chinese converts was not guaranteed. According to the Western powers, however, including the United States, the converts were protected by the treaties signed in 1858 and 1860.

Charles to the Ewing Family, April 1898, Peking

Dear Ewing Family:[1]

We have entertained a deputation from the [American] Board, the first representatives to inspect its work in China during the 68 years since it was begun. . . . They had only a day or two in any one place [because of the problems of travel] . . . Dr. [Judson] Smith, Board Secretary, always appeared at meals with a spotless white collar [in spite of a Gobi Desert dust storm]. . . . With these visitors I had my first experience of translating for a foreigner.

[1]Both Charles and Bessie wrote letters with the salutation "Dear Ewing Family." Such letters were intended to be distributed to all members of the Ewing family even though they were mailed to Charles's mother and father.

Charles to Dr. C. H. Daniels, Assistant Secretary of the American Board in Boston, April 15, 1898, Peking

Dear Dr. Daniels:

Perhaps I have previously written about the emperor's order for Christian and scientific books. As these were not in stock in Peking—some of them—the order had to be forwarded to Shanghai. His majesty was not pleased at being thus put off, and thought that he was being deceived by attendants who did not wish him to see such books. He accordingly had these men beaten, and when they next came to the book store, they were in mortal terror lest they should be beheaded if they could not take the books back with them. At least that was the story they told. To appease the emperor, they took with them a large number of Christian books that were on hand here. Very fortunately the Shanghai order arrived a day or two later. The palace eunuch who was sent to buy the books in the first place has attended church twice, once at each of our two chapels.

Charles to Edward and Ellen Ewing, May 1898, Peking

Dear Father and Mother:

Calling again on the man who was persecuted because he wanted to build a house for the church [see March 1898 letter], I found that his attackers have been punished and men in the village have guaranteed future good behavior. So the land has been purchased that was formerly refused, the church member has deeded it to the American Board, and the deed was given to me.[1]

[1]The letters of March and May 1898 not only indicate an anti-Christian attitude in a rural area of Chihli province but also the ability of the local authorities to find solutions to problems arising from that attitude.

Charles to Judson Smith, September 12, 1898, Western Hills

Dear Dr. Smith:

The weather here at the Hills, with the sky clouded over for several days in succession, has become quite cool and a bit raw, and as we have no fire, we shall be glad to go into the city again. But Peking is anything but a health resort at the present time. You will remember that when you were with us [in the spring of 1898] the long months without rain had left the great plain, both in the city and outside, deep with dust, and that a moderate breeze was enough to make cleanliness next to impossible. Well, after the rains came on, the inches of dust were changed to inches of mud. In the country the ditch-roads became running streams of yellow water, which flowed away into the rivers and left instead black stagnant pools to be stirred up by every passing cart, so that for a long time the only dry roads were the smaller paths not sunk in ditches.

In the city the effects of these summer rains are fully as serious as outside, because the water can not run off as readily. During the progress of the storm the water rushes out of the city gates to seek the moat without, but when the rain ceases, it appears that the roadway through the gates is too high to carry off the great masses of water inside the walls. This water must stand until the ground, already well soaked, can receive it, or until it evaporates. Often another rain comes before there is any respite in either of these ways. You will recollect that in Peking the streets are raised, and the result is that, while the roadway itself is deep with mud, the standing water is relegated to the ditches on both sides or to the courts and compounds. Such are the health conditions of Peking through the summer, and it is in such a city that those live who remain there through the hot rainy season. The heat is not intolerable, but the dampness breeds disease.[1]

. . . [T]he special topic of interest here just now is the opening this autumn of the Hall of Great Learning, the new Imperial University, of which Rev. W. A. P. Martin, D.D., L.L.D. is to be the president.[2] He has received from the emperor a red button, denoting the second rank, and the plans of the university have been revised in accordance with his advice. It is encouraging that this new school, the first of its kind, should have as its first president a man so widely known, both in China and the West, as a man of large intellectual ability, of broad sympathy, and of untarnished Christian character—a man who has himself been engaged in missionary work, has devoted many years already to the education of the Chinese, has done a marvelous work in Chinese literature, and has brought the ideas of Christendom and of Christianity to the attention of many Chinese literati. He has had much to say concerning the management of the new university: for one thing, there are to be no Sunday sessions—a great triumph for the Christian Sabbath. Dr. Martin has endeavored to select Christian men to be professors and instructors, so that while there will of course be no Christian instruction, the Christian character of the members of the faculty must be manifest in many ways. The imperial plan is that eventually each province shall have such a university, but the first is to be in Peking.

There is of course much opposition to the innovations, and much doubt as to the wisdom and the outcome thereof, but for the present this opposition and criticism is much quieter than would naturally be anticipated.

Another topic of much general interest is the proposed visit of the emperor to Tientsin early in November. He has never been to Tientsin, and the expedition is to be by way of the new railway. It is to be hoped that nothing will occur to interfere with the plans, and may we not also hope . . . that this will be one step more toward the casting off of imperial invisibility.[3]

[1]Malaria-bearing mosquitoes are what the dampness bred.

[2]Dr. William Alexander Parsons Martin was an American who had come to China as a missionary, mastered mandarin Chinese, translated a number of scholarly works into that language, and in 1898 taught at Peking University. His written work includes *The Siege in Peking: China Against the World* (New York: Fleming H. Revell, 1900) and *The Awakening of China* (New York: Doubleday, 1910).

[3]Something did occur to prevent the emperor's trip to Tientsin and the development of the Imperial University. On September 21 the emperor was seized by his aunt, the Dowager Empress Tzu Hsi, and imprisoned.

Bessie to Myra Smith, September 1898, Peking

My Dear Aunt Myra:

You have doubtless heard all the rumors that are current here. The young Emperor's plans for reform offended the Empress Dowager, she has made him a prisoner in a palace on a small island, and she continues to rule.[1]

[1]While keeping the emperor prisoner, the Empress Tzu Hsi reestablished herself as regent.

Charles to Edward and Ellen Ewing, October 1898, Peking

Dear Father and Mother:

You will perhaps have been somewhat worried at the news of anti-foreign feeling and disturbances in Peking. It is true that several foreigners, on their way from the railroad station [at Machiapu], passing through the most excitable part of the city, were attacked, mud and stones and bricks being thrown. Members of the British and Japanese legations were thus attacked, but no injury was done, except in the case of Rev. Mr. [George] Lowry of the Methodist Mission, who had one rib broken and was considerably bruised. The government was slow to punish the offenders but we felt sure that they would protect all foreigners properly and this proved to be true. Extra police force was stationed in the troubled area, a soldier guard was sent to the sections where foreigners lived (until they learned that we would rather not have them), placards were posted enjoining proper treatment, and lastly, came an imperial edict, in the name of the Empress Dowager, proclaiming that foreigners were to be protected as hitherto. But as anti-progressive edicts keep coming out day after day, the Chinese in general doubt the permanency of foreign residence in Peking. The native Christians are really standing the brunt of the persecution: outsiders point to them and say, "Soon, soon, your time is coming soon," or, "You will soon gain the happiness of heaven, of which you talk." What is to happen is surely unknown. . . . It did seem as tho China was waking up, but just now it is as if the light had dazed her eyes and caused her to shut them suddenly. If she refuses to wake up, there will be disaster of some kind, but we here consider she is too nearly wide awake already to get to sleep again. China is bound to come out into the wide awake life of the twentieth century, and if the present Manchu dynasty interferes, so much the worse for the dynasty, and for the Manchus in general.

Charles to Ellen Ewing, November 1898, Peking

My Dear Mother:

For a month thieves have been coming frequently within the bounds of our property. The police will do nothing, the head of the system says nothing can be done unless the American Minister sends a complaint thru the Foreign Office [Tsungli Yamen], and rumor says that the Empress Dowager has given notice that officials are not to incur the ill-will of the people, and especially the dangerous classes.

Charles to Judson Smith, November 26, 1898, Peking

Dear Dr. Smith:

Dr. Ament started early this morning for Cho Chow, planning to go part of the way by rail, thus reaching there this afternoon, in less than half the time it used to require by cart. . . .

There has been little in my own life and work for the last month that is worthy of record. Mrs. Ewing, after some fever which resulted in an early weaning of the baby, is feeling thoroughly herself again.[1] In spite of considerable sickness since she has been in China, and especially during the past year, when she had a prolonged tho not very serious siege with pleurisy, I think it is fair to say that on the whole her health has not deteriorated noticeably in these four years. The baby prospers and promises well, tho she does not grow heavy very rapidly. Marion, who is now 3½ years old, seems to be in the most vigorous and hearty condition that she has ever been. She has never been a sickly child, but now she is growing strong, more lively as the days go by, and is increasing somewhat in weight too.

My own health is good at present, but I seem to have lost, to a large extent, the mental vigor and exuberance in which I used to rejoice, so that I no longer feel capable of doing my best work, except by a special effort. This is probably the result, in part, of living and working in a land to whose atmosphere, customs, and people I have not been accustomed to from early days, but probably the principal reason is that I have been injudicious in the matter of working and resting, so that if I take a good vacation next summer instead of trying to keep at work, I will be all right again. Please excuse me for having said so much about myself, I did not intend to this time. . . .

Thursday was Thanksgiving day for Americans, even out here in China. The new American Minister [Edwin H. Conger] and his wife [Sarah Pike Conger] continued the custom of the Denbys[2] by inviting the Americans to Thanksgiving preaching and Thanksgiving dinner. I understand that there were about sixty present. Mrs. Ewing and I did not go, as we hardly cared to leave the baby for as long as would be necessary. . . .

The teacher of the North Chapel day school was married to one of the Bridgman School girls. Of the young man I have written something before this. He came from one of our out-stations, and was sent to Tungchow to study, some years before Dr. [Henry] Blodget left [the college]. He had certain peculiarities of disposition which led him to be on less cordial terms with the missionaries than most of the students are. For one thing, he had an exaggerated idea of independence, financial and otherwise, commendable in certain particulars only, and leading him to be "offish" in his attitude toward the foreigners. Perhaps if anyone had been able to divine the best way of dealing with him, he might have been somewhat different, but probably it was one of those cases that just has to run itself [sic] out. The effect, however, was such that when he graduated from North China College in the class of '97 he did not care to take the theological course, preferring to study medicine, but as there was no opportunity for pursuing a medical course then, he became teacher of the North Chapel day school, and he has continued there because the way has not yet opened for the study [of medicine]. . . . And now with no prospect of such an opening, he concluded that the time was ripe for him to be married. He was advised that in the West young men wait until they have earned the money to pay the expenses of the occasion, but he prepared to borrow the money and go ahead. He managed the affair with more than the usual expenses of such occasions, and it passed off very pleasantly. The young lady was one to whom, according to a frequent Chinese custom, he had been betrothed since they were both children. As her parents are not living, and she had only an old uncle to depend on, the mother of the young man, again following a frequent custom here in China, has taken her future daughter-in-law to live in her own home, in anticipation of the time when she would properly be under the constant oversight and authority of her mother-in-law. But the girl has been for several years a student in the Bridgman School. She is one of the prettiest of the girls, and one of the best singers. Now that they are married she is to be the teacher in the Emily Ament Memorial School, on Fifth Street. Since the summer vacation this school has been in need of a teacher. . . .

As to the wedding itself—well, I have written, and others have written, about Chinese weddings. At the risk of repetition I want to call attention to certain features of the affair. . . . Now, the wedding invitations had noted the day when the affair was to take place, but with no intimation as to the hour; and as the Tungchow ladies [who were friends of the groom], were anxious to start for home as early as possible, we sent to inquire at what hour the ceremony would take place. The answer came back: at eight A.M. the bride will enter the red chair, at nine the ceremony will be performed. Accordingly, we went at nine o'clock to the future home of the young couple. But tho we were a little late, the chair had not even gone to fetch the bride, but stood in the street beside the gate. This was not encouraging to the ladies who were in a hurry, but it was properly to be expected here in China, where men set watches, and not watches men. The woman who was managing the affair, and whose business it was to go to summon the bride, was not to be hurried. In China, at the best, haste is unseemly and indecorous. In America, a gentleman should not run on the street; in China, he should not wish to run. And so, the wedding festivities must proceed in due course. Accordingly, the missionary ladies were invited to partake of the wedding breakfast, which in China usually precedes the marriage, and of which the bride herself has no part. Two or three Chinese women sat to eat with the ladies, and one of them, the manager, could not be hurried, but was bound to take her time. Breakfast over, she seated herself in the bride's red chair and was borne away to summon that young person herself. Meanwhile, the guests inspected the rooms where the young couple were to live. The musicians, one of them a church member, after marching about the yard with the weird fifing, accompanied the sedan chair that went for the bride.

Now the bride had left Bridgman School about a week before to go to the home of friends in the city, not far from her future home. She was a scholar whose spiritual life, formerly not very deep, had received a serious impulse a few months ago, and as she was steadily growing in Christian character and in self-control, the ladies in charge of the school were sorry to lose her so soon. Both she and the young man whom she married have been commending themselves to us by their lives in the year that is past, so that we have good hopes that they will prove very helpful to the church life and work. . . .

At about 10:30, the bride arrived, hidden inside the red chair, and with her came the managing woman and her assistant, both church members, and the North Chapel pastor and his family. Soon after we were called to witness the ceremony. Under the blue cotton canopy that covered the little yard, a piece of red felt was spread on the ground, and on this the bride and groom stood. Beside the bride were the two women who had come with her, for in China it would not be proper for a bridesmaid to stand thus before the public gaze; while the groom was accompanied by two young men, one of them a college classmate, the other a neighbor. Instead of joining hands—another thing that would be improper here in China—each of the parties most interested held one end of a red cord while the native pastor conducted the marriage service. As usual, it was very hard to get any answers to the questions put the bride and groom; one reason is that it is foreign to Chinese custom for the two to speak, especially the bride; again they subject themselves to ridicule if they promise to love. And so we have sometimes to be satisfied with a mere nod of the head, and can seldom hear more than a whispered "yes."

The ceremony over, congratulations were in order. The bride, accompanied by the women folks, entered her new home, while those of the men who had not eaten before were invited to sit at the tables spread attractively with Chinese food. After satisfying myself, I went home, bidding the groom a courteous farewell. But some of the young men, especially fellow students from Tungchow, remained to pester the bride with the usual teasing. She is compelled to sit on the bedstead-platform, and neither smile nor speak, while the young men—a species of creature from who she has for years been sedulously kept separate, torment her and tempt her to break her sober silence, jesting, singing, asking questions, and every way making the best of their opportunity. On this occasion all their attempts were unsuccessful, and finally calling on her to pour them each a cup of tea, they made their truce. . . .

At the close of the committee meeting [of the North China Tract Society[3]] I hurried to . . . attend a meeting of the Peking Oriental Society, held at the American Legation. Sir Claude MacDonald, British Minister, is president of the society; Baron Arthur Von Rosthorn,[4] secretary; and Dr. [W. A. P.] Martin, the moving spirit. At the meeting I attended, Dr. [Devello Z.] Sheffield [from the North China College at Tungchow] exhibited and explained his Chinese typewriter, the first machine of the kind, and already quite famous. Dr. Sheffield gave some account of his experiences leading up to the construction of the perfected instrument, told something of its mechanism and capabilities, and showed its practical working by writing a short passage from the Sermon on the Mount and another from [the Chinese philosopher] Mencius at a rate twice as rapid as a Chinese teacher could be expected to attain. The typewriter was pronounced a success, all that had heard of it were glad to see it, and Dr. Sheffield himself was very glad of the opportunity to present it before such a gathering.

[We had a meeting] . . . at the house of Dr. Curwen of the London Mission.[5] Dr. Curwen's sister has given fifty copies of the English Congregational Hymn book for the use of the Peking Union Service;[6] and Dr. and Mrs. Curwen invited the foreigners to their house twice to rehearsals to familiarize us with the hymns and tunes in the new book. . . . Mr. Bondfield of Shanghai, the agent of the British and Foreign Bible Society for China, was present and was asked to speak briefly concerning his work. He sees much to encourage him and all of us. Up to four years ago, the average annual sales of his society's books (Bibles and portions [*sic*]) were 250,000, the highest point reached being 290,000. During the first ten months of the present calendar year, the sales were 795,000, and the prospects are that by the end of December this number will rise to one million, while the issues for the year will be a million and a quarter. Furthermore, it was evident from other things that he said that he is very careful in filling orders, not to overdo the matter for the sake of making a good show or for any other reason. For instance, he said that if an order comes for ten thousand books, he sends two thousand, taking it for granted that the missionary who orders is not aware how large in amount ten thousand books would look if he were to receive them, and besides, Mr. Bondfield considers it unwise ever to furnish a stock of Bibles which is not likely to be sold out within seven or eight months.

Speaking of Bible societies, you of course know that the American Bible Society's China agent has already been to the Philippines to open work there. The Peking agent of the society now lives in our [American Board] compound, renting the little house where Miss Russell once lived. He and his wife make a pleasant addition to our little community, and she assists in the woman's work of the station.

The North China Tract Society has had . . . experience, as you know, somewhat beyond that of the British and Foreign Bible Society. The sales in the past two or three years far exceeding anything previously, and the demand exceeding the supply. Even the recent troublous times have not made themselves felt very noticeably—tho it may still be a little early to speak with certainty. In the matter of the sale of Christian books, there has been and is large cause for encouragement. And the same may be said concerning other forms of missionary effort. Even our own work shows it. Of course there are cases now and again where we are grievously disappointed in some one or other of our native Christians, sometimes those whom we have trusted most. But I could offset every case with a case of marked progress in the Christian work and of growth in character, and there would still remain . . . the general improvement that is constantly going on in the church as a whole.

[1]A second daughter, Ellen, was born to the Ewings on November 10, 1898.
[2]Mr. and Mrs. Charles Denby were in Peking from 1885 to 1898, where he was the chief United States diplomatic representative to the Chinese government.

³The North China Tract Society was an American Board organization engaged in the printing and distribution of religious material in the Chinese language.

⁴Baron Arthur von Rosthorn was a member of the Austrian diplomatic mission to China.

⁵The London Mission was a missionary society in China that was made up primarily of British Congregationalists.

⁶The Peking Union Service was an English-language service conducted in Peking through the participation of a number of Protestant denominations.

2

The Boxer Uprising
and Subsequent Manchu Reform Efforts
1899–1904

A NEW world power had arrived at China's doorstep in the summer of 1898. That summer the United States had in just a few months defeated the Spanish in the Philippines and the island archipelago was about to be militarily subjugated. America, occupied with its new imperial possession, had not engaged in the China land grab of 1898, and its interests in China remained the same: commercial activities and the Protestant missions. However, in September 1899, Secretary of State John Hay circulated diplomatic notes to the various nations involved in China. These notes called for the safeguarding of the Open Door in China.

By the Open Door, Hay essentially meant the ability of all commercial and missionary interests to exist in China and not to have anyone excluded from a foreign-dominated zone, although Hay admitted that spheres of influence might exist. Critics of Hay's notes argue that they had not even been discussed with the Chinese and were only intended to protect America's interests and to make a claim for a stake if China were to be split up. Others have argued to the contrary that Hay's Open Door called for a self-governing China, and that it was a forceful restatement of the time-tested British policy of free competition in a unified and independent China. Britain supported Hay, and by such action indicated British desire to keep to its traditional policy in China.

Following the European land grabs of 1898 a large number of Chinese troops had been concentrated in the vicinity of Peking. Such a force was unusual, as the throne had long feared the presence of too many soldiers close to it. While the army units were well placed and numerous, they remained largely provincial militia and acted upon the whims of their commanders. Elements of the army were foreign trained and modernized but it was not yet a unified national army. As a modern historian has written, Chinese armies had "poor leadership, lack of training, a wide variety of weapons, and those persistent evils, corruption and inadequate pay."[1]

In addition to the acts to strengthen the Chinese army in the vicinity of Peking, the Dowager Empress had appointed the antiforeign traditionalist, Prince Tuan, to lead her government. Tuan was a member of the Manchu royal family and a first cousin of the emperor, whom he royally despised. Furthermore, Tuan was married to a niece of the Dowager Empress. Late in 1899 the son of Prince Tuan was named by Tzu Hsi as heir apparent to the throne. This highly irregular appointment exacerbated the dynasty's relations with the foreign powers. It appeared to be a defiant act meant to insult the foreigners, who had preferred the reformers during the summer of 1898. The Manchu dynasty was apparently turning its back on the soon-to-be twentieth century of the West.

Others in China were also to turn their backs against the West. In the fall of 1899, Dr. H. S. Porter, a missionary with the American Board in Pang Chuan near where the Grand Canal crosses from Shantung into Chihli, had written about a secret society which he called Spirit Boxers. He reported that in western Shantung the Boxers were "a company of young fellows who have gathered together for wrestling and general gymnastics, with the underlying purpose of combining against all foreigners within range.[2] In fact, the Chinese name of the society was I Ho Chuan, or the Society of Harmonious Fists. It was in the vicinity of the Shantung-Chihli border where numerous conflicts involving Christian converts and other Chinese had first taken place. Although the Boxers' most common slogan of 1898 was Down with the Ching [Manchus], sometime in 1899 the favorite chant changed to Death to the Foreigners.

As the spring of 1900 came to the flat land of Chihli, it brought out large bands of Boxers dressed in special red-ribboned head and arm bands. They quickly moved against Christian converts in the eastern Chihli cities of Hochien, Ichou, and Paoting. Many converts fled, and others were killed by the advancing Boxers. As the seemingly irresistible movement could, or would, not be stopped by local authorities, it acquired many new adherents. By mid-May they were no longer attacking just converts; the railway and telegraph lines around Paoting were also being destroyed. The Boxers soon turned to the destruction of the bridges and stations along the newly constructed railway. By the third week of May, the railway workshops and the station at Paoting, along with its European employees, were under attack.

[1]William J. Duiker, *Cultures in Collision: The Boxer Rebellion* (San Rafael, Calif.: Presidio Press, 1978), 74.
[2]George N. Steiger, *China and the Occident: The Origin and Development of the Boxer Movement* (1927; reprint, New York: Russell and Russell, 1966), 131.

The Europeans fled for safety to Tientsin and Peking. On May 28 the Fengtai station, only six miles from Peking, was destroyed.

It had not taken the Boxers long to get to the gates of Peking. The society's members no doubt had grievances against the Chinese converts and the assistance provided them by the missionaries and foreign diplomats. The Boxers believed the rail and telegraph lines to be devices that took jobs away from laborers. They even blamed the droughts that plagued the region upon the foreigners. The question was whether they could have gotten to the gates of Peking and Tientsin without the special consideration of the Manchu dynasty and the army. That special consideration no doubt came from highly placed members of the Manchu court. Prince Tuan was suspected as the culprit.

When the Boxer movement reached the outskirts of Peking, the eleven diplomatic representatives located there decided to request small detachments of military personnel from their warships in the Gulf of Chihli to guard their legation compounds. There had been a delay in requesting the guards in spite of Monsignor Favier's letter of early May to the French minister, Stephen Pichon, stating that the situation outside Peking had deteriorated badly and asking for a detachment of guards for the Peitang cathedral in Peking. Pichon, a small rotund man with somewhat pompous ways, had delayed the request in order to act in concert with his diplomatic colleagues. The British minister, Sir Claude MacDonald, had been reluctant to request marines or sailors, as his instructions from London were to keep the situation in perspective and under control. Britain was then involved in the Boer War in southern Africa and wanted no additional military conflicts. MacDonald had served in the British army in Egypt and Africa and was inclined to view the Boxers with condescension.

Other ministers had also agreed to delay their requests for legation guards. Among them was the American minister, Edwin Conger. Conger, a Civil War veteran, midwestern politician and former congressman, held his post in Peking because of his political connections with President William McKinley. After little more than a year in China, the fifty-seven-year-old Major Conger tended to follow the direction charted by the more experienced British diplomat.

When the request for the guards did go to the various fleet units, they responded in unison and quickly. On May 31 a force of marines and sailors representing eight nations[3] set out from Tientsin and reached Peking that same day. They traveled by train, as the line between the coast and the

[3]The eight nations that sent guards to Peking were Austria, France, Germany, Great Britain, Italy, Japan, Russia, and the United States. The legations of Belgium, Netherlands, and Spain had no guards.

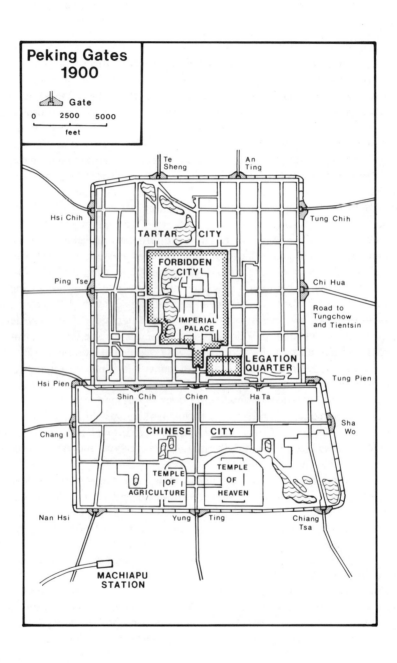

Peking Gates 1900

Gate

0   2500   5000
feet

Te Sheng

An Ting

Hsi Chih

Tung Chih

TARTAR   CITY

FORBIDDEN CITY

Ping Tse

Chi Hua

Road to Tungchow and Tientsin

IMPERIAL PALACE

LEGATION QUARTER

Hsi Pien

Tung Pien

Shin Chih   Chien   Ha Ta

Chang I

CHINESE   CITY

Sha Wo

TEMPLE OF AGRICULTURE

TEMPLE OF HEAVEN

Nan Hsi

Yung   Ting

Chiang Tsa

MACHIAPU STATION

capital remained open despite the burning of the Fengtai station. A few days later the guards were reinforced, bringing their total to over 400 men. The number of legation guards and their movement to Peking had been agreed to by the Manchu authorities. They considered the foreign marines insufficient in numbers to pose a threat to the Forbidden City but enough to protect the legations under normal conditions. But normal conditions were not to prevail.

On June 4, a party of Methodist missionaries, in Peking for a church conference, left by train and arrived safely in Tientsin despite large numbers of Boxers and Chinese soldiers gathered along the tracks. That train was the last to move between the two cities for more than three months. At about the same time Peking's missionary community learned of a massacre of converts near Tungchow. By June 8, Minister Conger felt it necessary to instruct all American missionaries for their safety to go to the Methodist compound near the Ha Ta Gate. That compound was large and less than a mile from the American legation.

As it was rapidly becoming apparent that Peking's foreign community was being cut off from the outside world, the diplomats sent a message asking for additional legation guards. On the fifteen foreign warships anchored off Taku Bar in the Gulf of Chihli, the senior officer was Britain's China Fleet commander, Admiral Sir Edward Seymour. Seymour quickly agreed to lead an international force of additional marines and sailors to Peking. The governor of Chihli, Yu Lu, gave his permission for Seymour's force to proceed by rail to Peking. By June 12, Seymour was at Yangtsun, some thirty miles from Tientsin, with four trains and about 2,100 men.[4] That day the trains moved toward Peking, only fifty-five miles away, but they soon found that the Boxers had torn up the double tracks.

With the telegraph line cut, the communication back to Tientsin was precarious; to Peking it was nonexistent. On June 14 the Boxers attacked the trains as the marines tried to repair the tracks. Although the Boxers sustained heavy casualties, they impressed the foreign marines with their courage and willingness to die. Admiral Seymour soon realized his supplies were running short, and he could not possibly fight through to Peking. He had to retreat to Tientsin before his force was trapped and annihilated. Seymour's relief force for Peking's legations had not only failed to reach its objective but, as a "show of force," had aroused the countryside and created a situation in which the enemies of the West in the Manchu court saw another example of how the Boxers could work to their advantage.

[4]Arthur H. Smith, *China in Convulsion* (New York: F. H. Revell, 1901), 439, lists Seymour as having 915 British, 450 Germans, 312 Russians, 158 French, 112 Americans, 54 Japanese, 40 Italians, and 25 Austrians.

While Admiral Seymour and his marines were under attack halfway between Peking and Tientsin, the Boxers were busy elsewhere. By June 14 they had entered the walled cities of Peking and Tientsin without resistance. The Boxers immediately began ransacking and burning property belonging to the missionaries and to Chinese converts. In Tientsin the Catholic cathedral was put to the torch. However, the foreign concessions bordering the Pei Ho River and outside the walls of the Chinese city were not immediately attacked. Those concessions, about a mile in length and only several hundred yards wide, were unwalled and vulnerable to attack. Fewer than 400 armed men protected them. The foreign inhabitants' fear that the concessions would be overrun by the Boxers was greatly lessened when 1,700 Russian soldiers from Port Arthur reached Tientsin on June 15.

The Boxers who had entered Peking's Tartar City not only burned the Tungtang (East) and Nantang (South) cathedrals but had trapped inside the Nantang several hundred Chinese converts, who died in the flames. Of the Catholic cathedrals in Peking, only the Peitang (North) survived the first night. The fortresslike Peitang, together with its compound, was guarded by both Monsignor Favier and his followers and a detachment of French and Italian marines.

The Protestant missionary facilities received the same treatment given the two Catholic churches. The Boxers and their accomplices burned and looted 34 houses, 18 chapels, 23 schools, and 19 dispensaries. Only the Methodist compound, where all the Protestants had taken refuge, was spared. It was, fortunately, guarded by a detachment of American marines. During the daylight hours of June 14, teams of marines and armed civilians went out beyond the legations and brought back with them into the Legation Quarter several hundred Chinese converts whose lives were in danger. A number of Boxers who were marauding near the legations were shot and killed.

The sixteenth of June was a day of decision for both the Manchu court and the foreign fleet in the Gulf of Chihli. The court issued a decree calling for the recruitment of the Boxers into the militia and ordering Governor Yu Lu of Chihli to resist all foreign military attacks. Yu Lu was now free to officially order his soldiers to attack the Seymour column even though he had given them permission to entrain for Peking. While the court was ordering its governor of Chihli to stop the foreigners, the officers in the fleet reached a decision to attack the Chinese forts at the mouth of the Pei Ho, which guarded the route to Tientsin. The officers who made that decision had apparently given little consideration to the political situation and had received almost no intelligence information about the size or disposition of Chinese forces between Taku and Tientsin. They did know that Seymour and the marines had been forced to turn back before reaching Peking and that the Chinese city of Tientsin seemed to be in the hands of the Boxers.

On the morning of June 17, nine shallow-draft warships of France, Germany, Great Britain, Japan, and Russia bombarded the Taku forts, which were then occupied by naval landing parties. The gateway to Tientsin was open although insufficient troops prevented the naval forces from advancing. Herbert Hoover, then living in Tientsin with his wife, Lou Henry Hoover,[5] considered the attack upon the forts ill-advised and thoughtless because it further inflamed a delicate situation. Hoover had good reason to believe the attack a foolhardy one since on the afternoon of the seventeenth the first Chinese artillery shells fell upon the foreign concessions in Tientsin. The siege of that settlement, with its 700 civilians (of whom 300 were women and children) and its 2,000 soldiers and marines, had begun.

In Peking the situation on June 17 remained vague. All foreigners were now in one of three locations: the Legation Quarter, the Methodist compound, or the Peitang cathedral. All were defended. Barricades had been put up, walls had been constructed, and entrances had been bricked up. Beyond the legation compounds a kind of neutral area or no-man's-land was established by the marines and their diplomatic leaders. The neutral area included the compound of the Manchu noble, Prince Su, which could best be described as a park with buildings. This park, the Su Wang Fu, or the Fu, became absolutely essential to the defense of the Legation Quarter. Other open areas around the legations were the Imperial Carriage Park, the Mongol Market and the Hanlin Academy. The Hanlin was China's seat of highest learning and home of the more than 11,000 volumes of the Ming Encyclopedia. In addition to the neutral areas, the Legation Quarter was protected on its south side by that part of the massive Tartar Wall between the Chien and Ha Ta gates. Inside an area of approximately 2,500 by 2,100 feet were the seven legations of France, Germany, Great Britain, Japan, Russia, Spain, and the United States. The other four legations were outside the defensible zone and eventually abandoned to the Boxers. In addition to the legations, the secure zone included three banks, two hotels, two general stores, the Russian post office, the International Club, and some offices belonging to the Imperial Maritime Customs. The secure zone did not include the Methodist compound or the Peitang cathedral.

Baron Klemens von Ketteler, the German minister and ex-army officer, had decided to go to the Tsungli Yamen (an office with some of the functions of a foreign ministry) to determine whether the diplomatic notes the legations had received proposing an evacuation of Peking by all foreigners were to be taken seriously or merely as a Chinese ruse. The ministers were

---

[5]The Hoovers were in Tientsin during the summer of 1900 because the future president, then twenty-six and married for one year, was in China to do geological exploration for a British mining company.

split over the proposed evacuation. A major issue was what to do with the Chinese converts now with the foreigners. The missionaries demanded to take them along if the foreigners evacuated Peking. On June 20, together with his interpreter, von Ketteler started off in sedan chairs for the two-mile trip to the Tsungli Yamen. They never reached their destination, as the German minister was shot and killed and the interpreter wounded. Their assailants were Chinese soldiers, and the apparently premeditated attack was instrumental in bringing on the siege that was to last fifty-five days.

On the day that von Ketteler was murdered, the Methodist compound was abandoned on orders from Minister Conger, as he believed that a withdrawal from Peking might be possible. Following the death of von Ketteler, though, the possibility of withdrawal under Chinese auspices had ended. In Peking after June 20 there were two besieged locations approximately two miles apart. In the Legation Quarter there were 362 marines; 473 other foreigners, including 149 women and 79 children; and approximately 2,400 Chinese Christians. The majority of the Chinese were women and children. At the Peitang cathedral there were 45 French and Italian marines; 100 other armed men, including Monsignor Favier and his priests; and over 3,300 converts, including 850 orphans and schoolgirls.

In Tientsin, with the Chinese army providing artillery fire, the Boxers assumed the task of trying to overrun the besieged concessions. Reinforcements for the besieged were sent toward Tientsin in an altogether unmilitary and piecemeal manner. Eventually, after fighting units of the Chinese army and struggling through a North China dust storm, an international relief column of 3,000 men entered the Tientsin concessions on June 23. Herbert Hoover recalled years later that the U.S. Marine buglers were playing "There'll Be a Hot Time in the Old Town Tonight" as they marched down Victoria Boulevard in the British concession.

On the same day that the relief column reached the concessions, Admiral Seymour and his badly mauled but still intact force were located at the Hsiku arsenal, just four miles away. Two days later, and after additional fighting, Seymour's marines and sailors joined with the main international relief force. Of the 2,100 men who had headed out from Tientsin by train only fourteen days earlier, 62 were dead and 238 had been wounded. Sir Edward Seymour, of Her Majesty's Navy, had had more than enough of infantry warfare and wisely returned to his ships in the Gulf of Chihli.

By early July over 14,000 foreign soldiers and marines were in the Tientsin concessions or between there and Taku. However, Chinese artillery continued to lob shells into the concessions, and the old walled city of Tientsin contained thousands of Boxers, as well as units of the Chinese army. The international command decided that before it could go to the relief of the besieged in Peking, it must first drive the Boxers and soldiers

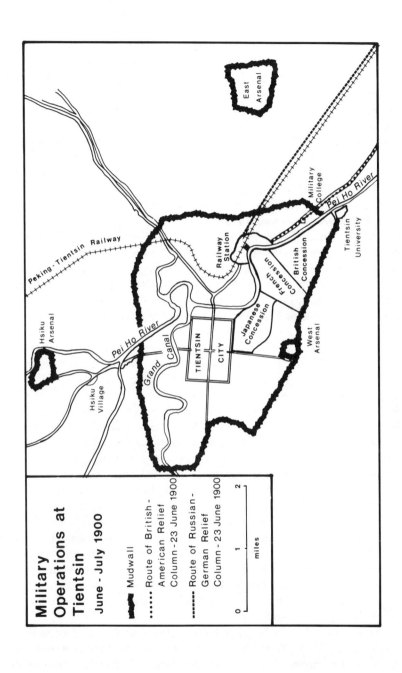

Military
Operations at
Tientsin

June - July 1900

Mudwall
Route of British -
American Relief
Column - 23 June 1900
Route of Russian -
German Relief
Column - 23 June 1900

0   1   2
          miles

East
Arsenal

Military
College

Pel Ho River

Tientsin
University

British
Concession

French
Concession

Railway
Station

Japanese
Concession

West
Arsenal

TIENTSIN
CITY

Grand Canal

Pei Ho River

Peking - Tientsin Railway

Hsiku
Arsenal

Hsiku
Village

out of the old city of Tientsin. On July 13 and 14, units of the Japanese army, Britain's Welsh Fusiliers, the Ninth U.S. Infantry and the First U.S. Marines—a total of 6,000 men—assaulted Tientsin, and the result was the heaviest fighting of the entire Boxer Uprising. More than 800 casualties were reported by the international army as it captured Tientsin. Chinese losses were believed to be equally heavy.

After the fall of Tientsin, the Chinese army and its Boxer auxiliaries retreated up the Pei Ho to Yangtsun. There Governor Yu Lu and his generals reported to the throne that the Boxers were "too wild to be trained,"[6] had pillaged everywhere, had no intention of fighting the foreign soldiers, had vanished during the fighting, and could not be reorganized. The usefulness of the Boxers was beginning to wane.

While combat engulfed Tientsin, the Peking legations were under siege and had lost contact with the outside world. The ministers did not even know the situation at the nearby Peitang cathedral. Between June 20 and July 17, artillery and rifle fire fell almost continuously upon the Legation Quarter, and the Chinese barricades drew an ever tighter ring around it. Heroic efforts were normal for the Legation Quarter's defenders. Special notice went to such individuals as Colonel Shiba and his Japanese marines who defended the Fu; Dr. Francis D. Gamewell, an American engineer turned Methodist missionary, who was largely responsible for the construction of the elaborate defenses of the entire secure zone; George E. Morrison, the Australian correspondent of the *London Times*, who was seriously wounded but continued to provide advice; Herbert Squiers, the American diplomat, who served as Sir Claude MacDonald's chief of staff after the death of the British marine commander; the women missionary doctors who served as both physicians and nurses in the temporary hospital; August Chamont, the Swiss proprietor of the Hotel de Pekin, who helped defend the perimenter, organized provisions for the besieged, and with his wife (born Mary McCarthy in San Francisco) never failed to find bread or champagne for the marines from his never-vacated hotel; and the Fighting Parsons, a group of Protestant missionaries who chose to defend themselves and their families. (Charles Ewing was one of the six Fighting Parsons.) By July 14 the defenders had lost fifty-seven men killed and eighty-seven wounded. The Chinese attackers, who had sustained heavy casualties, had pushed the legation guards out of most of the neutral zone and were at the walls of the legation compounds.

Beginning on July 17, the Manchu authorities allowed a truce at the Legation Quarter. They offered a second chance for the besieged to leave Peking, but the foreigners refused, fearing treachery. The exact motivation for

[6]Chester C. Tan, *The Boxer Catastrophe* (1955; reprint, New York: Octagon Press, 1967), 100.

the truce and the offer to leave Peking are not known, but a number of events may have led to those actions. One was the buildup of the International Relief Force. A second was the fall of Tientsin on July 14. A third event that may have caused the truce was the lack of response the throne had received from the regional viceroys and governors in its request for military assistance. Three men in particular were opposed to the Boxer activities in North China. They were Li Hung-chang, the former viceroy in Tientsin who in 1900 held the same office in Canton; Chang Chih-tung, the all-powerful viceroy in Central China; and Yuan Shih-kai, the governor of Shantung and commander of a well-trained and equipped army. These three men, all Chinese, sent a joint communication to Prince Jung Lu in Peking beseeching him to save the diplomats and others from being massacred.

A fourth event was the throne's awareness of the massacre of missionaries at Taiyuan, the capital of Shansi. There on July 9, thirty-eight Protestant and Catholic missionaries and ten Chinese converts had been beheaded despite the fact that they had been under the protection of the governor, the bitterly anti-Western Manchu nobleman, Yu Hsien. Unfortunately, the killings continued, so that by the end of August a total of 159 Protestant (including 46 children) and 12 Catholic missionaries had been murdered in Shansi province.

A fifth event that may have led to the throne's declaration of a temporary truce was the situation in Manchuria. Early in July the Christian missions in Mukden were sacked and burned and the Russian employees and guards of the South Manchurian Railway were attacked. Russia's response in mid-July was to send its army from Siberia into southern Manchuria to protect the railway and the leased territory at Port Arthur. Moderates at the court, including Jung Lu, must have seen the Russian move as one more calamity befalling the dynasty because of the Boxer outrages.

Notwithstanding the moderates' concerns, Li Ping-heng, who was a close colleague of Shansi's governor Yu Hsien, had been called to Peking to provide guidance and inspiration to Prince Tuan and the reactionary faction at the court. With Li's arrival the truce came to an end on July 27. Artillery and small-arms fire was renewed, and the Chinese barricades were pressed further into the Legation Quarter. During the truce, however, the besieged not only had obtained a respite, but the ministers had been able to send and receive messages from the outside world. They now were aware that a rescue operation would soon be mounted and in time the siege broken.

Preparations for the relief of the besieged in Peking had begun on the day following the successful operation against Tientsin. During the next three weeks the International Relief Force had to deal with more than a thousand sick and wounded who had been incapacitated as a result of the Seymour expedition and the capture of Tientsin. Next they had to await the arrival of additional troops before undertaking the move upon Peking over the hot and dusty lowland of Chihli against the still intact Chinese army.

With the arrival by August 1 of Generals Adna R. Chaffee (American), Sir Alfred Gaselee (British), Nicholas P. Linievitch (Russian), and Moto-omi Yamaguchi (Japanese), the time had come for action. Pushing for immediate action, General Gaselee of the British Indian Army held the day. On August 4 the International Relief Force marched out of Tientsin, headed for Peking. It was to take ten days to march and fight the way to the Imperial city, roughly one hundred miles. The international army followed the Pei Ho River to Tungchow and then went overland to Peking.

It was a polyglot army that left Tientsin under the agreed-to, but not always adhered-to, overall command of General Gaselee. As the campaign progressed, various national units operated more or less on their own initiative. The old Indian fighter and cavalryman, General Chaffee, seemed to enjoy that arrangement. The largest contingent, and about half of the entire Relief Force, was that from Japan. It numbered approximately 10,000 men and contained units who had fought the Chinese in the 1894–1895 war. Next in number, about 4,000, came the white-uniformed Russians from Port Arthur. Gaselee's British and Indians totaled some 3,000 and contained such varied units as Welsh Fusiliers, Sikhs, Bengal Lancers, Rajputs, Punjabis, and the Hong Kong Regiment. The three American regiments, two army and one marine, under Chaffee contained about 2,000 men and had come from the Philippines. The French unit, made up of almost entirely of Indochinese troops under General Henri Victor Frey, numbered 800. A small detachment of German and Italian marines made up the final unit. Each of the large national forces had their own artillery, which together totaled seventy pieces. The total strength of the International Relief Force was about 20,000.[7]

Two military actions of consequence took place during the advance upon Peking. The first was at Peitsang and the second at Yangtsun, where the railroad crossed the river. Both actions were made upon entrenched Chinese positions and were preceded by a desultory artillery barrage and followed by an infantry attack. The Chinese response was to fire a few volleys and then to retreat. The Chinese had lost their spirit to fight, but since all Chinese were believed to be potential Boxers, there was a great deal of indiscriminate killing by the men of the international army. Discipline broke down in the extreme heat, and there were more stragglers eating watermelons than there were advancing infantrymen. Marine Lieutenant Smedley Butler remembered that walking through the ten-feet-high fields of sorghum was

---

[7]Peter Fleming, in *The Siege of Peking* (New York: Harper and Brothers, 1959), 182f, believes that the actual combat strength of the Relief Force was between 16,000 and 17,000 men.

"like walking through a blast furnace. . . . [and being] eaten alive by mosquitos."[8] Between Tientsin and the walled city of Tungchow, which the Relief Force reached on August 12, the generals received a message from the legations with the information that the besieged were still alive but under continuous attack. The result was a footrace to Peking.

The attack upon the great walled city of Peking began on August 13 from Tungchow. Each national unit was to advance within a few miles of Peking and then halt. The plan was to have the Russians on the right flank force open the Tung Chih gate and the Japanese in the center move against the Chih Hua gate. Next to the Japanese would be the Americans, and finally the British on the left flank would attack the Tung Pien gate. The British and Americans were closest to the Legation Quarter and the Peitang cathedral.

By the morning of the fourteenth the plan had already gone awry. The Russians and Japanese both fought their way through the same gate and into the Tartar City. Meanwhile, the Americans and British found the Chinese City easy to enter. While the Americans, led by the army's Fourteenth Infantry, advanced cautiously along the street bordering the south side of the Tartar wall, the British moved freely through the Chinese City and soon came within sight of the flags of the legations atop the Tartar wall. The Legation Quarter's defenders were on top of the wall and signaled the British troops not to try to storm the Chien gate but rather to force their way through the Imperial canal's seven-foot-high tunnel under the wall. The Indians of the Seventh Rajputs broke down the canal's gates and barricades and after wading through the stagnant and filthy sewer water, were the first to enter the Legation Quarter. They were quickly followed by the Punjabis, the Welsh Fusiliers, and General Gaselee.

The Americans under Chaffee arrived later that same afternoon as did General Linievitch and General Yamaguchi. The siege of the Peking Legation Quarter had ended. Not so that of the Peitang cathedral. The French hoped to relieve the cathedral, but despite their best efforts it was the Japanese who reached the Catholic bastion on August 15. As one account of the end of the siege put it, "The Manchu Court had fled, the Chinese Government had disintegrated, the Imperial armies were melting away, [and] the streets were littered with scarlet trappings discarded by the Boxers."[9]

The International Relief Force was totally unprepared to be an occupying army and to govern Peking. Nonetheless, various national contingents divided Peking into sections and governed as best they could. The Americans

[8]Lowell Thomas, *Old Gimlet Eye: The Adventures of Smedley D. Butler* (New York: Farrar and Rinehart, 1933), 69.
[9]Peter Fleming, *The Siege of Peking*, 212.

and British became "Temple Soldiers" as they occupied the buildings and grounds of the Temples of Heaven and Agriculture. The great city was a mess, several of its major parts were badly damaged, and corpses still littered the streets and compounds. Much of the population had fled, and extensive looting had taken place. What the Boxers and Chinese soldiers did not get, the Relief Force did.

One of the most questionable features of the Allied occupation of Peking and Chihli during the remainder of 1900 was the punitive military expeditions that were carried out against those suspected of being or having been Boxers. The earliest such expedition, and one that did make military sense, was undertaken in Peking on August 19. On that day an international contingent found near the Legation Quarter a sufficient stock of artillery and ammunition to have destroyed the secure zone during the siege. The artillery had never been used. It had been under the control of Prince Jung Lu and gave rise to further speculation that he had deliberately held back equipment from those who were bent upon destroying the besieged legations and cathedral. Other actions were less defensible. A large-scale expedition was carried out against Paoting by the Germans under their commander, Count Alfred von Waldersee. Von Waldersee and the German army had reached China only six weeks after the siege was lifted. Having missed the combat, von Waldersee nevertheless deemed it necessary to demonstrate German military prowess to the Chinese and the International Relief Force. At Paoting a number of Chinese officials and suspected Boxers were summarily executed. In another expedition two American missionaries were active participants in collecting indemnity payments for Boxer outrages on behalf of Chinese converts. Those missionaries were taken to task by Mark Twain in a series of magazine articles that appeared in the *North American Review* in the winter of 1900–1901.[10]

The Boxer Uprising had ended almost as abruptly as it had begun. The Dowager Empress and her prisoner, the Emperor Kuang Hsu, had fled to the distant city of Sian, capital of Shensi province. Over 40,000 foreign troops occupied Peking, Tientsin, and Chihli province. The railway between Peking and the sea was open under the control of the occupying armies. In addition, the railway from Tientsin north to Manchuria was being run by the British and Russians. Chinwangtao, the ice-free port north of Tientsin, was administered by the British navy. The coal mines of Kaiping had also been taken. Manchuria was occupied by the Russian army. The Chinese Empire appeared on the verge of disintegration.

[10]The missionaries criticized by Twain were William Ament and E. G. Tewksbury. Both men had been through the siege of Peking. The anti-imperialist and anti-religious Twain argued that the missionaries were tools of commercial imperialism.

In order to partially extricate itself from the embarrassment of these occupying armies, the Manchu government ordered plenipotentiaries, including the elderly and ailing Viceroy Li Hung-chang, to North China to
negotiate with the foreign powers. On January 16, 1901, a protocol was
agreed to that contained articles for peace and the return of normal relations. While negotiations continued for a final treaty, the foreign powers
demanded that the court take action against those officials who had supported or encouraged the Boxers. While still in Sian, the Dowager Empress
ordered that Prince Tuan be exiled to Turkestan and that a number of his
collaborators commit suicide. Governor Yu Hsien of Shansi was ordered beheaded, and Li Ping-heng was posthumously degraded. Governor Yu Lu of
Chihli committed suicide.

On September 7, 1901, a peace treaty was signed by Viceroy Li and the
ministers of the foreign legations. Its main features were the payment by
China of an indemnity of 450 million taels (about $333 million); the prohi-
bition by China for two years of the importation of arms; the suspension for
five years of the official civil-service examination in cities where foreigners
had been mistreated; the reservation of the Legation Quarter in Peking for
foreign diplomatic missions, which would defend it; the razing of the Taku
forts; the establishment of foreign military posts at Tientsin; the amend-
ment of existing treaties of commerce and navigation; the improvement of
the river channels leading to Tientsin and Shanghai; the structuring of the
Tsungli Yamen into a ministry of foreign affairs; apologies for the murder of
the German minister; and the erection by the Chinese of monuments of
atonement in desecrated foreign cemeteries.

Three things stand out in the peace treaty. First, despite its humiliation,
the Manchu dynasty continued on the Dragon Throne. Kuang Hsu did not
abdicate, and Tzu Hsi remained the regent and the power behind the royal
facade. Second, China had not been divided among the foreign powers although Peking's Legation Quarter was greatly expanded and fortified, Tientsin's concessions were quadrupled in size, and Russia occupied Manchuria.
Third, the Chinese government was an indemnity-paying nation and would
be in debt to the powers for years to come. China's ability to control her
national finances was very limited, and revenue gathering was largely in provincial or foreign hands. The Imperial Maritime Customs under Sir Robert
Hart had become, in the words of Hosea Morse, "the collecting agent of
the foreign creditors of China."[11]

The imperial soothsayers selected January 7, 1902 as a date for the
court to return to Peking. Although utilizing traditional Manchu pomp and

[11]Hosea Ballow Morse, *The Period of Subjection, 1894–1911*, vol. 3 of *The International Relations of the Chinese Empire* (London: Paragon Book Gallery, 1918), 394.

circumstance, the court did allow Peking's residents to view the return. Tzu Hsi and her retinue had departed Sian in October and for nearly three months had proceeded in a triumphal way to "tour the provinces" before arriving in the royal railway carriage at Peking's Machiapu station.

Prior to her return to the capital, Tzu Hsi and her close associate, Prince Jung Lu, had taken a number of steps that set in motion a new direction for the imperial government. The new direction was intended to appease the foreign powers, modernize and strengthen the government, and, most importantly, maintain the Manchu dynasty in power. While the court was still in Sian, reform proposals had been collected and considered. To further show a new direction, modern army units commanded by the powerful governor of Shantung, Yuan Shih-kai, suppressed dissident and ex-Boxer brigands in Chihli. A number of these modernized battalions then proceeded to Peking. There they maintained order and impressed the foreign legations as the troops of the International Relief Force withdrew from the capital.

Upon the death of Viceroy Li, his protégé, Yuan Shih-kai, was named the acting viceroy of Chihli, with temporary viceregal headquarters at Paoting. There he began to train and build a new army, utilizing as a framework his small modernized force. Finally, before her return to the Forbidden City, Tzu Hsi took an action that dealt with the dynasty's succession and was meant to further appease the foreign powers. Since Prince Tuan had been exiled from the court, his son, the heir apparent to the throne, was stripped of his honors and sent to join his father.

While the foreign armies were withdrawing from Peking and establishing themselves in Tientsin, the Russians dawdled in Manchuria. Fearing Japan's presence in Korea, the czar's government concluded that the Japanese wanted a portion of Manchuria for themselves. The government of the emperor of Japan concluded that Russia wanted part of Korea. Both were right. The court in Peking could do little to force the withdrawal of Russian forces except to encourage Chinese migration into the sparsely populated homeland of the Manchus. However, the result of the suspicion between Russia and Japan brought about war that began in February 1904 and ended with the Treaty of Portsmouth on September 5, 1905. All the land battles were fought on Chinese soil in Manchuria, where the Russian armies were defeated and driven north. During the conflict, China had wisely remained neutral. The peace talks, held in Portsmouth, New Hampshire, under the auspices of President Theodore Roosevelt, required that both Russian and Japanese armies withdraw from Manchuria. However Dairen and Port Arthur were to be under Japanese control, as was the South Manchurian Railway from Port Arthur to Changchun. The rail line from Changchun to the border of Russia would be controlled by the Russians. Finally, both countries recognized the Open Door policy in Manchuria. Recognition was one thing; actual practice was something else.

The period from 1901 to 1904 saw an awakening in China. That awakening was set in motion by the aging Dowager Empress Tzu Hsi through a series of reform efforts. Those efforts can be viewed primarily as an honest last-minute attempt to change China into a modern state or as a final desperate effort to save a feeble and ineffective dynasty from the mandate of heaven. These belated reform efforts forced into the open the long-standing issue of provincial (regional or Chinese) versus central (Peking or Manchu) administrative control. In order to deal with foreign incursions into China, a stronger, more effective central government appeared to be a necessity. To accomplish this, Peking made efforts at reform in the fields of commerce, education, and the military.

In 1902 the throne provided Chinese businesses with a commercial code that gave them legal protection and permitted chambers of commerce to be established. A national primary and secondary school system was to be established and Western subject matter taught. The old, ineffective armies of Manchu Bannermen and provincial militia were to be replaced by a modern army, patterned on those of the European countries and Japan. Such efforts required increased centralization of the dynasty's authority. Generally, provincial authorities resisted the reforms as power plays by the weakened Manchus to obtain more control and finances at the expense of the authorities away from Peking. A latent Chinese anti-Manchuism had become increasingly evident. The struggle to increase centralized control at the expense of provincial or regional autonomy was to continue throughout the life of the Manchu dynasty and beyond.

Ewing Papers,
January 1899 to December 1904

Charles to Judson Smith, January 2, 1899, Peking

Dear Dr. Smith:

[A]nd now we look forward to the new year, knowing that there must be either a cutting down of the work, or more private gifts, perhaps both. Accordingly, I have agreed to find money from private sources for the carrying of the work at the North Chapel—which means about one hundred dollars gold, not including the pastor's salary. This means about sixty dollars for the school, and the remainder for chapel-keeper, light, heat, etc.

. . . Just now we are in the week of prayer, when union services are held every day, and the attendance is so large as to absolutely prohibit our having any of the meetings here [at the small American Board chapel]. Indeed even the London Mission chapel is too small, and the meetings are held in the new [and large] Methodist church. You would have enjoyed seeing yesterday's audience, about 1200 people. And it is inspiring when one stops to reflect that in the midst of this heathen capital there can be gathered so large a congregation for Christian worship. Probably very few of these were themselves not Christians, and the number of church members who were unable to attend would be more than enough to take their places. Reckoning the population of Peking at one million, the largest figure that any one claims, we should find that about one in eight hundred attended the first service of this week of prayer, and that there is a least that proportion of church members in this city where Confucianism, Taoism, and Buddhism, with all their rites and superstitions still hold sway.

. . . Dr. Ament was the preacher yesterday and held his audience well throughout his rather extended discourse. . . . I suppose there can be little doubt that Dr. Ament is the best Chinese [language] preacher in the city. The people like to hear him. And then, he is exceedingly good in personal work, taking an interest in men individually and winning them. This kind of pastoral work is just as invaluable here as it is at home. . . . In every way, it is a great advantage to have the senior member of the station [Peking] back on the field and at work again. And then, Dr. Ament is a great worker. How he gets through with so much work, I don't know. I always said that he could do two men's work. . . .

The American marines who are in the city [to guard the legation] are allowed sufficient freedom so that they can attend this week's prayer meetings, the foreign meetings being held in the evenings, at different missions in rotation. Some of the marines have taken a stand as Christians since coming to Peking, and it is hoped that more will follow. There were eighteen marines sent up to Peking; three of them have had smallpox (or varioloid), and one died, and five are to go back to Tientsin, but twelve will remain through the winter.

Charles to Myra Smith, January 1899, Peking

Dear Aunt Myra:

We are now in the Chinese twelfth month and the usual annual run on the native banks has begun. The cause of this is that near the end of the year the Manchus who are granted a government allowance, receive two months money at one time. Their allowance is in silver, and they immediately want to change it for cash, as their living expenses must be paid in cash, and there is not enough cash ready on demand to meet the call. Several banks have failed already. Two that suspended payment have been torn down by the crowd and everything of value taken away. . . .

We have now nearly completed one half of our first term. It has sometimes seemed as if I should not be able to stand the full period of ten years.

Bessie to Myra Smith, January 1899, Peking

My Dear Aunt Myra:

There are eighteen Marines stationed in Peking at the legation. This group is very nice appearing, owing partly to Major Conger's[1] request that no drinking men should be sent up here. There are a few Christians among them, one having been through college and taken part of a theological course.[2]

[1]The American minister to China, Edwin H. Conger, was usually referred to as Major Conger because of his Civil War rank.

[2]In the spring of 1899 the eighteen American Marines left Peking and returned to Tientsin. Their withdrawal seems most ill-advised in view of the events of the summer of 1900.

Charles to Judson Smith, January 18, 1899, Peking

Dear Dr. Smith:

. . . With the change to 1899, the oversight of the rest of the work [for the outstations] goes now entirely over into Dr. Ament's hands, and henceforth

I shall doubtless be left more free to do afternoon work at the North Chapel. And I am beginning now, when Pastor Jên is away. So each afternoon, after an hour or so of reading or letter-writing, I go to the North Chapel. Sometimes I let others do the preaching while I talk with church members or inquirers in the inquiry room. Sometimes, as this afternoon, I preach myself, anywhere from half an hour to an hour. There is a text on the blackboard each day: today it was John 3:16, and that of course gave one a fine opportunity of telling the simple gospel message, which is more delightful and satisfactory than any other kind of preaching. Today I took my cue especially from the Chinese character for "love" (愛), the middle part of this is a character by itself (心) meaning "heart," while the upper and lower parts combine to form (憂) the character for "suffer," and so it was easy to say that God's love meant (1) the heart of God is love (which by the way is the Chinese expression for "God is love," as translated in I John), and (2) God suffering for men. . . .

Today as I went to the North Chapel, the streets seemed even more interesting than usual, and I wished you were with me to see the people. They were out in greater numbers than usual. This, I suppose was because today is the first bright warm day (comparatively warm) after a cold snap. We had our first snow-storm last Thursday night, and good snapping weather since then. Among the people on the street today, I noticed many Mongolians: they come to Peking at this time of the year when the pasture lands of Mongolia are less serviceable than in the summer. You can see them dressed in their peculiar colors (sometimes a peculiar yellow, sometimes a faded maroon), stalking along with their great strides, men and women alike, or riding their sleek camels, astride between the two humps. Sometimes you hear them talking in their own language, seemingly as unlike to Chinese as English. Today, it also happened that I saw on the street a number of Russian sailors from the legation guard out for a stroll. Then there were large numbers of Chinese and Manchus, buying, selling, or on the go. Taken all together, the scene was more than ordinarily busy and interesting. . . .

Last week . . . several native banks suspended payment. It is reported by the Chinese that the missionaries of the Methodist Mission had a large amount of money in one of these banks. I know they deal with that bank very largely, and it certainly closed, the bankers absconding with all they could carry. Two of the banks that closed were set upon by the crowd, the buildings torn to pieces, and everything of any value carried off. The bank with which we deal, tho rather scared, pulled through all right. But even if it had not, we seldom deposit much money there. The cause for the breaking of the banks was, in part at least, the special demand for cash at the beginning of the twelfth month, the banks having issued more paper money than they were able to redeem. Silver was not quite as scarce, but people wanted cash, and so the exchange value of silver fell to the lowest point yet reached.

Charles to Judson Smith, February 17, 1899, Peking

Dear Dr. Smith:

. . . It is quite possible that the Western world knows things about the situation in the palace that have not yet been heard, or if heard have not been credited, by the foreign residents in Peking. And it is not at all impossible that some events that have caused very little comment may have some deeper meaning beneath. For instance, nearly or quite all of the Russian troops [guarding the Russian legation] left Peking one day in the latter half of January, and it was reported that they were going to Port Arthur. At about the same time, German troops were also called away, and it is to be supposed that they went to Kiaochow. Also, there have been rumors for a month now, and growing more definite, that the U.S. Marines stationed here and at Tientsin are to go to Manila very soon. As to the interpretation of these facts and rumors, there is of course some difference of opinion, and you at your distance, with a broader outlook, will probably be better able than I to judge whether these movements are important. My own opinion, doubtless imbibed from others, is that the Russians are intrenching themselves at Port Arthur and Talien Wan [also on the Liaotung peninsula in southern Manchuria] with the intention of remaining there permanently. Indeed, I suppose there can be little doubt about that, . . . However, Russia bears watching, and certainly not less at Peking than elsewhere. . . . It is said quite plainly here by some people that the Russians know how to make the best use of money and the Chinese, and that they do not scruple to do so, further, that in this way they not only keep their own plans secret, but also ferret out plans of other nations, which were intended to be secret.[1] Political acumen and diplomatic ability of no mean order, assisted by unscrupulousness in method, thus give Russia the inside track, as compared with other nations. It is quite possible that the czar [Nicholas II] may be eminently sincere in his desire for peace, and yet be definitely proposing to enlarge his borders. . . . But I think most of us feel that, even if Russia gains control [of Manchuria or North China], she will not be permitted to put a stop to [Protestant] Christian missions, nor drive out the missionaries as formerly in Siberia. . . . [Y]ou will hardly feel like revising your conclusions concerning the Chinese as a race, either: whatever may become of the Chinese empire and government [as a result of European land seizures], the Chinese as a people are not to lose their racial characteristics, and as long as they retain these peculiarities, they cannot be effaced, lost, or absorbed.

There is surely a future for the Chinese. What is it? God knows: and I surely believe that He intends better things for them than they have ever known, and I hope better than even the most sanguine of us can suspect. . . .

The people at Kalgan have been so situated as to have been thrown into some association with the Russians living there. Dr. [Elizabeth] Murdock in particular made several good friends among them. The family that she knew best moved to Tientsin at about the same time that Dr. Murdock came to Peking, which was the same year [1894] that Mrs. Ewing and I arrived in China. While spending our first winter in Tientsin, we became somewhat acquainted with them. Mr. Batouieff, while himself a member of the state church [Russian Orthodox], attended, and still attends, the Union church in Tientsin. His little (adopted) daughter was in the Sunday School class that Mrs. Ewing taught for several months. Mr. Batouieff is a very wealthy man. While his wife and child are in Russia, he has been building for them a most beautiful home in Tientsin. While he was in Kalgan, he built an exquisite little church for the Russian community, . . . and when the new Union church was to be erected in Tientsin, he contributed quite liberally. . . .

One of the ladies living at the Methodist Mission has been teaching English to a Russian lady, the wife of the gentleman in charge of the business of the Russo-Chinese bank. She finds the lady . . . of great culture and intelligence. She was for some years a teacher in a college in St. Petersburg, where her husband also taught for a long time. I was quite surprised to learn of the extent of educational facilities open to women in Russia, although perhaps I ought to have learned as much before.

. . . While I was [recently] in Tientsin . . . I was able to see a game of Rugby foot-ball, another foot-ball game played according to "Association" rules, a game of pony polo, and a game of bicycle polo (like pony polo, with bicycles instead of ponies). I also took time to go to the "Dewey Barracks"[2] and call on the American marines, two of whom I had previously met in Peking. On the last morning that I spent in Tientsin, I saw a review and drill of all the foreign troops in the city except the French. There were 35 Americans, 27 Germans, about 20 British and a still smaller number of the Tientsin volunteer corps (British). The American marines presented the best appearance, owing in part to the fact that they were larger men than the others, and in part to the more artistic uniforms. But in drill, the Germans excelled. The German uniform is perhaps more ornate than the American; the latter is very simple, but very appropriate. Of course, the great interest in the American marines was for the reason that, with not more than three exceptions, they all had been in the battle of Manila Bay.[3]

[1]Charles here refers to the widespread use of bribes to Chinese officials by the Russians.

[2]Charles does not state where in Tientsin the "Dewey Barracks" were located. Since there was no American concession there, the barracks may have been situated in another nation's concession or on board an American gunboat.

[3]The battle of Manila Bay took place on May 1, 1898, and for all intents and purposes ended Spain's control of the Philippines.

Charles to Judson Smith, March 4, 1899, Shun I Hsien, Chihli Province

Dear Dr. Smith:

Yesterday was "fair" day here, many people from surrounding villages coming into this little city [twenty miles north-east of Peking] to buy or sell. Among these were several of the church members. One of these is a man whom I had not met before. He only joined the church in November. He carried a pole on his shoulder, with a large box hanging from each end . . . , what struck me was that he had the courage to have a Christian motto written on red paper and pasted on his boxes. It is rather unusual to find a church member who is willing to let his Christianity be known so openly. . . .

As I sat in the street chapel yesterday afternoon, writing at a table there, quite a crowd gathered around to see the strange operation. They seemed quite interested, judging from snatches of their conversation. "How fast he writes." "We couldn't write like that." "Why, he doesn't write perpendicular." "No, horizontal." "What kind of pen is that?" (a fountain pen). "It isn't like ours." "No, he can write all day without using any more ink." One man sat opposite me, and watched very intently for a long time. When I came to a good stopping place, I asked for his honorable name and his place of residence. "In the temple nearby," he replied. "And whom do you worship there?" "The venerable Kuan." As nearly as I could make out, this was some revered man who was supposed to have gone to heaven. "But what do you worship him for?" "We worship the mud [*sic*] image." "But what power has the mud image? or what power has the venerable Kuan? Please explain your doctrine, as I should like to hear it and understand it. " The only reply to this was "What is your pen made of?" "Of rubber, which exudes from a tree. It is very useful. Now, if your mud image is useful, I should like to know, and if your doctrine is better than mine, I will change. Please explain." I said all this politely enough so that the man must have felt at perfect liberty to reply if he had anything to say. But his continued silence was sufficient to the crowd that he could not explain. This gave me an admirable opportunity for preaching to those men as they stood around, and for showing them that Christianity was glad of a audience and that we desired inquiry and were always ready to explain.

Charles to Judson Smith, March 22, 1899, Nan Meng, Chihli Province

Dear Dr. Smith:

The only matter of importance that I remember now [about the past week in Peking] was the departure of the American marines who had been stationed at Peking, and the decision by several of them to lead Christian lives. Some had so decided earlier, and enough were added to their number in the last few days to make the number of Christians eight, out of a total of twelve marines who had been at the legation. Most of the work with these marines was done by members of the Methodist Mission. Major Conger has complimented the men very highly on their character and conduct. He made them a very nice speech just before they started off, and I understand that he has written a letter of commendation either to Admiral Dewey or to the authorities at Washington.

Bessie to Myra Smith, March 1899, Peking

My Dear Aunt Myra:

Charles will be in the country [Chihli province] most of this month. There are trains now between Peking and Paoting, and they go thru two places where we have chapels, Liang Hsiang [Hsien] and Cho Chow.[1]

[1]Although the Tientsin-Peking railway opened in 1895 and was later extended south to Paoting, this is the first mention of trains operating from Peking in the Ewings' correspondence.

Charles to Edward C. Ewing, March 1899, Nan Meng

Dear Father:

You asked in a recent letter "to what extent freedom of speech is tolerated in China." In general I may say that there are no more limitations than in America. China is really democratic in many ways, and individual freedom is probably as little fettered by law in this as in any land. It is not law, nor government, or force that keeps China as peaceful as she is. Rather, the people are peaceable by nature, and the great restraining force is custom, not law. The Chinese officials, especially the censors, have the privilege of criticising the government, with them, too, the great sin is in breaking away from precedent. That was the serious mistake of the Emperor and his advisors [during the One Hundred Days of 1898]. It seemed as if he had gone mad in his "following the devils." And it was madness, that is it was foolish, to expect the leaders of China to stand quietly by while the young Emperor proceeded to introduce foreign customs. There are many mandarins who are trembling for fear that the sword may fall on their necks any day.

Charles to Judson Smith, May 11, 1899, Peking

Dear Dr. Smith:

An interesting feature in the work at Nan Meng is the way in which a few of the men do volunteer missionary work. Whenever they know that there is likely to be an especially large concourse of people in any neighboring village, there is nearly always some one who has leisure, and is glad to take some Christian books along to sell, and glad to improve the opportunity by preaching to the crowds. During the few days that I was there three such occasions [arose], . . . and they were not allowed to pass unnoticed. One was a large funeral, another was a theatre, and the third was a special public day at a temple. . . .

The large funeral was on this wise. The wealthiest man in a certain village died. According to Chinese custom, the body would probably be kept in a coffin in the house for a long time, perhaps several months, until a favorable day came—a day that was declared by those supposed to know to be a "yellow mark day" (like our red-letter day?). Then came the funeral. But by this time great preparations had been made. An undertaker from the district city eight miles away had taken a contract to furnish all the draperies, adornments, and other accessories that were required to make the occasion a memorable one, and honor to the departed man, and a lavish manifestation of the filial piety of his sons. Music was provided, feasts spread, and everything prepared on a large scale. The festivities continued for three days. Many people from the villages all about came to see the sights, eat of the feasts, and pay the voluntary contribution that is always expected from guests at funerals or weddings. It was at this funeral that the brethren had the best success at preaching.

At the theatre the success was not so good, and I ascribed the difference to my [Western] clothes. But I have learned from another missionary that he has generally found the theatre crowds too light-hearted and lacking in seriousness to give the best attention to Christian preaching. These theatrical performances out in the country are not held in halls, but out-of-doors, or rather under large mat awnings, to screen from the sun, wind, and rain. Sometimes the stage used is a permanent one of brick and tile-roofed, much like other buildings except that it is set higher up and is open at the front. Such permanent stages are erected in connection with temples, and a large open piece of level ground is left for the gathering of spectators, hard and smooth like a threshing-floor. It is over this that the awning is erected, on poles, and made of cheap Chinese matting. But most of the county theatres have no permanent stage, the travelling theatrical company being expected to bring its own stage, poles, boards, mat roof, and all. The theatre of which I have made mention was constructed in this way. No admission was charged; indeed those not under covering or on the seats could still see the performance, while those inside could keep an eye on what might be going on outside. It was this latter circumstance, together with the constant wandering about of the people, that made it impossible for us to attract a crowd. We stood behind the stage, about a hundred feet away; the noise of the beating of brass cymbals and other discordant music reached as far as our position, and compelled us to raise our voices if we would be heard. I had no opportunity of hearing or seeing what sort of performance was presented, . . . Some say that the whole tone of the performance is low, and that there is much that is vulgar or even vile. Others say that, while there are such theatres, most of them are simply full of jokes and laughable presentments, giving entertainment and relation to the auditors. You may wonder how the theatre pays expenses, without charging an admission fee. It is in this way: the people of the village take up a subscription, for the sake of having the theatrical performance just outside of their village street, and for the sake of attracting a crowd, and then they bargain with the histrionic company to come for several days and play each day.

The gatherings at temples . . . are of still another kind. Certain days are known as public days at the particular temple in question. Vendors, victuallers, side-shows, and so-forth all make preparations, and are on hand at the given time with the intention of driving a brisk trade. The public turns out partly because of the surety that there will be a crowd, partly because of the special opportunity for worship at the temple, and partly because they hope to buy or sell to advantage when there is so much trading going on. In this last respect, the scene resembles a county fair as much as anything in America, but still there are lacking the educational and other exhibits that we expect at such a time, and there is more of individual trading, buying, and selling. It is like the market days in a market town, but on a rather more extended scale.

Charles to Edward and Ellen Ewing, July 1899, Western Hills

Dear Father and Mother:

Dr. Ament and I have agreed on the division of the work, giving me the general oversight of the outstations. . . . During the last two weeks in June I visited over a dozen of the stations. I walked on this trip, covering in all 153 miles by foot and in another week making a hundred miles.[1]

[1] It seems remarkable that during June of 1899 Charles walked over 250 miles in rural Chihli province without incident. The following summer, that province was swarming with militant antiforeign Boxers.

Charles to Judson Smith, August 26, 1899, Western Hills

Dear Dr. Smith:

Please forgive me for allowing June, July, and so much of August to pass without writing you . . . we came out here to the Hills on June 9. My brother and his family [from Paoting] accompanied us and remained here for ten days, . . . After my brother left on the 19th, Mrs. Ewing and the two little girls [age four and one] were the only foreigners on the hill . . . [Charles having left on a visit to nearby outstations].

. . . On the way home [to Peking before returning to the Hills], I was stopped by a day of rain. I had started out from Nan Meng to walk the twenty miles to Ping Tang, but had gone only three or four miles when the rain began to come down so heavily as to send me for refuge to the nearest place where cover could be found. This was a temple, where I was compelled to stay the rest of the day, and to spend the night also. It was a somewhat mixed company of which I was one member there. There were two Buddhist priests and a lama. Besides, a neighbor who came in had worked for the Catholics, not many miles away. The cook provided extra food, and I ate of the same mess that was prepared for the priests. When I went, I insisted on paying, tho they protested. But I overcame the objections of the priest in charge by saying: I have not refrained to tell you what I think of your church and its sure decadence in the near future, nor have I scrupled to express my opinion of you, a priest, spending your time in smoking opium, that destroyer of all that is good in man; and how can I eat of the food provided by the temple for you, and give no money in return? They took no offence at what I had said, and finally allowed me to leave them a fair compensation for my food. The food was good, but of the night's lodging I cannot say as much. The priest offered me the privilege of sleeping in the same room with the others, but as the room was close and had been occupied by the opium smokers all day, I delined with thanks. I slept in another room, on a bundle of split reeds, a rather unsatisfactory bed that seemed to become lively after nightfall. The next morning, I made an early start and plodded on through the mud to Ping Tang. . . .

Charles to Edward and Ellen Ewing, September 1899, Peking

Dear Father and Mother:

We returned from the Hills earlier than usual for two reasons. First the summer has been quite cool and second there has been very little rain, in fact a drought. Our cisterns on the hill top were all empty and the well below failed. The village would not sell us [water] from their wells as they feared they would not have enough, so we were reduced to the river water . . . The drought has had a bad effect of the autumn crops, but not entirely spoiled them. We hear that some of the temple priests are praying for rain. For this they sometimes draw an idol through the streets on an open cart to let him feel how hot and dry the air is. Another ceremony is to scatter a great amount of dirty water all over the street. When that was begun in one town where Bible booksellers had their wares spread out, they asked the men to wait until they could cover their books. The priest asked what books they were, and when he knew, the water was thrown on them and the crowd called out, "These are the devil's followers." Having spoiled the books they then attacked the two Christian booksellers, tore their clothes and beat them severely with clubs. An appeal was made to the official, who did not seem disposed to do anything. However, the people realized that the thing had gone too far, and they tried to make some adjustment by giving the men one or two new articles of clothing.

Charles to Judson Smith, September 22, 1899, Peking

Dear Dr. Smith:
The return from the Westen Hills was made rather earlier than usual this year. We were the last to leave, on September 5. The summer had been so cool and so dry and the city was so cool and dry that we ventured to return early, . . . there is no mud, there are no shiny pools filling the ditches, there is no green scum. But instead there is dust.

Such a dry summer has been hard on the farmers. Their crops are not full and rich, and in some cases the loss is quite serious. But the first crop, reaped in June, was so exceptionally fine that, on the whole, this year has been far more prosperous than last year.

Bessie to Myra Smith, October 1899, Peking

My Dear Aunt Myra:
The ground is so dry that farmers don't even want to plant their precious seed, unless rain comes. Rumors are rife at such times as these, that it is the presence and schemes of foreigners that keeps back the rain.[1]

[1] The drought in North China, mentioned in the letters of September and October 1899, has been cited by some historians as one of the reasons for the success of the Boxer movement in that region during the spring and summer of 1900.

Charles to Edward and Ellen Ewing, October 15, 1899, Peking

Dear Father and Mother:
And now, we have made up our minds to do all that we can to get you out here [to Peking]. I hope that you already have it in mind, and that you are only waiting for a renewed assurance of welcome, and will start right off as to arrive here early in the spring. Why not? . . . Yes, come in the spring, via Honolulu, come early, to arrive here the first week in April. There is a place for you in our house, a place for you at the Western Hills in the same house with us, and a still larger place in our hearts.[1]

[1] Charles listed fourteen reasons that his parents should visit Peking and apparently was little concerned in the fall of 1899 about the antiforeign troubles or the possibility of a Boxer uprising.

Charles to Edward C. Ewing, November 1899, Wen An, Chihli Provine

Dear Father:

This outstation, our farthest one to the south, is my headquarters for three weeks. Before coming here I went to the farthest outstation to the north, Shun I Hsien. I was there over Sunday and received nine people into the church. . . . There are about forty members in this region and we ought to have a helper stationed here.[1]

[1] In departing Wen An, Charles walked for three days, about sixty miles, and then caught the train at Cho Chow, less than fifty miles from Peking.

Charles to Edward C. Ewing, November 25, 1899, Peking

Dear Father:

You will hear, doubtless, of the serious trouble in the neighborhood of our Pang Chuan station,[1] where the Porters and Smiths live. I have been with others to our U.S. Minister, Major Conger, to make sure he is doing all he can to protect our work. He impresses me as a frank and sensible man, ready and desirous to do all he can for those who appeal to him, no matter whether missonaries or others. I think his experience in Brazil led him to regard the missionaries there as largely engaged in a fight with Roman Catholicism, and as a man of the world who knew the best side of Catholicism, he thought that rather small business. Perhaps he accordingly expected not to be favorably impressed with mission work in China, but there has been no appearance of prejudice in his action or his attitude. He is cordial to all, a good type of the sensible manly American, as it seems to me.

[1] Pang Chuan is located on the Grand Canal southeast of Peking in Shantung province. The trouble Charles refers to was caused by the Boxers, but he does not mention them by name.

Charles to Judson Smith, December 12, 1899, Peking

Dear Dr. Smith:

I hardly need to tell you that the persecutions in Shantung have made us all more than usually prayerful for the work of the Pang Chuan station. The new governor[1] is an energetic man, but it remains to be seen what he can and will do. The central government grows weaker, and there is scarcely any one who dares to predict that there will be any improvement. Dr. [W. A. P.] Martin said to me a few days ago, "There are troublous times ahead," and no one would venture to contradict that statement.

[1] The new governor of Shantung was Yuan Shih-kai.

Bessie to Myra Smith, December 1899, Peking

My Dear Aunt Myra:

Charles took Marion to Paoting[1] for a week and the change has been of great benefit [as she had been sick from malaria].

[1]As late as December 1899, Charles felt that it was safe to take his four-year-old daughter to Paoting (or Paotingfu, as the suffix *fu* indicates a district capital) to visit his brother Henry Ewing. Henry at that time was with the American Board mission in Paoting. Although Bessie does not mention the mode of transportation for the hundred-mile trip, it would seem most likely that Charles took Marion on the train.

Bessie to Ellen Ewing, January 1900, Peking

My Dear Mother Ewing:

As to the political situation there is certainly a great deal of trouble in the neighborhood of our Shantung province and our [Chinese] Christians have both real and threatened dangers. Some families have lost house, grain, and everything portable or that could be destroyed. The Catholics have suffered the most and are the first objects of attack. The society of "Boxers,"[1] by whom all these outrages are committed, is spreading into other provinces and has received but little hindrance from the government. The feeling is strong that the Empress Dowager is secretly encouraging them and if she does not do something to punish them quickly the foreign powers will probably interfere, and perhaps China as a government will soon be a thing of the past. All seems quiet about Peking.

[1]This is the Ewings' first mention of the word *Boxers.*

Charles to Edward C. Ewing, February 1900, Peking

Dear Father:

The Empress Dowager has kept the young Emperor imprisoned since last September [1898]. Word has gone out that he is in very poor health but foreigners were very suspicious, it being quite generally believed that reports were sent out in order to prepare the public for his death, indeed, but that when he died it would not be from disease. Accordingly a foreign physician,[1] connected with one of the legations, was allowed to see him and have a report. It then became known that he was a sick man. Another announcement in January said that he would be unable to go through with the usual [Chinese] New Year duties and later an edict was issued saying that he must give up his imperial office and that a youth of royal blood had been selected to succeed him.[2]

As to the outrages of the Boxers, in addition to the robbing and persecuting of [Chinese] Christians, they have now murdered a young Englishman of the Episcopal Mission.[3] As for church property, in some places, doors and windows have been stolen and all books and personal property made away with. As far as we can see there is no redress in view, and if the people know this, it is scarcely likely that the Boxers and their sympathizers will stop, until they are made to do so. When? God only knows. The movement has been gradually coming northward. In some of our outstations inquirers are afraid to come near the chapels, church members are timid even, and it is thought wise for the missionaries to remain away. In other parts of our field, however, the rumors have been less intimidating, and foreigners can visit these places freely. Miss [Nellie] Russell is in Cho Chow now.

[1]It is not known which doctor Charles is referring to here. At the time there were two doctors associated with the legations. These were an Englishman, Dr. Wordsworth Poole, and Dr. Carl Velde, a German.

[2]The youth of royal blood was Pu Chun, the son of Prince Tuan. The diplomatic corps refused to recognize Pu Chun as the heir apparent and in so doing increased the animosity of Prince Tuan toward the foreign community.

[3]The young Englishman, S. M. Brooks, was killed at Feicheng in Shantung province.

Bessie to Myra Smith, March 1, 1900, Peking

Dear Aunt Myra:

Charles had planned a country trip this month but because of the growing feeling against foreigners the Chinese church members advise us to stay at home. Our Nan Meng pastor has moved his family to a quiet place in a village while he stays "an orphan alone" as he explains it. In Shih Ko Chuang the helpers and members are reviled and threatened, whenever they appear on the street. "In a few days," they say, "we will kill you and tear down your chapel."[1] Major Conger is trying to get a promise of protection but none of the other foreign ministers seem to put much importance to the movement of this society of "Boxers."[2]

[1]Both Nan Meng and Shih Ko Chuang are in Chihli province, southeast of Peking.

[2]Bessie here expresses a common missionary concern, i.e., the foreign diplomats' seeming lack of concern for the Boxer Movement.

Charles to Edward and Ellen Ewing, April 30, 1900, Peking

Dear Father and Mother:

The illness of Mr. Mateer[1] proved very serious wth little hope of recovery . . . [and he] died on April 23. . . . This was the first death that I had witnessed, the first coffin I ever helped to make, the first death that has ever meant the changing of my plans.

[1]Mr. John L. Mateer was an American Board missionary.

Bessie Smith Ewing Diary

Saturday, June 9, 1900, Methodist Compound, Peking

I went to Tungchow with the children[1] on Saturday, May 26th to attend Mission meeting. Charles could not go then, but walked down early Sunday morning and returned on Monday morning. There had been a few refugees[2] coming in, but the principal reason for Charles being at home was his oversight of the new church building. The reason for his going on Sunday was that he had to preach the annual sermon in English. He expected to go down again later for some part of the meetings but the continual coming in of the refugees prevented this. It was not until the burning of Fengtai,[3] the railroad junction, on Monday [May 28], that the foreign legations seemed really to be aroused. As threats of attack in Tungchow continued more numerous, we hoisted the American flag as a sign of protection and also mounted a telescope on the roof turret of one of the houses. This telescope had been up there nearly all last year for astronomical classes and some of the Chinese had been frightened, thinking it was a big gun. Every opportunity was taken to undeceive them, but still with no effect. Now was the time to use this telescope as a scarecrow, and it proved a good one. The story was soon going around that when that big gun went off half of Tungchow would be destroyed. This reminded me of the yarns we were told when children about the bronze dogs in people's yards.

Several gentlemen [from the American Board] visited the Governor of the city [Tungchow] to demand protection. His promises were many and his personal intentions were undoubtedly good, but he had no soldiers and could do nothing. He had sent to Tientsin for several hundred soldiers and when they arrived we were promised a guard. But the Governor was just as anxious for protection as we were, and begged the gentlemen over and over not to fire off their big gun. The soldiers did not come and we had one or two scary nights, thinking that the "Boxers" were going to attack us, but all passed off quietly.

Charles could not come to us, and I did not know as we were going to be able to go to him, but it was finally decided safe, and a number of us planned to start on Tuesday morning, the fifth of June. Although the jour-

[1]The Ewing children were five-year-old Marion and nineteen-month-old Ellen.

[2]By "refugees" Bessie refers to Chinese Christians who had fled from their homes as a result of actions by the Boxers or rampaging mobs.

[3]Fengtai was the junction city, only six miles from Peking, where the two railway lines met. At the time, the Peking-Hankow or Lu Han line terminated beyond Paoting, and the Tientsin line continued on to Chinchou on the Gulf of Chihli.

ney was decided safe, I was fearful. The rest were all to go in carts, but Ellen and I had to go in a sedan chair, and could not go by the same route.[4] The bearers I knew, and they were good, trusty men, but I must confess I was afraid to start on that fifteen mile ride with only my baby and four Chinese for company. The bearers were given very positive orders to keep with the carts, but in many places that is almost impossible. As soon as we were fairly on the way I felt all right and as though there would be no trouble, and everything was as quiet as possible. We found Peking pretty well excited, and with reason. Each day brought news of fresh outrages, and refugees came in large numbers from our country church districts. On Thursday [June 7] Mr. F. [Franklin] M. Chapin and family came up from Tungchow. Their home is in Lin Ching,[5] but they had been attending the annual meeting. They arrived early in the morning and in the afternoon word came that the Tungchow friends had decided that they must all leave. Carts were hired and Mr. [William] Ament went with them. They reached Tungchow about eleven o'clock at night and the party left at three in the morning, twenty-four foreigners and a number of Chinese helpers, students and church members. They had only a short time to pack the necessities and to bury silver, etc., and space for baggage was very limited. They felt sure that everything would go as soon as the foreigners left, but did not feel safe to stay longer. The sudden change for the worse was due to the arrival [in Tungchow] of seven hundred Chinese soldiers from Tientsin, foreign drilled. Instead of giving protection, as we had hoped, they proved to be a set of ruffians and stirred up the people more and more. About eight o'clock the friends [from Tungchow] arrived, but only a few came to us. The rest went to the Methodist compound.

At a general meeting in Peking on Thursday, it was decided that in case of serious danger all missionaries with their native converts, refugees, should collect at this place [the Methodist compound], so the Tungchow people thought it better to come here at first. It was well they did, for danger signs threatened so fast that by Friday night, June 8th, all American missionaries were here and some five hundred native Christians.[6] It all seemed so strange to be packing up to leave our home. I tried to take as few things as possible, expecting that we should have to run to the Legation at the last. So we packed only our two extension bags with a change of under-clothing around, a warm outer suit apiece and two or three thin suits. We piled

---

[4]Observing proprieties of the time, Bessie does not mention her pregnancy. Suggestions of it surface occasionally in the diary.

[5]Lin Ching is thirty miles north of Peking.

[6]By "all American Missionaries" Bessie refers to Methodists, Presbyterians, and the American Board members.

everything into one cart; the children's two mattresses on the bottom, the two bags at the back. I curled up in front with Ellen in my lap; the small spaces held two hand bags and cooking dishes for Ellen's food. Marion was on the outside with the driver, and Charles walked by the side to be near and to see that nothing fell out. In this way we left our home after ten o'clock last night. Ellen had been asleep four hours, but Marion did not get any rest until about midnight.

We were sent to Mr. [Francis] Gamewell's[7] house into an empty room. They had just cleaned out ready to go home to America. With the two mattresses and a Brussels carpet that Mrs. [Mary] Gamewell brought out for us, we lay down for a few hours. Charles had expected to return home last night but the Methodists protested, saying it was not fair to leave us all here for others to protect in case of attack. Although we did not think it likely the "Boxers" would come, this argument had force and so Charles stayed. By half past five this morning he was up and had started for our home for more things.[8]

Monday, June 11, 1900, Methodist Compound, Peking

We found on reaching here that we must keep house, so Charles spent Saturday morning in packing up a few dishes and cooking utensils and some provisions. He sent down our dining room table, all the common silver and table linen, the greater part of the kitchen things and just enough of our crockery to get along on for ten people. The kitchen where we were was used to make the soldiers' food for we had a guard of ten American marines.[9] But the stove was a large one and had places for two separate fires, and under the circumstances we thought we could manage very nicely. My cook was with me and was able to buy meat, rice and string beans. I had crackers and jelly and we made out quite a meal. The Chapin family, numbering four, and Miss [Ada] Haven boarded with us and we expected Mr. Ament but he did not get down. He is loath to leave our property [the American Board compound], fearing looting by idle fellows, and thinking no

---

[7]Mr. Francis (Frank) Gamewell, an engineer trained at Rensselaer Polytechnic and Cornell University, was a Methodist missionary.

[8] The American Board Compound was about a mile and a half from the Methodist compound. The latter was located on Filial Piety Alley just inside the Tartar City and a few hundred yards from the Ha Ta Gate entrance.

[9] Later the number of marines at the Methodist compound was increased to 21. The Americans numbered 56 out of a total of 337 officers and men from the marine and naval detachments of Great Britain, France, Italy, Japan, Russia, and the United States that reached Peking on May 31 to guard the legations. On June 3, an additional 89 German and Austrian marines also reached Peking.

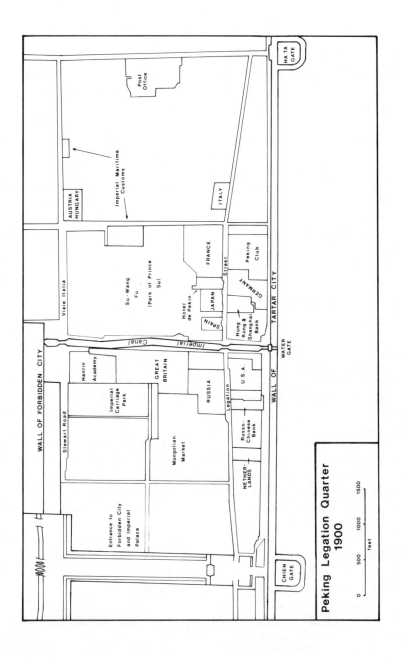

Peking Legation Quarter
1900

0   500   1000   1500
feet

one will dare trespass as long as a foreigner is on guard. That afternoon the cook bought potatoes and collected a few more kitchen utensils from our house, but before he returned, it had been decided that we should move and board with Dr. George Lowry. We moved in the afternoon and Charles sent down both the children's beds and our double mattress. In Dr. Lowry's house we have a large room furnished and are very comfortable. Dr. [James] Ingram and family are in the next room. Dr. Lowry's family is in Tientsin.

Saturday morning at a general meeting it was decided to sift out the Chinese as there were too many for the health of all. Therefore, any who had homes in the city not on Mission property were asked to leave. About one hundred were thus sent away. This of course was a very hard thing to do but it seemed the wisest course and nearly everyone thinks there will probably be no general uprising in the city. Our cook had to take back his family, wife and six children and so asked leave to be gone a day, promising to come back and help me with the washing. During Saturday the church was provisioned with everything we could get that could be eaten without cooking and I did not retire until after two o'clock staying up to boil kettles full of water for drinking. This was carried to the church and placed in large earthen jars.

The men are all very busy fortifying our position. The work is so urgent that they kept at it all day yesterday even though it was Sunday. Mr. [Frank] Gamewell plans and directs everything and the Chinese also assist, no matter whether college bred pastor or humble coolie. A service was held in the morning in Chinese and one at five in the afternoon in English. The ladies were able to keep a quiet Sabbath until about sundown when the gentlemen all asked for cartridge belts.

We have about fifty London Mission[10] converts with our refugees and two Englishmen with them, also one English woman. In view of this, the British Minister, Sir Claude MacDonald, sent ten rifles with ammunition to help us out with defending. So we bought Chinese strong blue cloth and set to work to make belts for the cartridges as fast as possible not knowing but that they would be needed last night. But all was quiet and we think the troops from Tientsin must come soon.[11] I fear when they do come that the ladies and children will be sent to Tientsin, and a good many of us do not wish to go. But just here we are glad that we are Americans for no one will order us away. Our minister can only advise.

[10]The London Mission was a British missionary effort that maintained a school for the blind in the Chinese City of Peking.
[11]Here Bessie is referring to the relief column of more than 2,100 men under the command of Admiral Edward Seymour of the British Navy. Seymour's column never reached Peking.

Thursday, June 14, 1900, Methodist Compound, Peking

Our property in Tungchow, both in the city and at the college outside the city, was looted and burned Saturday and Sunday [June 9 and 10], with a loss estimated at $150,000. It does not seem possible that the beautiful college building where we held our annual meeting only two weeks ago, is all gone and the homes of our dear friends gone too. The new church at Tungchow was roofed and the flooring all laid. We are much concerned now about our friends in Paotingfu. There are Miss [Mary] Morrill, Miss [Annie] Gould and Mr. [H. T.] Pitkin of our mission, the Bagnall family of the China Inland Mission and eight in the Presbyterian mission.[12] There is no possibility of their escape by themselves, the foreign force of marines is too small to send for them, and no Chinese guard is to be trusted. We simply must wait for a larger force and pray God to protect them. Henry [Ewing] and his family are at the shore with a British gun-boat in the harbor ready to take them away in case of danger.[13] Every day we look for more troops from Tientsin as twenty-five hundred are said to be on the way. But they are coming by the railroad, repairing as they come, and their progress is slow.

I get pretty tired each day as the baby's nurse did not come with me. I was surprised that she did not come for I thought nothing would persuade her to leave Ellen. But the moment I spoke of leaving home and said she could do as she pleased, she spoke up quickly, "Enough, hire a cart and get away." It seems she had agreed with two other women that if there was any serious trouble they would all stick together. So we gave her wages for the full month and a little extra and left her. But after trying for four days, without success, to get carts to take them out of the city, she sent word to me on Monday asking if she might come back to me. I was getting along very well and curing Ellen of some bad habits, and it seemed as though the sleeping and feeding of another would trouble others so much. I knew the woman was comfortable at our place [the American Board Compound], and there seemed no immediate danger, therefore I sent back word that she need not come unless as a refugee with the other Christians. She did not come and now it is too late. Oh! I have felt so badly that I did not say, "come" but we thought we were doing the best thing at the time.

Last night [June 13] began the terrors in the city. The Boxers set fire to our property and to many other mission premises.[14] The Christians who

[12]Paoting was not relieved, and the missionaries Bessie mentioned were unprotected by the Chinese army. The result was the deaths of the missionaries and many Chinese Christians.

[13]Henry Ewing had gone with his family to Peitaiho on the Gulf of Chihli and thereby escaped the Paoting killings and the Siege of Peking.

[14]The Boxers and others not only looted and burned missionary property but also that of the Imperial Maritime Customs.

lived near had to run for their lives and our woman must have been among the numbers. Some have reached us but we have heard nothing from her [Ellen's Chinese nurse]. Ellen cries for her a good deal and clings to me all the time. The cook came to me on Monday and put a few clothes to soak, but I could not get any soap that day so he went home again. Now I suppose he and his family are wanderers if they have not already been killed. I had to do the washing myself yesterday but shall not attempt much ironing.

I have the use of Dr. Lowry's kitchen to prepare food for Ellen and also for our orphan girl Martha.[15] She, with her little sister and the old lady who looks after them, came here the same night we did. Martha has been very poorly since the warm weather came on. Her cough is bad, she cannot sleep and can only be tempted to eat. The refugees have only millet, rice and cornmeal cakes and these not well cooked, so I prepare for Martha [food] twice a day and take it to her. Dr. Lowry's cook buys vegetables and eggs for me to give her and I can sometimes get her a little bread and jelly or fresh fruit.

Charles went up to see our house several times on Monday and Tuesday [June 11 and 12] and saved a good deal. He packed and sent down here practically all our clothing, also my good table linen, sheets and pillow cases, best silver and church communion service and our small gold clock. My silver pudding dish was the only large silver piece Charles sent. Our other double mattress was brought down for one of the officers and the bedding was brought with it, but not my best quilt that Auntie Ellen[16] pieced for me. Charles did not have time to pack Mamma's tea-set and that is gone. I feel the worst about losing that. On the last trip Charles brought down all the deeds to our mission property both in Peking and in our out-stations and also brought all the account books, Mission, Press and personal. These had been in the Press safe and Charles sent the books to our Legation to be placed in the safe there.[17] He saved the book of Marion's baby pictures, the record books of the two children, a small album containing pictures of Mamma[18] and of us four children, several of Marion's best picture books, a few playthings and my Chinese primer, over which I have spent so much time and thought.

Dr. Ament had been very bold all along and he did not like it that everybody left their places for it only invited the Boxers to burn and pillage.

[15]This is Bessie's first reference to the Chinese orphan girl whom she called Martha. The Ewings' correspondence does not mention how Bessie came to find Martha or anything about her age or background.
[16]This aunt is Ellen Smith, a sister of Bessie's father.
[17]During the Siege of Peking, the books were misplaced and were lost.
[18]Bessie's mother was Mary Hough Smith, who died in 1875, when Bessie was only four.

In spite of protestations from all, he stayed up at our place [the American Board Compound] until yesterday afternoon [June 13] coming down for a short time other days. But when he came yesterday in time for supper, he said he would stay all night. He came away none too early. As far as we know all our houses are destroyed and also those of the Christians who lived near. The walls to our new church are still standing but every stick of timber was burned or carried off. Charles has worked so hard over that building and the iron [tin] roofing was just being put on when we left.

We all slept in the [Methodist] church last night being hustled in about seven in the evening when the street chapel in connection with this mission was set fire by the Boxers. We did not know but a general attack on us would follow but a few shots from our marines scattered the rioters and there was no more trouble. The gentlemen all have their posts of guard duty and so could not help us. We had not carried much over to the church and so I tried to take all I could in what might be the last chance. Six ladies and nine children slept on the church platform and the rest on the floor between the rows of seats or just inside the altar railing. There are about one hundred school girls who live in the South compound[19] who came over to the church to sleep last night. They spread their cotton quilts on the floor between the rows of seats. The seats are the folding chair style and give a little circulation of air underneath. Twenty of the Chinese girls are from our school, the rest are Methodist school girls. We had nearly seventy but were able to send many of them home to their parents before matters grew so serious, but many of the Methodist girls' homes are too far away.

Tuesday, June 19, 1900, Methodist Compound, Peking

On Monday of last week [June 11] Major Conger sent us ten more marines. He is very kind to give us protection here dividing his own small force, but he is willing to do all he can to help us care for our native Christians.[20] He sent us the marines against the will of the captain and could really have been reprimanded for so doing. We feel very grateful to him for doing so much for our Christians.

By Thursday [June 14] the work of fortification had made good progress.[21] Besides the twenty marines there are twenty-one foreign gentlemen

---

[19]The South compound adjoined the Methodist mission.

[20]This may not be altogether the case, as evidence indicates that Mr. Conger and the other ministers debated the possibility of leaving the Chinese converts in Peking in order to save their own foreign nationals through an evacuation.

[21]The work on fortifying the Methodist compound was directed by the missionary-cum-engineer Frank Gamewell.

and about twenty-five trusty Chinese, all armed with rifles and doing sentry duty. Many other Chinese are armed with spears. Under orders of Captain Hall[22] and under direction of Mr. Gamewell, the sentry lines have been advanced outside the compound on all sides covering all the street approaches; the compound itself has been strengthened against attack and the church has been converted into a small fort. This church will seat about fifteen hundred people and in case of general attack all foreigners and Chinese are to repair thither. Since the burning of the mission compounds many more refugees have come to us so that now there are about seven hundred [Chinese]. We foreigners all told number seventy.[23] The windows of the church have been removed and wire netting put in their place, some are entirely bricked up more than half way leaving loop holes for shooting. Doors have been made of iron roofing to draw up after we enter our fort. Large jars are kept filled with drinking water and water is in readiness on the roof in case of fire. Large sacks of grain, hundreds of eggs, salted meat, cases upon cases of condensed milk, and many kinds of canned goods are piled on the platform to be used in case of siege.[24] Short pointed sticks have been driven into the ground just inside the compound walls, beyond these is a barbed wire fence. In some places a deep trench has been dug inside the fence and a second fence of barbed wire put up on the inner side. The brick walks have nearly all been torn up to make new walls within our compound, cutting off a small enclosure around the church from the rest of the premises. The two large vestibules of the church are filled with trunks, six or eight deep. Our things are all there including a case of milk and a ten pound tin of oatmeal for Ellen.

We had just settled ourselves for the night at about eight o'clock on Thursday when such a din arose as I never heard before in my life and hope never to hear again. The terrible noise was the shouting of a mob just outside the Ha Ta Gate. One continuous yell of "Kill, kill, kill the foreign devil." We were so close that it seemed at first as though the mob were surely inside the gate and would be upon us any minute. But some of the gentlemen came in quickly to relieve our minds and say that the city gate was safely locked between us and them. Still we did not feel very secure, fearing that the gate-keeper would unlock the gate without much objection if the "Boxers" wished to come in. The hideous yelling kept up for two hours and we learned afterwards that the cause was the dividing of the spoils obtained from our foreign premises all over the city.

[22]Captain Newt Hall commanded the U.S. Marine Corps detachment.

[23]This number excludes the twenty U.S. Marine defenders.

[24]Bessie does not mention where the supplies of goods came from, but a considerable amount had been bought or "requisitioned" from nearby vacant Chinese shops.

The next night [June 14–15] we took the precaution to have the key to the big gate in our possession and just here lies one of the great jokes in the midst of all this tragedy. Four of the gentlemen[25] with their guns went and asked the gate-keeper to lock the gate. This he did without hesitation. It was a spring lock and did not need a key for the fastening. Then the gentlemen asked to see the key. When it was brought (an iron bar about two feet long with a peculiar crook at one end) Dr. [James] Ingram took it in his hand and said, "We want this." The gate-keeper demurred but after a little parley gave it up and our gentlemen brought it away, a thousand and more Chinese soldiers standing by and not saying a word. The next morning two gentlemen with four marines went and unlocked the gate and have continued this performance night and morning each day. Sunday a request was received for the Chinese foreign ministry asking us to relinquish the key to the proper authorities and not to take it again, but Major Conger advised us to pay no attention to this request. Nothing more was done.

I continued to sleep in the church at night, but put the children to nap in Dr. Lowry's house, as it was so much quieter there and I could darken the room. One night when it rained I slept in the house, for I was afraid we should take cold in the church with all the windows out. One large skylight had been removed and the rain poured in there besides leaking in many other places. We did not expect an attack in the rain, either, but our guards had to keep at their posts just the same. Umbrellas were bought for the Chinese sentries and the foreign gentlemen managed to get extra covering of some kind. Charles wore his ulster and borrowed a pair of boots. His hours of watch are from twelve to three at noon and at midnight. We can buy provisions every day but many of the servants are afraid to go out. The shops are all shut, but the side doors are open. Several times our gentlemen have had to force sales at the mouth of their guns. The second Sunday [June 17] was more noisy and work-a-day than the first as each day seems to bring an attack nearer. We are now so well fortified that we do not fear the Boxers but only the Chinese soldiers.[26] The latter have not made any open attack as yet, but one of the generals has expressed it as his avowed purpose to prevent the foreign troops entering Peking, and has said that he does not intend to fire on the Boxers. This general alone has command of ten thousand soldiers.

Our American Marines were started off for Peking in such a hurry that they did not have time to get their thin clothes and were sweltering in their thick flannel suits. Our ladies offered to make some thin suits out of blue

[25]The four men were Charles Ewing, John Inglis, Dr. James Ingram, and E. G. Tewksbury.
[26]The Chinese soldiers mentioned here were Moslems for the western province of Kansu under the command of General Tung Fu-hsiang.

drilling and the marines accepted the offer gladly. We have made twenty suits for those who are guarding us and the poor fellows were very grateful and so proud that they want a chance to show off their new clothes to their comrades at the Legation. We did not offer to make a suit for the captain but Dr. Lowry gave him a white duck suit.

Tuesday, June 26, 1900, British Legation, Peking

Tuesday night June 19th just after we were in bed, a note came from Major Conger saying that he with all the other ministers had received word from the Chinese foreign ministry that all foreigners must leave the city [of Peking] within twenty-four hours. The Chinese claimed that some foreign troops had fired on the forts at Taku, just below Tientsin, and that this was a declaration of war, and if we did not get out they would fire on us. The foreign ministry said that they had not declared war, but that the first shots came from the foreigners. Major Conger demanded transportation of course, one hundred carts for one hundred and six Americans. That was an anxious night but I felt sure we would not have to go. We did not believe the story but felt it was a ruse to get us out within easy reach, as our present positions were too strong for the Chinese to attack.[27] Major Conger said we were to wait until his reply came from the foreign ministry. The reply was a refusal to his request.[28] About nine the next morning the German minister[29] was killed and the interpreter shot and then we were all ordered to the American Legation to start at eleven. First we were told we could take all we could carry for baggage, next that nothing could go except what the ladies could carry, next that the ladies and children were to go first and the gentlemen and the Marines would wait until all baggage and provisions had been sent over. With all these conflicting orders it was hard to pack for flight. I could not do much except to attend to Ellen. Her morning lunch is at ten and not knowing when or how she would get another meal I felt this one was very important. She went right to sleep after eating and then I had time to do a little, but everything was so uncertain, and still we thought we should certainly get our trunks, that I had not the heart to pick out much. The day before Charles had packed everything very carefully in view of a possible journey to America. Our small extension bag I filled with necessary articles for myself and the children and Charles got out his clothes, just one

[27]Apparently, Bessie refers only to the Boxers and not the Chinese army commanded by General Tung.
[28]In fact the reply was not a refusal, but a further request to evacuate. At one time a number of the ministers were prepared to evacuate their nationals and leave the Chinese converts behind in Peking.
[29]Baron Klemens von Kettler's wife was an American and was with him in Peking.

change of underclothing. The word came and we formed in line more than fifty ladies and children and a few gentlemen as escort. A number of German marines were in advance carrying the German interpreter on a litter. He had been brought to our compound as he was shot nearby.

I did not carry anything as the two children were enough for me to look after. I took hold of a hat that was in the trunk but Charles said, "No, wear your big sun hat." Mine was badly torn so I put on Marion's, thinking thus to save her hat and feeling sure of getting mine later. Miss [Nellie] Russell and Miss [Elizabeth] Sheffield[30] took turns with me in carrying Ellen, a walk of about a mile while I carried their things. We had been at the Legation only a few minutes when our gentlemen and marine guard came in. Captain [Newt] Hall was afraid of an immediate attack following the murder of the German minister and would not stay [in the Methodist Compound] after the ladies left, so of course the gentlemen had nothing else to do but come too and leave our things. Charles and our orphan boy[31] brought over two hand bags, the small extension bag, our afghan and double shawl. You see our worldly belongings will almost go into a red cotton handkerchief.

We were at the American Legation about two hours and Mrs. [Harriet Bard] Squiers, the wife of the first secretary very kindly prepared and served a lunch for us of crackers, sardines and tea. Then we were all ordered to the British Legation. This had been decided upon as the final place to defend for all foreigners in Peking. Another walk of a few minutes brought us to our last stage. When we feared we might have to leave the Methodist Mission it was doubtful what would be done with the [Chinese] Christians. Several meetings were held when we expressed our determination not to leave them. They must go with us or we would stay. We felt after all they had been through after finally reaching a haven of refuge, and after all they had done for us in the way of fortifying our place, that it could not be that we should be called upon to desert them at the end, but still matters looked pretty dark. Major Conger was very urgent representing that the foreign soldiers [the Legation Guard] could only protect foreigners and that nothing could be expected of them for the [Chinese] Christians. He has been influenced largely by Sir Claude MacDonald, who has been the most backward of any in taking measures against the Boxers, and would not believe there was or could be any very serious trouble. Now that trouble has come he will do nothing for the native Christians. He said his own subjects must come to the Legation if they wished protection but the brave English missionaries would not desert their Chinese brethren, neither would they ask their minister for more favors, saying it was no use, and it was two

[30]Nellie Russell and Elizabeth Sheffield were missionaries with the American Board.
[31]This is Bessie's first mention of "our orphan boy."

American missionaries who interviewed Sir Claude and finally obtained the loan of ten rifles. When the order really came that we were all to go to the Legation we were again in doubt as to the fate of the Christians and did not know surely until the last moments that they could go also. Some days before a number of German marines had rescued a large party of [Chinese] Catholics who were being attacked in one of their cathedrals. Large grounds belonging to one of the princes,[32] were secured and the Catholic refugees placed there. These grounds are situated just across the street from the British Legation and on the other side of the canal.[33] Our Christians were allowed to come away with us and go into the same grounds. Many of them saved their bedding and what few clothes they had. Our orphan boy has no change of clothes. He had a good supply and put them in the church one day when all were suddenly ordered into the fort. We had to stay in only a short time and the Chinese went right out to work again and our boy forgot his clothes. When he went back for them they were gone and no trace of them could be found. Martha's brother carried her over here and saved her bedding. The old woman did not stay with the two children and I am glad. She is seventy-two years old and is not very well and complains all the time that in all her life she never has seen such troubles as these. She has been provoked at me because I did not give her Martha's food money just the same now, even though she is at no expense and has her own food provided besides. She has vented her spite on the children and one night I found Martha crying because the old lady had been scolding at her so much about me. The children are in a room now with a kind woman who takes a great interest in Martha and there are others near by who do for her also. I sent her a can of milk the first day but we are not allowed to go across the street.

As everything remained quiet Wednesday afternoon [June 20] about ten gentlemen and a hundred Chinese went back to the Methodist compound. The looters had been at work and had opened everything that was not fast locked, but a good deal was saved. As neither of our trunks were locked (one lock being broken and the other having the key bent) we lost all. There were great quantities of goods scattered all over the church and these our Chinese gathered up into sheets and quilts as best they could. We had discarded quite a large pile in repacking, thinking the articles selected would do the Chinese refugees more good than they would us, but many of these old things were brought over. Nothing ever appeared from our trunks or big box. About all we gained from the scatterings were my very old winter coat, Charles' old overcoat, one white suit and an extra pair of white trousers, a

[32]Prince Su and his compound, the Su Wang Fu.
[33]The Imperial Canal drained the lakes in the Imperial City and exited through a tunnel under the Tartar Wall midway between the Ha Ta and Chien gates.

flannel underskirt, a torn shirt waist, a crocheted sack of Ellen's, a few soiled clothes, my silver pudding dish without the cover, our gold clock and some bedding. The latter consists of the children's mattresses, Ellen's pillow, one thin quilt, one mosquito net, three large sheets and four small ones and three pillowcases. Charles has one thin suit besides the old white one and two sets of underclothing. I have three wash dresses and four extra shirt waists. Marion has six wash dresses and a skirt without blouse waist. Ellen has seven dresses. We each have a change of underclothing and a little flannel for cooler weather. Ellen's thin coat and mine are also saved. Handkerchiefs, ribbons, brushes and combs, etc., we had in our bags but we have not a Bible to our name. They were beside my bed and when I started for them I was interrupted and then they slipped my mind. The only book we have is Marion's primer, which she began reading in the Spring. Ellen has one cotton night dress and I have my two wrappers for night wear. Someone has given me a flannel nightdress for each of the children and loaned me blankets, for the first night was quite cool.

Well we reached here Wednesday afternoon with the purpose expressed by the minister to stay and fight it out. Word was received that night from the Chinese foreign ministry expressing their deep feeling for the foreigners and saying that the utmost protection would be afforded. They said as it was impracticable for us to leave the city we should receive protection here and the Chinese soldiers had orders not to fire on us, and they hoped that we would feel no alarm and that our soldiers [the Legation Guards] would preserve the peace. Acting, as we suppose on this avowal, Prof. James[34] were out of the compound just before dark and unarmed. He had been with the native Christians trying to help them get settled in their new quarters and we think he may have gone out to do more for them. A British soldier on guard saw all that followed. Prof. James walked as far as the bridge to the north and there a few [Chinese] soldiers rode up. Some three hundred had passed a few minutes before and these were the stragglers. One soldier raised his gun to fire but Prof. James threw up his hands to show that he was unarmed. The soldier lowered his gun and Prof. James started to run. He was again covered with the rifle and this time the soldier dismounted, laid his hand on Prof. James' shoulder and led him away. Our men had strict orders not to fire the first shot and so they had to obey and a brave man must lose his life, perhaps after severe torture. We know not the end but cannot but think he was killed in some way. Prof. James has shown a very helpful spirit through all. He predicted serious trouble and promised to stand by the missionaries and the Chinese to the end and did as much to

[34]Professor Huberty James was a faculty member of the Peking University and a Sinophile whose compassion for the Chinese cost him his life.

gain protection for the native Christians as any of the missionaries. He was very busy all the time collecting reliable news, assisting Dr. Morrison.[35] The latter has been really the only correspondent whose words have had weight in England. He has been very careful only to tell authenticated facts and his care has been rewarded. Ten minutes after Prof. James was led away firing commenced, the first shots from the Chinese soldiers. This firing has kept up almost without intermission but without apparent aim or purpose except to frighten us. The Chinese do not dare to show their heads, but point their guns up into the air and bang away. We soon got used to this. After a few days of firing most of the soldiers [marines] and citizens left their respective legations and came here for combined defense, but the next day Sir Claude sent the soldiers back with orders to hold their legations as long as possible.[36] In this way we cover territory about sixty acres in extent, while the civilians occupy the least exposed compound [the British Legation], covering about seven acres.

Yesterday a flag of truce was hung up on the bridge and a messenger sent. The purport of his letter was that the Chinese were very sorry that our soldiers had opened fire and they sincerely wished that hostilities might cease. Strict orders were being given to their own soldiers to stop all firing and they hoped that our soldiers would be given the same orders. Of course we said we would be glad to stop if the Chinese did. Just about midnight we were wakened by rapid firing and the fiercest attack followed with the first cannonading of the war [i.e., the siege]. It lasted about half an hour and then quiet reigned. That ended the truce.[37]

Saturday, July 7, 1900, British Legation, Peking

We seventy American missionaries were given the chapel for our residence. The main room is about forty feet by twenty-five. Here forty people sleep every night. There are two closets at the front which we use for bath rooms. The children have a small room at the back. There is a larger room at the rear of the church which is used as a pantry. We sleep on the floor and on the settees. The altar is the china closet. Dishes and canned goods have been taken from the foreign stores. A number of gentlemen sleep in the loft and some sleep out doors in open pavilions. Charles is among the latter number. Several ladies sleep in Lady [Ethel Armstrong] MacDonald's ball room.

[35]George E. Morrison was the correspondent for the *London Times*.

[36]At this point in the siege of the Legation Quarter, Sir Claude MacDonald had been recognized by the ministers as their military leader.

[37]Bessie does not refer here to the truce at the Legation Quarter that lasted from July 17 to July 26.

There are thirty-five of our [American Board] mission including ten children, nineteen of the Presbyterian mission including the Reids[38] and Mr. [William B.] Stelle and sixteen of the Methodist mission. We have our meals by denominations this being a natural division. The Congregational [American Board] hours are 6:00 A.M., 11:30 A.M. and 6:00 P.M. I am glad we have ours first, even though the breakfast is pretty early. But some of the children wake by four o'clock and there is not much sleep possible after five, so I can generally get myself and Marion ready in time, though her hair is not always combed until later. Ellen cries so if I leave her that I often make my toilet in my own corner without going to the bath room. We have two settees placed together under a large west window just in front of the pulpit. I have three chairs at one end where Ellen sleeps, and Marion and I lie on the single mattress with our heads at opposite ends. We generally have to untangle our feet several times during the night. As we eat in the same place, seated on our bed, and have to get through in time for the next table to use the dishes, I can't be late even though that means breakfasting with untidy hair. To such a pass we have come that we wonder whether we will ever recover from the demoralization or not. Gentlemen and ladies all have to sleep in this room without even curtain partitions. A good many do not undress at all except to pull off their shoes. The gentlemen must all be ready to go on duty in case of sudden attack.

The flies are something terrible in numbers. The room literally swarms with them, and all possible means cannot keep them out of our food. Because of [their] feeding on so many [animal] carcasses that are lying dead all around, it is a marvel that this does not cause disease among us. The flies wake us all at the first streak of dawn, and it is amusing to hear the sudden buzzing that starts up in the night when the cannons commence to boom.

The housekeeping arrangements are to a large extent in the hands of our committee. This consists of three ladies, one from each mission. They make out the menu each day and vie the orders to the [Chinese] cooks. Our bread is all baked by the Hotel [de Pekin] manager and of course we do not have cake or pastry. Everything in the way of food material has to be carefully measured out and all left-overs kept for the next meal. A famous dish we have is siege pancakes. These are made out of the remnants of cereal, rice and stale bread with baking powder to raise them. At first we ate molasses on them but now that is gone we use sugar. As there is very little canned meat in our supply and only a few sheep which must be saved for invalids food and the cow's [sic] milk is more valuable than their flesh, we have begun eating horse flesh. This is in reality not such a hardship as

[38]Dr. Gilbert Reid was a Protestant missionary who was not affiliated with a major church denomination.

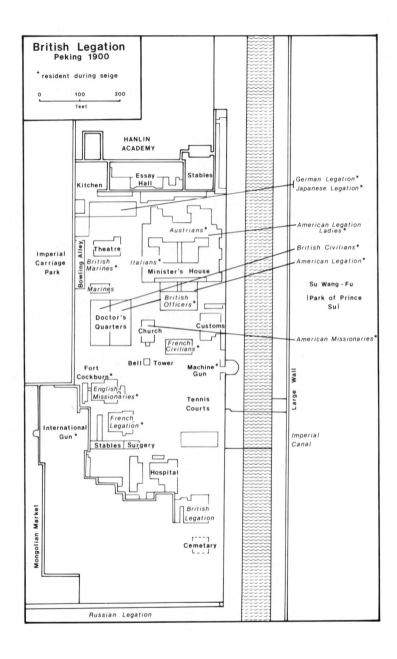

British Legation
Peking 1900

* resident during seige

0   100   200
feet

HANLIN ACADEMY

Kitchen   Essay Hall   Stables

German Legation*
Japanese Legation*

Imperial Carriage Park

Bowling Alley

Theatre

British Marines*

Marines

Austrians*

Italians*

Minister's House

American Legation Ladies*

British Civilians*

American Legation*

Su Wang - Fu
[Park of Prince Su]

British Officers*

Doctor's Quarters

Church   Customs

French Civilians*

American Missionaries*

Bell □ Tower

Fort Cockburn*

English Missionaries*

Machine Gun*

International Gun*

French Legation*

Tennis Courts

Large Wall

Stables Surgery

Hospital

Imperial Canal

British Legation

Mongolian Market

Cemetary

Russian Legation

one would suppose. It was rather hard to most to muster courage for the first taste, but now that we have become accustomed to the diet it is not easy to tell the difference between horse flesh and beef.

There are two cooks and they have to prepare everything on a small Chinese range. Two of our ladies act as housekeepers each day, making the tea and coffee on oil stoves, cutting and spreading bread, preparing dishes of butter, sugar and milk and serving the rest when all is ready. We each take a plate, cup, knife and fork and spoon and sit down wherever we can find room. Two others assist the housekeepers in waiting, and they are kept busy I can assure you. The housekeepers are changed each day. There are eight Chinese servants belonging to our whole party. They wash the dishes (nine times each day), bring the food from the kitchen which is on the opposite side of the court, draw water and do the hard work of cleaning the chapel and the court.

We Congregationalists have charge of cleaning [the chapel] every third day and the Presbyterians and Methodists attend to the other days. We also have the care of the bath rooms and the court around the chapel. There are so many more of us that of course it is fair for us to do more of the cleaning. Most of the carpet has been taken up and put in the loft, but the church cushions will be used as table seats for the children and to fill up the depressions in the settees so that our beds will be even. These cushions must be beaten, all the settees and everyone's baggage moved, and the floor all swept and mopped each day. There is not much chance for quiet.

Breakfast lasts from six to nine followed by prayers then an hour for the cleaning and dinner for half past eleven to half past two. Supper begins at four and keeps up until seven and then people begin to retire. We are not allowed lights in the evening, except a candle for a short time, as the enemy could more easily locate us, and as we must rise so early we try to get to bed early.

Nearly every day since the siege began attempts have been made to burn us out. On some sides there were open spaces but there were many buildings adjoining us and these have nearly all been burned now. At the time of the fires every one was busy, even the ladies forming in lines from the wells to help pass water. But none of our own buildings caught [fire] and we were thankful after every fire that there was one more clear space next to us. Many of these burned buildings were shops and large quantities of confiscated goods were collected. Some food and coal was thus added to our stock, but many of the goods were cloth and garments. The latter were carefully distributed among the native refugees and the former was made up into sandbags. These bags are made seventeen by thirty-four inches in size filled with common dirt found in the yard and piled up to make barricades. The ladies work all day at this sewing, and some of it is pretty hard.

We have two machines in the chapel that are buzzing away most of the time. At Mrs. Conger's and other houses they are equally as busy. The material that has gone into these sandbags would make a fortune. Most elegant silks and satins, beautiful figured goods, legation curtains and damask, fine bed spreads, woolen blankets of the soldiers, whole pieces of foreign cloth and large quantities of cotton cloth have been among the variety. Some of us exchanged strong cloth, such as sheets, pillow cases and bed spreads for thin silks, embroideries, and dress goods. I put in two large sheets and received six yards and a half of very fine black cashmere. Mrs. Mateer will give me skirt lining and I was given enough odd pieces of legation chair covers for a waist lining. I have hooks and eyes from the same source. A beautiful piece of light blue grass cloth came in about ten yards but very narrow, and I made another exchange for that. Now Marion can have a nice dress.

Last Sunday [July 1] we made arrangements for a service in the chapel, but just before the time for the service word came in that our American marines would have to leave their positions on the City wall unless they could have several hundred sandbags within two hours. The losing of this position means almost certain destruction to us, so you may be sure the needles flew on that Sunday and we made the necessary number. I say we, for I was able to make three or four bags while Ellen slept. The Chinese women and school girls also help in this sewing. When the sandbags are not in urgent demand, there is bedding for the hospital to be made, and trousers for the rest of our American marines.

What a queer Fourth-of-July we passed! We hoped very much that the troops would arrive by that day, and Sir Claude promised to celebrate with us Americans if our hopes were realized, but again we were disappointed. Rumors have come that the first party [Admiral Seymour's relief force] had to go back for reinforcements and that the larger force has not yet started. That means at least another ten days of suspense.[39] We all wore badges in honor of the day, a red, white and blue bow made out of heavy Chinese silk cord. Mrs. Squires invited all the American children to a little treat. We received souvenirs in the shape of cancelled meal tickets which the Chinese had used. In order to be just and not let the lazy ones get out of all the work, each man is given a meal ticket after his day's work, and if he has no ticket to show he receives no allowance of food. The foreign gentlemen have each ten to twenty Chinese in charge who work on fortifications and they have to keep a sharp look-out to see that none of them run off. Some of the Chinese [students] are detailed for laundry work, but they are green hands. I am thankful to get my clothes through soap and water, although I

---

[39]It was actually forty more days of suspense.

cannot be sure that they will be much cleaner when they come back than when they are sent. There is only starch enough for collars and nothing else seems to be ironed.

Yesterday Charles cut Ellen's hair. Oh! I did feel so sorry to do it but it is best for the poor little thing. It is so hot that after her nap her head looks as though it had been put into a basin of water and she rubs and pulls her hair a great deal when trying to go to sleep. I have saved the two cunning little braids that were tied on each side of her head, and also a few ringlets, marking the package, "Relics of the siege of Peking." Today I have engaged one of the Tungchow women to help me with Ellen. Ellen is not at all well and frets so much that I am about tired out. She cannot bear to have me out of her sight or do anything but amuse her when I am near. I have to fan her and sing to her to put her to sleep and when she is quiet there are so many things to do that I don't feel as though I could lie down and rest then.

Sunday, July 8,1900, British Legation, Peking

Today is more quiet than for several Sabbaths past. The ladies do not have to sew but most of the gentlemen are as busy as usual. We had a short service this morning at which a number from the Custom House [Imperial Maritime Customs] and from our Legation were present. Last night a stray shell struck one corner of the chapel taking off one of the little ornaments from the roof. These midnight attacks, though generally short, are much worse than in the day time. To be awakened out of a sound sleep by a storm of shot and shell is something terrible. Several times the big bell has been tolled as the signal of a general attack. This added to the cannonading of the enemy and the return fire from our men makes even me shudder. In the day time there is so much confusion that one does not always distinguish sounds, but when all else is quiet these sudden onslaughts are appalling. It seems as though we must surely be overcome and when a lull comes in the storm I dream of a Boxer sword poised over my neck. That first night of fierce firing I could not help asking myself if I was willing to die. I did not feel afraid to die but I would rather live longer. I feared most that Charles might be killed and that I should be left alone with the children. I tried to be willing for whatever God thought best, but prayed that we might not be taken from our dear ones at home in such a terrible manner. Now even these night attacks have lost much of their terror. Of course I waken but often fall asleep again before the firing ceases.

We had a Bible reading this afternoon on the Ninety-first Psalm. How true and real every verse is to us now! Later there was a quiet sing out in front of the chapel and then I took a little walk with Charles and we had a quiet talk together. This has seemed more like a real Sunday than for several weeks past and has been indeed a rest to my heart.

Monday, July 9, 1900, British Legation, Peking

Our "International" cannon has been making itself heard today. The Russians had some big shells but no gun to fire them. A cannon was found in a Chinese junk shop which fitted these shells. It was evidently of English make and was probably brought over in 1860.[40] It was brought here, mounted on an Italian ammunition carriage, fired by an American gunner into the Chinese Imperial City from the British Legation. Because of this history the gun has been given its present name. Its first shell went over into the Forbidden City (the palace grounds) and so surprised the Chinese that they immediately popped up their heads over their barricades to see what had happened. Our rifle shots soon stopped that.

Charles was busy all the morning from seven until noon superintending the building of a ten foot wall beside the house of the British minister. In fact Charles did a good deal of the brick laying himself. The bricks had first to be torn up from the walks and from the flooring of the pavilions. Sir Claude's house is very much exposed and has received a good many shots. There have been narrow escapes but no serious accidents. One day after the table was all set for lunch a large cannon ball pierced the wall just over the Queen's picture and the scattering plaster very much disarranged the table furnishings. Last night about one hundred Christians were brought over to this side and lodged near the American Legation. This place has been seized since we came into siege and the residents sent away. Here our Christians are very comfortable, having small courts and houses by themselves. Each family is given its supply of food raw and so can cook it to suit themselves. More families have come today and also all the school girls. There were fierce fires all day yesterday next to the Chinese quarters across the canal and it was thought best to remove the people before any imminent danger. The Japanese are rather glad to have the place burned but still they probably cannot hold all the ground [of the Su Wang Fu] that they now have.

I am not feeling very well this morning. The steady diet of horse and mule does not agree with most of us. Ellen seems nearly well but has not eaten very much today. When we came from the Methodist mission I brought enough milk to last Ellen ten days, hoping to get our whole case over later, but still thinking the smaller amount would be all that would be needed until the troops should come [from Tientsin]. But a second ten

[40]In 1860 the British and the French occupied Peking for a short time.

days has almost passed by and still no relief. I have to use milk from the general supply now and there are but a few cans of the unsweetened, so I have to use all sweetened. I brought one cup and two spoons to use in preparing the milk, but as the supply of dishes is small I put my few in with the general stores and now one of the spoons has been lost. It was one that was Mamma's, the other is one of my solid silver spoons. This afternoon I prepared some thick gruel for Ellen's supper and she ate it very greedily. It is the first she has had since we left the Methodist mission. A gentlemen gave several mothers each a tin of oatmeal. I exchanged for barley from the common stock, and can generally find some time when the oil stove is not in use when I can prepare the gruel. Ellen drank one cup full with hardly a stop for breath then said "Mamma det um more." A second cup followed with the same refrain, and then a third with still a request for more. But there was a little left in the third cup and she did not quite finish it after all. The woman is doing very nicely, but Ellen cries for me a good deal. Today I have made her a silk shirt.

Tuesday, July 10, 1900, British Legation, Peking

Today the barber clipped Ellen's hair close to her head, she does look so queer but it is so much more comfortable. Charles did not get it cut very even and we have been waiting to have the barber complete the trimming. It is funny to see Ellen try to pull her hair now, and as she finds she can't get hold of it she has begun pulling out her long eyelashes. Today she has felt poorly again, has not slept well and has cried for me all afternoon. I lay down with Marion for a little rest and wake to hear Ellen crying. Then I had to leave her with the woman a while longer so that I could make her gruel. Tonight she ate a good amount but the gruel curdled in her stomach and she was sick in half an hour after eating. Then she went to sleep quietly. The Chinese woman asked to go back to her friends for a day or two as she came away in such a hurry. All her clothes were soiled and she borrowed from someone else to come. There is no chance here to wash, and so she wanted to go back and get cleaned up. She is not very well herself and Ellen crying so much with her, I feel doubtful about her return.

Wednesday, July 11, 1900, British Legation, Peking

This morning Dr. Ingram said I better not let the Chinese woman return as there had been scarlet fever in the court where she had gone. We are more afraid of pestilence than of bullets. A great many, both children and older people have diarrhea or dysentery. One family has lost their two children from the latter disease. Ellen ate her breakfast at quarter past six this morning and would not eat again until four this afternoon. She asked for food once before but when she tasted that it was only milk and not the gruel she would not eat it. Miss Sheffield took her for about an hour after dinner to give me a chance to get a nap.[41] I had charge of cleaning the church this morning. I have not been able to help much before, and even with a Chinese woman [helping me] it was doubtful whether I could be depended on for the house keepers work, so I have been put in charge of the cleaning every day of our turn with one other lady to help me. There are four Chinese to do the hard work but with all the picking up and arranging the ladies have to do a good deal too. I took our mattresses out for an airing and beat all the cushions, besides wiping off a number of shelves and small tables. As Ellen did not go to sleep as early as usual Miss Sheffield took care of her while I cleaned house. Ellen likes Miss Sheffield best next to mamma and papa. She has been happier today than for a long time.

Thursday, July 12, 1900, British Legation, Peking

We had a very quiet night, scarcely a shot, but the weather was so hot that many could not sleep. I was thankful that the children slept. I woke very often to fan myself and the children until drowsiness overcame me again but the sleep was not very restful. This is the third very warm day, the thermometer was nearly 100° in the shade. This, our sixth [wedding] anniversary, is being passed in a strange manner. We have a great deal to be thankful for. Our health as a family has been very good. Ellen is much better, though very likely she will not be entirely well as long as we are here. I am all right now and Marion had only one day of trouble. She regularly loses two hours sleep each day and it is a wonder that she keeps up. Poor little Miriam Ingram[42] has some kind of skin disease. She was bitten on her face, then scratched it, and then the sores spread. Her face on one side is covered and more sores are coming on her body. The doctor gives no hope of cure until we get to a better place where the air is purer. Miss [Ada] Haven[43] has been very poorly all the time, probably malaria, though if so, it is the first time she has ever had this disease. Martha Fenn[44] was very low with dysentery but is much better now. She is a month younger than Ellen. Charles is very tired but keeps up all the time.

[41]Again Bessie avoids mention of her pregnancy during the siege. The Ewing's first son, Edward Alvord Ewing, was born December 26, 1900, in Connecticut.

[42]Daughter of Methodist missionaries Dr. and Mrs. James Ingram.

[43]Following the Boxer Uprising, Ada Haven, an American Board missionary, married Calvin Mateer. She would later write a book, *Siege Days* (New York: F. H. Revell, 1903) with contributions from many of those present in Peking.

[44] Daughter of Presbyterian missionaries Mr. and Mrs. Courtnay Fenn.

Friday, July 13, 1900, British Legation, Peking

Last evening Ellen went to sleep early and I thought I should have a quiet time with Charles. However she woke up again and Charles was asked to go to some work at eight o'clock. I felt very much disappointed for we have very few chances together, and I did want to talk on our anniversary evening. Ellen did not get to sleep until five minutes of eight, but five minutes before that Charles came to the window and said he did not have to go to work after all. So we did have a quiet time after all. We are all awake so early every morning and are disturbed so much in our nights sleep that I have to go to bed early too, and am asleep nearly every night by half past eight. Some nights the firing is very bad and some baby is pretty sure to have a crying spell and waken all the grown people if not the other babies.

Sunday, July 15, 1900, British Legation, Peking

Today has been quiet and we have not had to make sandbags. Just as last week there were devotional exercises at half-past nine and a Bible reading at three. There was also a Church of England service at Sir Claude's house. Besides these there were separate services for the hospital patients, the sick Chinese, the school girls and for other Chinese.

Ellen has been very languid for three days and has not eaten half her usual amount of food. She had a high fever two nights and is cutting her double teeth [molars]. She cut through one while we were at the Methodist mission, and now one and a half more are through. This with all the commotion and crowded quarters and in the midst of a summer in Peking is enough to make her miserable. She just moans for me or her papa if we go out of sight. Charles says she is fully as well here as she was last year at the "Hills" and I think he is right, although of course we think she would be better in better conditions. She has not apparently lost weight before, but this fever is telling on her and her little arms are no longer hard and firm. I have tried the housekeepers work and enjoy it. Charles is not quite as busy now at meal times and can often amuse Ellen for a while. The waiters eat after all the rest are through and I like that, we know how much there is left and can have a second help without fear of robbing others. I ate all I wanted on those two days that I served as waiter. I generally do get enough but have such a greedy feeling all the time. Many of the ladies cannot eat the coarse food, brown rice and coarse graham bread, but I have been well enough so far to eat anything. We have a number of delicacies obtained from the foreign stores, such as sardines, extract of beef, canned fruit, jellies, etc., but these have to be dealt out sparingly. One Sunday dessert consisted of one large macaroon or two small ones, two nuts and two candies for each person. These had all to be divided out into dishes beforehand, for it would never have done [*sic*] to pass them around in quantity.

Monday, July 16, 1900, British Legation, Peking

This morning Rev. Arthur Smith[45] led prayers and recalled our attention to the many special Providences of our situation. First, we have been able to protect our native Christians after many refusals at the beginning. And our having them with us gives a force that makes it possible for us to fortify our grounds and to fight the fierce fires. The few foreigners could not have done this alone. Second, the foreigners have been able to collect in a body in a defensible position. Third, this vast body is being fed. We number a little over eight hundred foreigners of all the large nations (including the four hundred marines) and nearly three thousand Chinese, two thousand being Catholics.[46] Mr. Smith brought out the facts about so many of our number (the party from Tungchow) having come from outside the city without a particle of food and still food was to be had in abundance. We have already been sustained here in siege twenty-seven days and could probably go on another month without much trouble. Even when we came from the Methodist mission we had to leave nearly all the provisions with which we had stocked the church. Only a small proportion was saved, and when there we had bought out the foreign stores in some lines. On the day of our arrival here [at the British Legation] a Chinese shop was found supplied with foreign canned goods. The owner had left and our committee seized the goods, keeping a careful account in order to pay in the future. A large grain shop was also found and the proprietor asked us to clean out his stock without pay. Of course he expects pay later, but he knows that his countrymen would take all he had now whether grain or money. In another grain shop were found several tons of wheat in the kernel, this year's growth. Grist mills were also ready to our use and the grain has been ground and bolted. Though not very fine it is eatable and nourishing.

The abundant water supply is also remarkable. There are eight wells in the compound, five of them containing good drinking water. In all Peking we never should have expected to find water safe to drink without first boiling, but one of these wells [the most centrally situated] has delicious water and most of us drink clear and cold just as it is drawn.

[45]Arthur H. Smith was an American Board missionary. Following the end of the siege he would write *China in Convulsion* (New York: F. H. Revell, 1901).

[46]There are varying figures for the number of besieged foreigners and Chinese in the Legation Quarter. However, Bessie's figures are close to other reliable estimates except for the number of marines. Her figure is high, since forty-five French and Italian marines were at the Peitang cathedral compound.

At first old buildings near us, from which there was danger of fire, were torn down and the wood used for fuel. Later coal was found in great abundance, enough to last for months. Although part of the premises occupied formerly by the Christians has had to be given up, the new quarters are much safer and more comfortable. Before the people were huddled together and many had only open pavilions for shelter. When the rains came on ten days ago, this shelter was of course insufficient. Now nearly all have good houses, some even better than their original homes.

Another special Providence is the comparative good health of all. When every one would naturally predict sickness and pestilence, on the whole all keep well and some who were very low have largely recovered. Only the babies do not get better. Still another thing that is so remarkable, and nothing else but a miracle can explain it, is the great preservation of life in the midst of constant firing. Of course during any special attack we stay indoors (the ladies and children) but stray shots are coming all the time. Men, women and little children are continually passing back and forth through the compound, and yet not one citizen has been seriously hurt. Charles stood in the doorway next to where a shell burst mortally wounding a young girl, broken pieces of shell and spent bullets have often fallen near him, and one bullet fell just beside the baby carriage when Ellen was riding in it. Shells are bursting over our heads and falling in fragments. Solid balls from four to fourteen pounds in weight have entered dwelling houses and pierced many walls, but in all this compound only two persons have been killed and these were marines.[47] Even the soldiers [marines] who know God's name only to take it in vain, have borne testimony that nothing but the power of God could thus preserve life. In their own posts of danger where many have been killed they recognize the same power as keeping them from being entirely wiped out. Just think of it! Not five hundred trained men holding out here for nearly a month against thousands and thousands of Chinese soldiers, besides many Boxers, and with no artillery until the finding of our "International."

For fear that cannonading should greatly increase, bombproof shelters have been built for a final retreat. Large pits have been dug roofed over and covered with several layers of sandbags. From ten to twenty-five people are supposed to crowd into each of these, if necessary, but we all hope we shall not be driven into such suffocating holes.

On Thursday [July 12] a return messenger of ours came in with evidence of a severe beating. He claimed to have been caught just outside the wall

---

[47]Bessie refers here only to the British Legation compound. By the end of the siege a total of 79 men had been killed and 190 wounded within or very near the Legation Quarter.

and taken to the palace of Prince Tuan.[48] There he was given a letter proposing peace to the foreign ministers and was sent back with another messenger from the palace, the latter to wait for our answer. The letter was a piece of bold impudence in its tone, and our ministers simply replied, "Impossible." The messenger could give no word whatever of foreign troops, but said the first relay of three thousand had gone back to Tientsin on account of an attack there. He said that Tientsin was burned on the sixteenth of June and that the foreign troops had captured the forts at Taku.[49] The almost daily rumors of the near approach of the [Western] troops have about ceased. Even the sure evidence of the distant sound of foreign cannon and the sight of the well known flash light from one of the English gunboats, we have had to doubt as the days go by. I am afraid our hopes furnished most of the material for these stories. Now any such rumors are received with scorn. We will believe the foreign troops are a reality when we see them. However, we do believe in our final deliverance. After all that God has done for us so far, we cannot think he means us as a whole to be swept out. His way and His time will surely see us safely through. Only a small proportion of missionaries can remain here,[50] but our rescued converts must be provided for.

Tuesday, July 17, 1900, British Legation, Peking

There was a new sensation this morning in the form of a letter from the foreign ministry containing a telegram for Major Conger in the private code of the State Department at Washington.[51] The letter said that a reply from us would be transmitted. The telegram was "communicate tidings bearer." The last word was puzzling and Major Conger sent back a letter of inquiry. This evening came the reply that the telegram was from Washington and dated July eleven. We suppose it must have been sent through the Chinese minister. Major Conger sent the following cable in cipher, "Surrounded and fired upon by Chinese for a month. If not relieved soon, massacre will follow." Another letter from the palace states that the firing was begun by our soldiers and requests us to cease. It also says that there are some American soldiers on the City wall who are making a nuisance of themselves and they

[48]Prince Tuan, a Manchu prince and cousin of the emperor, was an anti-Western adviser to the Empress Dowager.
[49]Part of the Chinese city of Tientsin was burned by the Boxers on June 14, and the Taku forts were taken on the seventeenth.
[50]Bessie's dire prophecy about the future number of missionaries proved wrong. Within two years after the end of the Boxer Uprising there were more missionaries in China than ever before.
[51]This telegram arrived during the truce that existed from July 17 to July 26.

hope that these [men] will be withdrawn. Another private letter to Sir Claude mentions some change in the palace and promises another letter tomorrow. Evidently there is a split and two forces are working for power, for at the same time with these peace advances the shot and shell continue to pour in.[52]

Ellen slept all night and has slept six full hours today, only waking for food. After her third nap this afternoon she seemed quite a little brighter.

Monday, July 23, 1900, British Legation, Peking

Yesterday afternoon I went to see Martha and some of our other Christians. Now that they are on this side of the canal we are allowed to visit them. Poor Martha, she has changed fast and is evidently in the last stages of consumption. It makes me feel so bad not to be able to do more for her. The milk supply is getting so low that it is all reserved for the babies, and, of course, I cannot take any to Martha.

There has been a sort of half truce since the letters from the palace and some Chinese soldiers were induced to come near enough our lines for conversation. The result is an egg market, the soldiers bringing the eggs concealed on their bodies. Even with this precaution we know that several have been killed by their officers for thus helping the enemy. But what a Godsend these eggs are to us. Ellen was almost wild over hers. I am allowed to buy three a day but only children or sick persons have permission to eat these luxuries. I saved two to take to Martha but felt almost guilty in doing that. Now I have seen her I don't know as she will be able to eat even eggs.

The little Inglis baby[53] died yesterday. She was not quite a year old and had cut five teeth since we came into siege. She kept well the longest of any of the children, but just faded away when she was taken sick. The last few days the only thing she could keep on her stomach was the whites of eggs.

Wednesday, August 15, 1900, British Legation, Peking

At last the troops [of the International Relief Force] are really here. The first ones, swarthy Indian Sikhs,[54] came into the compound yesterday afternoon about three o'clock. All the night before we heard heavy firing and knew without a doubt that our relief was at hand. I think that I was the

[52]Bessie may have meant that prior to the truce "shot and shell continue to pour in," since during the truce it was relatively calm.

[53]Elizabeth Inglis was the daughter of Presbyterian missionaries Dr. and Mrs. John Inglis.

[54]Here Bessie may have her British Indian soldiers confused, as the first to enter the Legation Quarter were Rajputs.

only grown person who slept any after eleven o'clock. I woke before then and realized the good news, but was too tired to get up.[55] Several came to my bedside and asked me if I heard the firing. I sleepily answered "yes," hoping they would soon quiet down but the talking only increased with much passing back and forth through the room. It did not seem as though I could have the children wakened, and I did need the rest so much for another day. When for the third time I was disturbed by "Have you heard the good news?", I said yes but I don't see why you want to talk all night about it and wake up all the children. Finally I said "Thank the Lord and go to sleep in peace." I was so nearly worn out as to have no more enthusiasm or sympathy than just that. Even through the day I did not get worked up to the situation. When everyone else rushed out at the last to greet the soldiers as they entered, I stayed behind with my sick baby who was trying to go to sleep. But as the "huzzas" rang out on the air a thrill ran through my heart and I did feel the excitement of the day and the relief from the long strain.

The last three weeks have been the hardest. I was quite sick for one week and the doctor tried to keep me on liquid or low diet. That treatment cured me but left me very weak. The low diet would probably have been all right if there had been any material, but beef extract was about all that could be obtained. I had mutton broth twice and a very little white rice towards the last. I did have one or two eggs but then the market closed. Some of the egg peddlers were shot by the French guard, and of course, that put a stop to the business. When after two weeks of starvation I was allowed to go back to pony steak [horsemeat] and coarse brown rice I felt much better. However I cannot eat the graham bread any more. In fact it is very painful now for me to eat at all as my mouth is filled with cankers.

The [Chinese] woman whom I had [for Ellen] did not return but her younger sister has helped me a good deal. She is the widow of our Tungchow pastor and it is very kind of her to come to me. Ellen took to her at first and they got along very nicely, but lately no one but mamma will suit her. The poor little thing has had a terrible sore on her left shoulder, an eruption just like Miriam Ingram's. She did not scratch it and so carry the poison to other parts, but the sore enlarged until there was a raw place about an inch and a half in diameter. A smaller one broke out on her cheek, and one commenced in her hair but these did not spread. The dear child tried not to cry but moaned, "baby hurt, baby hurt, mamma put on medicine." The summer complaint has become chronic with her and no medicine has any effect. She is too weak to stand on her feet and wants petting

[55]Between July 24 and August 14, Bessie was quite ill and hence made no entries in her diary during that period.

all the time. She screams "go way, go way" at sight of the [Tungchow] woman, and so this last week I have only asked her to do some washing and have not worried Ellen. Charles has helped me a good deal, but he has had to work on the fortifications just the same although we did know our rescue was near.

The Chinese redoubled their efforts to exterminate us the last few nights and it did seem as though they were going to succeed on Monday night [August 13]. They made six distinct fierce attacks on all sides at once, and how our alarm bell did ring.

Since the attacks have been less numerous, the gentlemen have had time to make matters more comfortable in the chapel. The loft has been cleaned up a good deal and room made for a number of ladies to sleep. Other ladies have been accommodated in some of Lady MacDonald's rooms, and when it did not rain some of the gentlemen slept outdoors. In that way we have not been so crowded in the main room. Several tables and benches were brought into the chapel and placed together making room for over thirty to sit down at once. Since then we have eaten in two messes instead of three, and had the Chinese wait on us more so that the house-keepers eat with the rest.

Charles slept on one of the long tables right beside our bed when I was sick and took care of the children at night. I have been obliged to give Ellen her milk weaker than she needed on account of the short supply and so she has had to drink once in the night. The morning the troops came I opened the last can in the general stores, but there are a few more cans to be had from private parties.

Another comfort has been the punkas (large swinging fans). For these the theatre scenery was used with fringe of newspapers to help scatter the flies. We could not have them pulled all the time, but to be able to eat without a swarm of flies on the table was comfort indeed.

Monday, August 20, 1900, British Legation, Peking

Today we expected to leave Peking, but no, the expectation had to be postponed. We were making preparations on Saturday when word came that we could not start until Tuesday, so Charles did not go out again that night. He had been trying to buy some necessary things for our journey but every shop in this region has been looted and there is no business anywhere. Then the commissary department ceased acting for us as soon as the siege was raised, and we were in more danger from scarcity of food than during the siege itself. So a foraging committee was appointed, Charles being one of the members. We have had beef once and quantities of chickens, but no eggs, fresh vegetables or fruit can be obtained. The farmers are all too

much afraid of the foreign soldiers to venture into the city. When Charles
was out one morning he heard a hen cackle and followed the sound, hoping
to get an egg. No egg was found and the hen got away too, but he spied
one squash and brought that back as a prize. With this foraging Charles
could not do much else, but on Sunday word came that we were to start
after all the next morning, so then we had to hustle around. As we could
not buy anything, the next thing was to confiscate. From the prince's house
where our Tungchow friends have moved, we got a trunk, some cotton bat-
ting, a piece of old cloth for a strong bag, and a fur garment. Perhaps when
matters are settled we shall receive the bill. From one of the foreign stores
we secured a heavy coat for Marion, and a lady gave me one for Ellen
which her girls had outgrown. Another friend gave me an old white straw
hat and a third trimmed it with some Chinese blue silk. Mrs. Inglis very
kindly gave me some of her baby's things for Ellen, and others contributed
a few articles of which they had a surplus. I had made a thin flannel shirt
for each of the children and two thin dressing sacks for myself, one out of
material I had saved from home, and Mrs. Mateer had cut and partially
made my black skirt. Everyone is very kind, and under these circumstances
we cannot be too proud to accept such help.

At ten o'clock last night [August 19] word was sent to us that we were
not to go until Tuesday the 21st. Of course all the guests at the British
Legation had to find other homes as soon as possible after the troops came.
After considerable looking about each mission decided upon a location
which would accommodate the missionaries who are to remain and also the
native Christians who have been saved from massacre. A few escaped ones
have come to us since Peking was taken by the allied forces, but of most we
only hear of cruel torture and murder.

The children's nurse is alive, but not the other two women who fled
with her. Our cook's family is all gone except one little boy. I went over to
the grounds where our Tungchow friends are settled and there we held a
second mission meeting. There were several matters discussed, but the
general opinion was that no plans could be formulated, everything would
have to be worked out according to the wisdom of those left in the field and
as circumstances allowed. Miss Grace Wyckoff [56] was asked to stay in Peking
and take charge of the Bridgman school. These girls and our Peking church
members are in another place very close to our old compound. Dr. Ament,
Miss Russell and Miss Sheffield will remain. We asked for our furlough
home as we have been out the longest of any [missionaries] at our station.
Then when peace returns and mission work can again be resumed in its
many forms, we shall be rested and ready to return to our chosen field.

[56]Grace Wyckoff was an American Board missionary.

On Sunday [August 19] a thanksgiving service was held for our deliverance. The Church of England service was first read, followed by a brief address by Rev. Arthur Smith. The meeting was held out of doors, and the British and American soldiers were in attendance, besides most of the English speaking civilians.

Martha died a few days before the troops arrived. I was not able to attend the funeral. It made me very sad to think how little I had been able to brighten her last days. She is at rest now, and it was better that she should go before the Christians had to move. Our orphan boy we leave in charge of Dr. Ament. I have been very brave until the last week. My own weak condition and Ellen's failing strength almost overcame me. She is so poor that the skin draws tightly over her little legs, and I began to fear that I should never get her home even though she had held out through the siege. Then in my Sunday reading came this verse to strengthen me, "For God hath not given us the spirit of fear, but of power and of love and of a sound mind," and I took courage and prayed for more faith. Although the siege is over and communication with the world once more possible, I will not venture to mail this lengthy diary but bring it when I come home.

September 7, 1900, On board the U.S.S. *Indiana*

The last day at the [British Legation] chapel with the disappointment of delay was almost the last straw for us all. We dreaded to think of another possible day there. But Tuesday morning [August 21] carts came for the baggage and we were told that the hour of starting was six, and that the wagons would go then whether we were ready or not. We hurried, but doing our best were a little late. We were all to start from the American Legation as this first party was an American convoy, but on arriving there we saw no wagons. There was one broken wicker chair in the yard, and this, with a Chinese water cart, a bench and seats around a big tree accommodated several of us for about an hour of waiting. The first wagon drove in at just about seven o'clock, a huge heavy lumberbox with canvas covering drawn by four horses. One wagon drove inside and loaded while another was being loaded outside the gate. Our family piled into number six, Charles having arranged boxes and mattresses so that Ellen and I could lie down. There was room left for Marion to curl up in the front part and for Charles to sit at the back. There were thirteen wagons in all, and by the time the long [wagon] train was ready and we were really off it was about eight o'clock.

As we did not know just what [U.S.] Army wagons were like and whether they would be an improvement to Peking carts or not, some of us thought of going by sedan chair to Tungchow. But a report assured us that the wagons were very comfortable with fine springs and not to be compared with Peking carts. Well, his words were true, I suppose, in regard to the ambulances, but those luxuries were not for us. The driver had a spring seat and some of the ladies rode outside, preferring the hot sun to the jolting inside. I lay down all the time and traveled fairly comfortably except when they got in a hurry and trotted the horses. As I answered Charles when he asked me if I was getting along all right, "Yes, because I have to."

We reached Tungchow at three, but it was four o'clock before we were stationed on our boats.[57] We had breakfast at half past five on bread and jam and coffee and had a lunch on the way of two sandwiches apiece with a few fancy crackers. We were all ready for "rations" you may be sure. However the Marine officer who had charge of our expedition was too drunk to care for us. The other boats, seven in number, managed to get their supplies, but for some reason ours were not forthcoming. We included the [F. W.] Walkers, the Misses [Elizabeth and Emma] Martin, the Fenns and ourselves. There was a guard of eight marines on each passenger boat. There were forty-one passengers on three boats, the other boats carrying soldiers. The order came to start, but our guard objected as there were only four days' rations for eight people on board while there were twenty persons to be fed. The only answer was swearing from the commanding officer and threats of court martial if he was not obeyed. We had seen our friends provided with Irish potatoes, sweet potatoes, and foreign onions besides army rations, but willing as they were to divide they could not have the say, as we were all guests of the American government. The marines very gallantly offered to share with us as long as provisions lasted, and said we must surely be allowed to stop at the next army post down the river and get rations.

Oh! how good that supper was! Canned salmon and hard-tack is most delicious after Peking siege fare. The fried bacon the next morning just melted in our mouths! But we were still on rations and two slices was the limit. There was plenty of hard-tack and coffee, however. The Walkers had two servants with them, who foraged for sweet potatoes and corn, and we were invited to share with them. In answer to all our inquiries beforehand we could not find out that we were expected to provide anything for the table, and so none of us took dishes or made preparations for cooking. When too late to make other arrangements we found that our rations were given out in the tins, and we must get them into eatable condition as best we could. There was a very small charcoal stove at one end of the boat at which the marines kindly gave us the first chance. As Charles was taken sick with fever as soon as the strain of the summer was over and was barely able to sit up, and as the two mothers had nothing to boast of in the way of

[57]The trip by wagon to Tungchow and by boat to Tientsin was necessary because the train was not operating, the Boxers having torn up much of the track.

strength, and their children were a positive factor, it fell to Mr. Fenn's lot to be cook for our end of the boat. By beginning an hour before meal time and using one of the marines frying pans, he was able to prepare a tin of bacon. Tin box covers and our fingers were our dishes. The second day we did get our supplies and several times the gentlemen foraged for corn and melons and so we fared sumptuously. Beans, tomatoes, roast beef and corn beef completed the list of "rations." One night we boiled potatoes and the next morning had fried corn beef hash. A cracker box full on the charcoal stove, a sardine box full on Mrs. Fenn's alcohol lamp and a frying pan full on the boatmen's stove served our family of six.[58]

One morning Mr. Fenn fried Saratoga chips [potato chips] with the bacon, but he voted that was too much of a good thing to repeat. Our boat and one other ran races and kept well ahead of the rest. We were congratulating ourselves in getting into Tientsin early Friday afternoon [August 24] when orders came to anchor and wait for the other boats. Because of this delay we did not reach our landing place until about nine o'clock Saturday morning. An army officer was on hand to show us where to land and to request that we hurry as they wished to send the boats back with more soldiers. But he was much put out when we asked where we were to go and how we and our baggage were to be transported.

Our mission compound was two miles from the landing and all wheelbarrows, small carts and jinrikishas were under military control and it seemed impossible to get either information or conveyance. After two hours the most we secured was a hand-cart for our baggage and I decided to try the walk rather than wait longer. But just at starting we met a jinrikisha which had been secured for Mrs. Ingram and had just returned. Mr. Gammon[59] who had come to meet us was in charge of the vehicle and the two children and myself all rode to our mission.[60] There we found Miss [Elizabeth] Porter waiting to receive us. She had rooms ready for the [Franklin M.] Chapins, the [Howard S.] Galts, the [James H.] Ingrams, the [Chauncey] Goodriches, Miss [Mary] Andrews and our family. The old familiar scenes where we spent such happy months on our arrival in China, the homelike feeling and Miss [Mary] Porter's welcome were all too much for me and I could only cry for joy. What a luxury to have a room to ourselves, to sleep between sheets, and to sit down to a civilized table with white linen and all the other proper furnishings! Here [in Tientsin] we rested for a week, waiting for a transport to take us to Japan. It was a real rest for me, although I

[58]The "family of six" that Bessie refers to are the four Ewings and Mr. and Mrs. Fenn. Why Bessie does not include the Fenn's young daughter, Martha, is not known.

[59]Mr. Gammon was an American Board missionary at Tientsin.

[60]Bessie refers here to the American Board mission compound in Tientsin.

kept very busy. The quietness of home was what affected us all the most. It was as though a sudden silence had fallen after the endless buzzing of heavy machinery.

At the Tientsin stores we were fortunately able to buy many necessary articles. A soft hat for myself, an umbrella, dark woolen goods for a dress for Marion, a cap and flannels for Charles and an alcohol lamp for heating Ellen's food were some of the principal purchases. Charles bought a khaki suit from the army supplies, also shoes and colored shirts. His other clothes had given out with the summer's hard wear. We came across an unexpected surprise in the shape of a box from San Francisco plainly marked for us. On opening it we found a smaller box inside for Dr. [H. S.] Porter and fifteen yards of cotton cloth. How that cloth came to be sent to us is still a mystery, but there being no other claimant I soon had most of it cut up for necessary garments. I kept four Chinese women busy sewing for several days. They completed my black skirt, made Marion's dress and helped on a number of other pieces.

Charles was very sick all the week we were in Tientsin, high fever and hard chills day and night. Medicine seemed to have no effect and how we longed to get out on the ocean. Ellen has picked up wonderfully in general health and ate like a half starved child as she really was. When a week had gone by with daily inquiries about a transport, the appropriate officer found out our presence in the city and came to call. He had received a letter from General [Adna] Chaffee telling of our departure from Peking and had been wondering why we did not arrive. After that we received very good attention and the rest of our journey so far has been very comfortable.

This is a pleasant steamer and there are not more than half a dozen other passengers besides we fifteen Peking refugees. We enjoy the fare especially because it is American cooking in contrast to French or English. Filipinos do all the serving, but they know only a few words of English and we have to point to the number on the menu when ordering our meals.

Sunday, September 9, 1900, Nagasaki Harbor, Japan

Our journey home thus far has been as much in delays as in goings. Again we have just missed [a connection]. We are being transported by the United States Government and they do not plan to make connections. Five of our party were Methodists and went to their mission here last night. We [the American Board] have no station here, and as we could stay on board over Sunday, preferred that to hunting up a boarding place. This steamer goes no further and when the next transport for America will come is uncertain.

When we boarded this steamer Charles was positively too weak to lift our small trunk, and even Ellen's weight was more than he wanted to carry.

However the sea is doing wonders and we shall all get well from our strain before reaching home. I think that Ellen is the slowest to recover.

Sunday, October 7, 1900, On board the S.S. *Duke of Fife*

Once more we are in sight of land but not of our native land even yet. In about twelve hours we expect to reach the quarantine station outside Victoria [British Columbia]. Then some time on Tuesday [October 9] we shall probably land at Tacoma [Washington]. The transports were so uncertain that we decided not to wait, and as we did not wish to go by way of Honolulu we let the S.S. Coptic go without us, although nearly all the rest of our friends took that steamer. Charles always remembers the fever that came on as we neared the tropics on our way out and did not leave him until we reached Japan. Therefore we could not feel it right to risk that route after such an experience as that of last summer. I wrote from Nagasaki that Charles was better. We remained there five days and then took the train for Kobe. We had found out about this line of steamers, but none of the boats stopped at Nagasaki. This steamer left Kobe on Tuesday [September 18] and we were all pleased to secure passage on her.

While in Kobe we were very kindly entertained by the Stanfords [Arthur W. and Jane H.] of our own mission. Charles' fever came on again there, and in a much worse form. The fever was very high and was accompanied by a severe headache. He could eat nothing. As medicine had apparently no effect before, Charles would not take any this time, thinking the sea was all he needed. But three days so weakened him that even after we got to sea again he was no better. His headache continued so bad that he was half delirious a great deal of the time and I was much afraid that he would have a long run of fever. There was no physician on board, but the steward, who is also purser, has had some medical training, and he did his best. The two days to Yokohama were very hard to bear. I hope I may never see Charles so weak again and so sick. He was so discouraged too, to think that the sea air had not effected a speedy cure. A Japanese doctor was secured at Yokohama, but he could not speak English and no one on board could speak Japanese. So we still trusted in Mr. Bishop, the steward. When we really were out on the broad Pacific, Charles' fever left him but his head did not clear for several days after. Oh! I think those days when Charles was so sick were worse to me than the two months of siege. Ellen did not begin to pick up either until we were out of the warm weather region. She was quite poorly while in Japan. This last week has been very cold and we have all enjoyed it. I cannot be too thankful that we chose this northern route. This line does not carry many passengers, but the boat is comfortable and the service good through not stylish.

The captain's wife is on board and also their little girl Elsie, aged six. She and Marion have had fine times together. The captain and officers are all very pleasant, the steward has been most kind and obliging, the captain's wife is good company, the weather has not been as bad as we feared and I have proved to be a good sailor. I think there have been only three days when we could not be on deck. A grate fire in the saloon has made us quite comfortable, but we have needed winter clothing. I could not have managed to keep warm without my fur garment. We have heard no word from our family since the sixth of June and are anxious to know whether or not they are all well. In Nagasaki I learned of papa's[61] death through Dr. [Devello] Sheffield. I had feared from the last letters that we might not see him, but did hope that he would live until we reached home. We can almost count the days now when we shall meet our family once more. For a long while my thoughts of home were visions of rest when I could just see everyone, and then have no care for anything for at least a week but just to go to bed and rest. I am about over that now and am also over the half starved feeling of the summer, and so I hope to appear like a rational person.

Monday, October 15, 1900, Bristol, Indiana

Finding that we could not reach home [New Haven] for Sunday we decided to come here and visit Charles' brother, Addison. We left Tacoma Tuesday night [October 9] going from the steamer to the train in a drizzling rain. Traveling by train we find more tiresome than on shipboard, but the scenery is more varied. We had forgotten that the United States was quite so beautiful a country, but after six years of absence we are better able to appreciate its merits.

Friday, October 19, 1900, New Haven, Connecticut

After two months of wondering we are at last really home and my summer is ended. Looking back over all the events since we left our home in Peking, we cannot but be thankful for what we did *not* suffer. These words of the Psalmist best express my thoughts: "Blessed be the Lord, for he hath showed me his marvelous kindness in a strong city" [*sic*].

Charles to Judson Smith, August 15, 1900, British Legation, Peking

Dear Dr. Smith:

We still have enough to eat for 800 foreigners and 3,000 Chinese. We are quite used to curried horse, pony steak and "cheval hash"; baked beans have

---

[61]Bessie's father, George Walstein Smith.

not given out; coarse brown rice is a staple and good wholewheat bread continues. Coffee and tea are plenty, sugar and butter running low, and milk almost gone. There has, of course, been a good deal of sickness, though the Lord has tempered the Peking summer beyond all belief. The Chinese children have suffered mostly and five foreign children have been laid away. . . .

I have been on duty a good deal, especially in fortification work. The hottest weather will be over in a few days and we are expecting our release soon, and so we feel that we can hold on a little longer. We have had no sort of news from Paoting for two months, but it is easy to suspect the worst. We left our home on June 8, and in the few succeeding days I got much of our most valuable and portable property away to the Methodist mission, where we were staying. On June 14 our place [the American Board mission] was destroyed; on June 20 we left the Methodist mission and came to live here in the chapel of the British legation. We left our two trunks and one big box, but succeeded in saving some of our bedding and as much clothing as we could bring in an extension bag. But we were all safe here before the firing began in the afternoon. You can see we have almost nothing left, but we have enough for present use, and the Lord will provide. We have been making out our bill for indemnity, it will be between three and four thousand dollars. When the siege is over probably half of us who have been through it will be in danger of a breakdown unless there can be a complete change, and so it seems decidedly best that we Ewings start for home at the first opportunity. I feel that this is further justified by the fact that my time in the field will be of much more value in two or four years, when I might take my furlough, than now.

As I write the bullets are snapping and singing, from our line at the west some of the enemies' shot fly over us, cutting through the leaves of the beautiful trees. A few moments ago one struck a tree a few yards from our door and fell heated to the ground. It was amusing to see a venerable Scotchman jump from his seat, pick the bullet from the ground and shake his burning fingers, and then try again and again, only the third time succeeding in holding it. Our men are replying to the fire of the enemy and every half minute or so we can hear the five big bullets of the British Nordenfield cannon go out with a gentle thud on their parallel courses against the enemy. For the past three weeks we have been nominally having a truce; there has been much less shot than previously, but still some bullets every day and much new fortification work done. But the last few days have witnessed a renewal of the fighting and this we may expect to continue with increasing vehemence till the troops arrive. Some think they will be here tomorrow or next day.

Wednesday, August 15. Hoorah! But it dies out in a gulp that is almost a sob. I wanted to cheer when the troops came in yesterday, but you will

The Ewings in the fall of 1900, back in the United States after enduring the Boxer Uprising. Marion stands in front, and Ellen is held by Charles. Bessie gave birth to Edward the following December.

know what I mean when I say it was a physical impossibility. I had not expected them before today but they came and gained such control of this part of the city that we had a quiet night and we knew how to be thankful for that after the recent nights.

But we realize now more than ever we have all along that your sufferings must have been worse than ours.

Charles to Judson Smith, December 21, 1900, New Haven

Dear Dr. Smith:

Herewith I am sending you a copy of a letter that was sent to Major Conger on August 20, having been written perhaps a day or two before. I send also copies of resolutions passed by a meeting of the American missionaries. You suggested that you might wish to see at least one of these documents. . . . Please use them as you choose.

"Honorable E. H. Conger, Our respected and beloved Minister,

Your very kind note of yesterday reminds us anew of the appreciation that you have manifested and the interest you have shown in all the work of American missionaries. Nor can we fail to recall the constant kindness and attentive care that you have always accorded to us personally. We assure you, it shall never be forgotten.

And we shall remember also the sincere interest that you have taken in the welfare and preservation of Chinese Christians, at a time when, but for the noble stand you took, perhaps even the remnant would have perished.

Please accept for Mrs. Conger and yourself our thanks for your personal interest in all that has concerned us at a time when the strain on yourselves was peculiarly severe."

"At a meeting of the American missionaries in the British Legation chapel at Peking, on Saturday, August 18, 1900, the following votes were passed:

Voted, the following resolutions presented by Mr. A. H. Smith, be adopted:

The Americans who have been besieged in Peking desire to express their hearty appreciation of the courage, fidelity, and patriotism of the American Marines to whom we so largely owe our salvation. By their bravery in holding an almost untenable position on the city wall in the face of overwhelming numbers, and in cooperating in driving the Chinese from a position of great strength, they made all foreigners in Peking their debtors, and have gained for themselves an honorable name among the heroes of their country.

Voted, to draft this resolution, and present it to Major Conger.

Voted, to adopt the following resolution, and send a copy to Sir Claude MacDonald:

The missionaries who have been in the British Legation during the siege that has just ended, desire to express their appreciation of the uniform courtesy and kindness that have been shown them by Sir Claude and Lady Mac-Donald and all others connected with the legation, and we would recognize with gratitude the heroism of the British marines and those of other nationalities, together with the civilian volunteers, who, against such fearful odds, risked, and in many cases laid down their lives, in defense of the many who were committed to their care. Charles E. Ewing, Clerk of the meeting."

Charles to Judson Smith, February 16, 1901, Springfield, Ohio

Dear Dr. Smith:

Thank you for the China letters, which I now return. . . . The case that Mr. [George D.] Wilder presents, or rather, the cases of those who made insincere recantation, remind one of Peter, not at all of Judas. The essence of the sin was in the lie, not in turning away from Christ; and so the sin is less, not greater. All of us seemed to feel that these cases must be settled severally.[1]

What Dr. Ament has been doing may not have been wise, but the newspapers misrepresent its spirit and tone, as well as the probable effect on the Chinese. Mark Twain has been well answered by John Kendrick Bangs,[2] from his point of view.

[1]Charles writes here of the cases involving Chinese Christians who during the Boxer Uprising denied their Christianity to the Boxers and others.
[2]The humorist John Kendrick Bangs was editor of the influential *Harper's Weekly* in 1901. His response to Twain was that American missionaries were not tools of big business.

Charles to Judson Smith, March 25, 1901, St. Paul, Minnesota

Dear Dr. Smith:

Your proposition, the vote of the Prudential Committee, took me quite by surprise. I shall not know what to answer definitely until I see my wife, which I hope to do next Tuesday evening.

I have never quite decided whether the Lord, who sets the solitary in families, ever intended that there should be such separations. We shall seek His will, and do it.

I do not know how you were informed that my family is so situated that I can leave them without special anxiety. My wife is not strong, especially after the experiences of the last year; and I am not sure that it will be right for me to leave her with the care of three children all under six years of age. She would live with a widowed sister and with no man in charge of the household.

You also speak of my health as being firm. The fact is, I was so nervously broken down at the end of last summer that I could not control myself for a long time after leaving China. Moreover, I have given myself no rest since my return; and I still feel the nervous effects of the siege, and have not begun to rest from the work of the years before.

In view of all these things, I said, two months ago, that if the Prudential Committee[1] voted me back to China, I should not feel it my duty to go—at least, not without several months of rest first. I do not say that now, but I must see my wife before replying definitely. If I had thought of my return this spring as likely to be called for, I should certainly have wanted to take some rest.

If I do return to China, I shall very likely ask to have an understanding that my regular furlough may come not far off; for I do not count this time in America as a furlough, by any means. I doubt if I can, without the furlough, and without my wife, stand the nervous strain very long.

. . . I have been looking forward to returning to China, but I have felt that I should be doing wrong to go this year. Your letter, however, makes it necessary that the question be met and decided.

I am quite well aware that it would be next to impossible for me to name anyone else who could go instead of myself, among the ordained members of the Mission. . . . The call from the field is imperative and if the Lord shows me that He intends it for me, I shall go. Pray for us.

[1]The Prudential Committee of the American Board, which was located in Boston, determined overseas assignments for the missionaries.

Charles to Bessie, March 28, 1901, St. Paul, Minnesota

My Dearest Bessie:

As with you, so with me; I can think of scarcely anything but the threatened separation. . . . If the Lord decides for me to go [to China], then nothing else would make us happy, and we should bitterly repent not having followed his guidance. . . . Think of what the possible alternatives would be: (1) stay in this country another year or more, and then all go back to China, with no houses suitable for you and the children[1] to live in; (2) stay in this country a year or more, and then I leave you here, while I return to Peking, in which case I would have had my furlough and would not . . . ask for another within five years; (3) give up the China work entirely, which would never satisfy us unless we were compelled to it.[2]

[1]At this time the Ewing children numbered three, Edward Alvord Ewing having been born on December 26, 1900, at New Haven.
[2]Here Charles is struggling with the question of their return to China to complete a scheduled ten-year tour.

Charles to Judson Smith, April 9, 1901, Boston, Massachusetts

Dear Dr. Smith:

While in St. Paul, two weeks ago, I received your letter announcing the vote of the Prudential Committee, authorizing and instructing me to return to China as early as possible. The wording of the vote seemed to call for and expect a definite acquiescence, but that I was not able to give immediately.

This vote, as I understood from your letter, was based on the supposition that I could leave my family without anxiety. Since my return to New Haven from the West, a week ago, I have been trying to find some way in which I might leave my family, but no suggestion has met with success, and I am at last compelled to reply definitely that it will be out of the question for me to go to China without my wife and children—for the present at least.

Charles to Judson Smith, June 19, 1901, North Haven, Connecticut

Dear Dr. Smith:

You may remember that soon after my return from China, anticipating that my visit in this country would probably be longer than the furlough ordinarily allowed, I mentioned taking up some pastoral work in this country, but it was not thought best for me to do so then. Again, in April, when Mrs. Ewing and I were in your office, I made a similar suggestion, feeling that it would be better to have that question settled before we rented and furnished a house. Your reply seemed to settle it that the Board would not care to have me take a pastorate, and so we purchased a controlling share in my father-in-law's estate, furnished the house so far as was necessary, and have settled down here. . . . I shall be quite ready to take up some work in this country, provided I can make an arrangement that will not interfere with our return to China at the first favorable opportunity, and provided also the place is open to me without solicitation on my part. To satisfy the first condition, perhaps it would be best to make arrangement for not more than one year, to end not later than Sept. 1 of next year. As to the second condition, I can, without making any solicitation, let it be known what my plans are.

Charles to Judson Smith, November 16, 1901, North Haven, Conn.

Dear Dr. Smith:

Mrs. Ewing and I are eager to return to China as soon as the leading of the Lord shall be in that direction. That it was quite out of the question for us to go this year, we were and are fully persuaded. . . .

It occurs to me that you know the most about my work in the field, and Dr. [C. H.] Daniels[1] the most about my work in speaking at home; and perhaps one or both of you may know of churches where I would be likely to fit, if so, I should be very glad indeed to avail myself of your suggestions.

[1]Dr. Daniels of the American Board in Boston was responsible for arranging Charles's speaking engagements throughout much of the northeastern part of the United States during 1901.

Charles to Judson Smith, April 17, 1902, North Haven, Conn.

Dear Dr. Smith:

Can you tell me what the prospects are for new buildings in Peking? Will they be ready by autumn? And would there be suitable residence for us if we were to return this year?

I raise these questions, because I hope that our return is not out of the question. Mrs. Ewing has come through the winter in much better health, strength, and spirits than I ventured to expect. If the next two months are equally satisfactory, we may be able to plan for return late in the autumn, and to start for Peking in October if nothing should occur to hinder. But I do not feel at all sure that it would be wisdom on our part, nor economy on the part of the Board, for my wife and children to undertake living in a Chinese house, even the best.

A recent letter from Dr. Ament seems to mean that none of the new houses will be ready this year. I had supposed otherwise. Can you tell me?

. . . Every letter from China has made us more eager to return. The certainty of the need of workers there, together with a growing knowledge of the over-supply here, has made it more evident that I am wanted there and that I am not wanted here. . . . I have indeed been wondering if it is not the Lord's definite intention to keep me out of the work here and open the way for my return to China. For that, we hold ourselves gladly ready, whenever it shall be manifestly proper.

. . . I can see now that my furlough has been of great benefit. The nervous strain had affected my spiritual development more even than I myself was aware; and it has taken a long time to restore that equanimity of spirit without which I should be an undesirable fellow-worker and a blunderer. My return last year, even if possible, would have been unwise. When I do go, I think I shall have learned some lessons that will make me a more loving laborer.

Charles to Judson Smith, May 8, 1902, North Haven, Conn.

Dear Dr. Smith:

Your opinion seems to confirm me still further in the hope for return to China in 1903 at the latest. As for a return in the autumn of this year, that is apparently dependent on two things—the health of my family and proper residence for them (us) in Peking (or possibly at some other station). Concerning the latter point, I shall do what I can to inform myself, writing especially to Dr. [James] Ingram, whose advice I value highly, both as a physician and as a man of good judgment and the right spirit. As to our health, I have every reason to hope that it will be so firmly established by next autumn that it should form no obstacle to our return.

Mrs. Ewing gave birth to a fourth child, a son, on Tuesday, May 6. She is under the best of care, at Grace Hospital in New Haven, and her condition, as well as that of the little one, is all that could be desired. The name of the boy is Andrew Goodyear, a family name on my wife's side of the house.

. . . Our own feeling and preferences then, may be stated briefly: (1) an eager desire for a speedy return to our work in China; (2) the hope that we may do what we can for that work while we remain in this country; (3) entire readiness to relieve the Board of our financial support, if any such opening is presented. If this view commends itself, I should be on the lookout still for some place where I might be able to relieve the Board of my salary. But I should also hope that my name might be restored to the list of those who are available for missionary addresses.

Charles to Judson Smith, May 23, 1902, North Haven, Conn.

Dear Dr. Smith:
A call is coming to me next week from Unionville [Connecticut], inviting me to become pastor there for one year; and I shall doubtless accept it. It is an opportunity that is in every way satisfactory; nothing could have suited me better, judging from what I now know of the situation and prospects. . . . It seems providential that the first opportunity of any kind should be so attractive, and that it should come just at the time when, as a result of my correspondence with you, it seemed finally necessary to abandon all hope of returning to China this year.

Recognizing that I may be tempted to remain in this country beyond a single year I nevertheless hope and propose to return to China when the way shall be clear. I should relish having a part in the work of reconstruction there. . . .

I want to thank you for your constant kindly interest and sympathetic counsel, I assure you that I value and appreciate it, and to put myself at your service whenever it may be possible for me to assist you . . . [in] the work of the Board . . . in China.

Charles to Judson Smith, September 16, 1902, Unionville, Conn.

Dear Dr. Smith:
The place where I am is just the kind that I have wanted. It requires patient, careful work. It is very enjoyable, and my year here is sure to be of great pleasure and benefit to me personally. Mrs. Ewing and the children enjoy it here also. It is already evident that Mrs. Ewing could not wisely have undertaken the trip to China this year; she has her hands full with the four children. . . . I feel very uncertain about the feasibility of our return, even after another year, the nervous effect of the China experiences (which

I felt at once, and from which I recovered soon) did not appear in Mrs. Ewing's case at first, but it seems to be more lasting. Our attitude toward the work in China has not changed, our desire to join in it remains the same as ever. If obliged to remain here we shall try to do what we can. . . .

Do you hear anything more definite about the payment of the indemnity?

Charles to the Prudential Committee of the American Board, October 3, 1902, Unionville, Conn.

May the Lord bless His work in China. Mrs. Ewing and myself rejoice that we have had a humble part in that work. We have hoped to resume it, after our enforced furlough. But the nervous strain of the Peking siege, together with the care of four little children, is too much for Mrs. Ewing; and all plans for our return must be dim and distant.

We hereby tender our resignations as missionaries of the Board. Our interest in the work will continue. We shall hope to do all that we can for the Board and for China while here at home. It may be that, at some future time, our return to the foreign field may be possible.

Charles to Judson Smith, October 1, 1903, Unionville, Conn.

Dear Dr. Smith:

[C]an you send me any very recent news of our missionary work in China—more recent than appears in the *Missionary Herald*? I am to give the annual report on China at Plymouth Church in New Haven next Tuesday evening. If you can lend me any recent letters . . . they would help. The report of [the annual] Mission meeting in Tungchow would be helpful. . . .

Mrs. Ewing has a recent letter from Miss [Nellie] Russell, written on her return to this country. Also, I received a good letter from Pastor Jên of the North Chapel in Peking. Like all our letters from China, these have aroused new eagerness for the work. Moreover, the possibility of our going to China again seems greater and nearer than hitherto. Mrs. Ewing is largely regaining her vigor, and we are cherishing a more definite hope that we have before ventured to hold that we may be able to start for Peking next year, availing ourselves of the privilege, suggested by Miss Russell, of going in company with her.

It has seemed to me advisable that some physician who knows Peking (Dr. [C. A. W.] Merritt or Dr. [Willis C.] Noble or some one else) should give his professional opinion as to the wisdom of our return. . . .

I have just been reading proof for the book, "Siege Days," compiled and edited by Mrs. Ada Haven Mateer, with contributions from nearly all of the American missionary ladies and children who were in the Peking siege. It is a graphic portrayal, which will make the experiences of those days more real to readers than anything yet published, and will be especially appreciated by ladies.

Charles to Judson Smith, December 23, 1903, Unionville, Conn.

Dear Dr. Smith:

Mrs. Ewing has just had the reading of the "round robin" that the ladies of the North China Mission always send home at Mission meeting time. Being her husband, I have availed myself of the privilege of reading these letters. . . . The reading of these letters has had the same effect on us as does the reading of every letter from the field—the renewal of our eagerness to return. This desire has risen so high now that it hardly diminishes between letters. We keep in mind almost constantly the hope that we may be back there within a year. I am writing now to say that we shall be glad if you can see that we receive the proper blank forms for application for reappointment.

Charles to Judson Smith, February 26, 1904, Unionville, Conn.

Dear Dr. Smith:

We are delighted at the prospect [of returning to China]. Our plan will probably be to start for China early in August. As my year with this church [in Unionville] closes with June 1, that will give us two months for final preparation. . . .

The grant of $325 for refit will, I hope, be sufficient. I should gladly do without that, if it seemed wise; but much of my indemnity money [from the loses sustained during the Boxer episode] is either spent already or tied up for the present, so that it will probably be necessary to spend the $325. I take it for granted that, unless the Board calls for my services before the start for the field, my salary will begin when we reach Peking, and all other arrangements will be as on the occasion of our first going. . . .

[A]fter these pleasant years in the home land, I think that we shall feel, more than ever before, the value of the interdependence of the two ends of the work. There are many ways in which I should like to render service to the Board in this country, if it were my lot to remain here, but this blessed part in the work we must leave to others, since there is granted to us the higher privilege of engaging in the seed-sowing which is the wise Master's quiet and unostentatious way of introducing his kingdom, using as seed-sowers those who go to fight as soldiers on "the far-flung battle line." The experience here will increase our fitness and readiness for the service in China, so different and yet the same.

Charles to Judson Smith, July 23, 1904, Northford, Conn.

Dear Dr. Smith:

A postal from Miss Russell received this morning, intimates that the North China Mission, at its annual meeting, stationed Mrs. Ewing and myself at Tientsin. As this reverses the action of last year, we are somewhat incredulous. There occur to me certain reasons which might lead to such a decision, even tho such action is entirely unexpected by us. Our plans and purchases[1] have been made with Peking in view, and that is of course the station that we should naturally choose. However, if the Mission desires otherwise, we shall acquiesce cheerfully, especially as I have always felt quite strongly that the judgment of the Mission ought to be considered decisive in such a matter, unless indeed the objections are such as to interfere with the efficiency of the work. Please inform me what action the Mission took.

[1]Since the Ewings knew Peking and may have expected to occupy their former house in the American Board compound, it is likely that purchases such as rugs, drapes, and furniture were made with that location in mind.

Recollections of Bessie, September 1904, On board S.S. *Empress of China*

[T]his time [to China] we took little furniture as we knew it could be made by the Chinese at low cost, both work and materials being probably less than the freight expense from America. But the comfortable black walnut rocker that was my mother's was shipped abroad. . . .

We moved from Unionville in May and spent the summer at Cousin Clara's in Northford [Connecticut]. In August we started again on the long journey to China, staying first a few days in New Haven, from where we took the train to Springfield, with through reservations from there to Vancouver. . . . In St. Paul we were joined by a new missionary for Peking, Miss Jessie Payne. . . . [1]

Our steamer [the *Empress of China*] set sail on Monday, September 5. The girls were in a stateroom with Miss Payne, Charles and I were in another, with the two boys on a long couch under the porthole, sleeping with their heads at either end.

[1]Jessie Payne was an American Board missionary from South Dakota.

Charles to the Ewing Family, September 4, 1904, Vancouver, Canada

Dear Ewing Family:

[W]hen we woke up on Thursday morning [September 1] the largeness of the farms was still apparent. We were in North Dakota. . . . We . . . did not pass into Canada until about breakfast time. The boundary station is double; first Portal, North Dakota, then North Portal, Assa. (Assiniboia) [Saskatchewan]. Our trunks were bonded through to Vancouver for customs examination, and the Customs officer merely walked through the train without stopping to look at our bags. . . .

Friday proved to be the greatest day of my life for sightseeing. I have never experienced anything like it in the past; and I venture to question whether there is anywhere else in the world a similar opportunity of riding on one train for a whole day through such a marvelous succession of massive, grand, sublime scenes. . . . If you have occasion to cross the country, take this route. If you want mountains, don't go to the Alps, but to the Canadian Rockies and the Selkirks.

Charles to the Ewing Family, October 12, 1904, Peking

Dear Ewing Family:

The heading of this letter does not mean that Peking is our residence—we are Tientsinners. . . . [While enroute here] we anchored at Kobe [Japan] and took the [shipping] company's tug for the shore in the rain, . . . and had a ride in covered rikshas to the Kobe college compound. . . . There was much loading and unloading at Kobe, principally the unloading of machinery, to be sent to Korea or beyond, and of twenty thousand bags of flour, the destination of which was probably not officially announced, altho we understood very well that it was intended for the Japanese army [in Manchuria]. . . . [1]

During that Wednesday [September 21] we passed through the Inland Sea, and how glad we were that the weather had changed. It was a beautiful day for this most charming part of our whole journey. . . . At ten in the evening we passed through the strait of Shimonoseki, and the sight was more beautiful than it could have been in the daytime. . . . The next day (Thurs. Sept. 22) we reached Nagasaki at about eight in the morning. The passage into the harbor is so picturesque that Bessie wanted a picture, but we were warned that the [Japanese] government permits nothing of the kind at present. . . .

On Saturday, Sept. 24, we anchored off Woosung in the early morning, and embarked on the company's little transfer steamer to go up the Whangpoo River to Shanghai. There we were met by Mrs. Edward Evans of the Missionary Home, who found rooms for us in two private boarding houses very near to the Home. We spent three days in Shanghai, sailing on Tuesday [September 27] on board the steamer Hsin Yu of the China Merchants Steam Navigation Company.

[We] reached Chefoo [on September 29] . . . went ashore, made some purchases at the silk goods store of the Presbyterian Mission, mailed letters, and walked through the native city to the Presbyterian Mission where I found my college friend Cornwell and his wife. . . . We had very little time to visit as it was necessary to hurry on board again. The children, being rather tired, were carried down to the shore in an open chair on poles, while the rest of us walked. . . .

It was refreshing to get back to where I could talk Chinese; I had tried it in Shanghai, but most of the natives there do not speak the Mandarin language [*sic*].

On Friday morning [September 30] at about seven o'clock, we reached the bar outside the entrance of the Pei Ho River, and went on board a tug-boat. There was a light rain falling much of the time as we went up the river, past Taku, to the railway station at Tangku. There we had to wait . . . for the train to Tientsin. We got dinner in the station hotel. At three oclock we reached Tientsin. We were not expected until Saturday, but Mr. [James H.] McCann was at the station to meet others, and he helped us with baggage, etc. We took rikshas to our mission compound, where we were entertained by the McCanns. Contrary to even our most sanguine expectations, our freight was there already. But the house that is to be ours was not yet vacant. . . .

We are the guests of Dr. and Mrs. Ament [in Peking] arriving on October 4. Last Saturday our [the American Board's] beautiful new church was dedicated. . . . I have preached in Chinese both Sundays, first in Tientsin, then in Peking. Last Sunday I preached also at our English service. I plan to go with Dr. Ament to one of the out-stations tomorrow, and to spend Sunday at another. After that we all go to Tungchow. There I leave the family, while I go back to Tientsin to settle the house.

[1]At this time Japan and Russia were at war in Manchuria.

Charles to Judson Smith, October 24, 1904, Tientsin

Dear Dr. Smith:

We reached Tientsin on Sept. 30, after an unusually short trip, having left New Haven on Aug. 29. . . . As no notice had reached the people here as to our time of arrival, until within a few days before we came, the house which is to be ours (the ladies' house) was still occupied. The tenant was Mr. Harvey of the Y.M.C.A., but he moved out as soon as he could. Meanwhile, we have spent our time in visiting, at Peking and Tungchow.

I am carrying out my plan as I stated it to you in Boston, of visiting the other stations before I settle down to my own work in the Tientsin field. This visiting must of necessity be brief at each station, but I believe it is worth while.

In response to the invitation of Dr. and Mrs. Ament, Mrs. Ewing and I took our four children to Peking to see our old friends and our old work. We went by train on October 6. . . . During the following days, we were able to see something of the city, visiting the American legation, the different missions, and some other places. On Oct. 13, I went with Dr. Ament to the out-station at Shun I Hsien, returning on Saturday. Then I immediately took the train for Cho Chow, spending Sunday there, and visiting Liang Hsiang [Hsien] and Pu An Tun. . . . I returned to Peking on Tuesday. . . . My object in seeing as much of the Peking field as I could was two-fold, both to renew my fellowship with the friends of former days and to see for myself the changes of which I had heard so much.

The first change to attract my attention in Peking was the fact that the train runs up to the Chien Men [Gate]. . . . it was a delightful experience to walk in through the Water-gate on a well paved road, where four years before the relief column had waded in the mud to rescue us. Inside the Tartar city, the most noticeable change is in the Legation quarter,[1] which has been greatly enlarged, strongly fortified, and separated from the Chinese buildings by a broad open space, at least a hundred yards in width, from which all buildings have been removed. Wherever foreigners reside there are new buildings, finer and more satisfactory than those in use "before the siege." As I remained in the city I noted also numerous changes in Chinese buildings, some two storey structures, countless signs in the languages of the West, streets newly macadamized or even now in the process, street lights that really shed radiance, rikshas as the most frequent vehicle in many parts of the city, silver coins replacing the old brass cash—these and other things mark a change among the Chinese themselves. Last, but not least, an almost incredible improvement in the matter of cleanliness in the main thoroughfares.

How much of a change has come over the people themselves it is difficult to say without further study. There are ominous mutterings that make themselves heard in some parts of the country, and there are . . . those among the foreign residents who predict renewed troubles. But in Peking and the region all around, the Chinese have no fear of anything of the kind, the native Christians report that there is no evidence of any bad feeling, and I myself could see no signs of hatred toward the foreigners. The suspicion that all evidence of animosity is restrained through fear does not appear to be justified, as no one appears to be afraid. The relations between foreigners and Chinese are quite as free as at any time in the past, and everything indicates an indefinite continuance of this condition. In Peking, at least, it is to the interest of the merchants, the marketmen, the builders, the laborers, and indeed the people in general, to have the foreigners there [as] prices have risen and prosperity has increased. . . .

As one enters the gateway of the American Board Mission compound, he sees before him a hundred yards away, a church building of gray brick, fit to be compared with churches in the home land [the United States]. The approach is by pathways through an open space about fifty yards wide, with the missionary residences at the east and west sides. This open space is eventually to be planted with trees, bushes, and flowers, but at present it is barren and bleak. The church itself is ecclesiastical in appearance, much more so than any other Protestant church in North China. A graceful tower on the south-east contains a sweet-toned bell. The high gabled front of the building is pieced by an arched window above, while below are the porch and entrance. There are other doors halfway up each side of the building, one facing the gateway of the Bridgman School, the other affording access for men only; thus all parts of the audience room are easily accessible. The interior is lofty, and maintains the ecclesiastical aspect of the exterior. . . . All the walls are of the beautiful gray brick of China; and the ceiling is of Chinese matting held in place by reed strips, producing a graceful ornamental effect.

[T]he [church] seats 800 people [and] it is estimated that over a thousand were present [at the dedication service]. Among the foreign guests were Major Conger, the American minister, and his wife, also representatives of the other missions in this part of China. Among the Chinese were some notables, altho the number of invitations had been purposely limited in order to guard against the great display of gifts that is sure to be attendant on such a festal occasion. Of the presents that were received, the most notable was a large tablet with the Chinese characters for "Faith, Hope, Love" written large by the hand of a Chinese lady of rank and education, who herself attended the service. Seated just below the platform were several notables—among them Chen Pi, president of the new Board of Commerce, a man who is doing more for education in Peking than anyone else; Hsu Shih Chang, a member of the Foreign Office and a progressive; and Hsi Pei Lo, the Mongol king whose palace nearby was occupied by our Peking station after the siege. . . .

My trip to Shun I Hsien was in company with Dr. Ament. I remained for two nights and a day, while he stayed longer. The full day that I spent there included a visit to the imperial district school, an interesting opportunity of seeing and talking with many men who had come in for market day in the city, an afternoon walk to visit the Christians in a village two miles out, an evening visit to the district official, and his speedy return of the call.

The imperial school [in Shun I Hsien] has excellent buildings, but poor equipment otherwise. There is no adequate supply of books, the result being that much of the work has to be copied by hand. The teacher, like many of his kind, after a partial course in the provincial college at Paoting, has been sent out to teach for a year or two before proceeding with his own study. The students have dwindled in number, until there were only three in attendance when we were there. The school is under the patronage of a man who was the backer of the Boxers in that city in 1900. Probably in part as a result of this, both this man and the teacher appeared to be terror-stricken at the visit of the foreigners. The school is hardly a brilliant success, but to have such a school at all is a step in advance, and the equipment will be likely to improve as time goes on.

[M]any of the children [at Shun I Hsien] . . . seem afraid to come to the chapel, and a similar feeling affects adults as well. The reason for this seems to be the memory of the great slaughter of Christians in that district, less than a dozen being left of the more than sixty church members of former times. As this is the only one of the Peking out-stations where such fear prevails, I tried to find whether the people had been terrified by the missionary, as had been reported in America from some places. All I could find was that the indemnity received has been barely enough to give us a place about like the old one, and that Dr. Ament saved the official of the district from having serious trouble with the German troops who raided the place, by lending him money (from the recently paid indemnity) to help meet the exorbitant German demands. Except in the case of the Boxer leader, it seems that the people are less afraid of the missionary than of being associated with him. . . .

In the edge of the evening, we went to call on the newly appointed district magistrate, principally in order to make his acquaintance. Within half an hour after our return, he did us the honor to ride into our chapel court in his official chair, to return the call. He brought as presents to Dr. Ament two quacking ducks and a jar of wine. I can imagine what would be done with the ducks, but I have been wondering what has become of that wine.

Cho Chow . . . is the largest of the Peking out-stations, has its own native pastor and its fine premises in the heart of the city, and carries on its work without expense to the Board, partly by native contributions, partly by income from invested indemnity funds, rents, etc. Cho Chow was one of the great storm centers of the Boxer uprising, and when the foreign troops came, it was only the prompt action of Dr. Ament that saved the life of the official, who had tried to enforce order and had become the innocent victim of over-powering circumstances. It was on account of the gratitude thus inspired that the Mission was given its choice of property in the city, the choice falling on a large place that had been one of the Boxer headquarters. Cho Chow has practically the equipment of a regular station—church building, street chapel, boys' school, girls' boarding school, Bible women,[2] etc. The native pastor is proving himself a man of good sense and good management.

. . . I went by train to Liang Hsiang, the district city lying between Cho Chow and Peking. Our work had not been opened there very long at the time of the [Boxer] outbreak. Only a few families had been won, but they were of sterling worth. They achieved martyrdom. The work has to begin afresh. . . .

Since writing the first part of my letter, I have heard new evidence which bears out some previous suggestions, and also certain suspicions of my own, as to the real attitude of the Chinese toward foreigners. I see no reason to change what I have written, because it referred to only a limited region, and also because I wrote of what "seems" and "Appears" to be the case. Appearances are sometimes deceitful, especially among the Chinese.

The real attitude of the Chinese toward foreigners has probably not changed essentially in the last ten years. As one of my Chinese friends, a man who is willing to speak frankly, put it, if there has been any change, it has been an increase of animosity, forgetting the persecutions and re-membering the humiliating experiences of the foreign military occupation. The people recognize the power of the foreigners, and so the animosity smoulders; but it is still there. Outwardly everything is serene, there are eager professions of friendship, and people of the two races are brought into new and close associations, but underneath the change amounts to practi-cally nothing.

On the basis of this, there are not wanting foreign residents who predict a renewal of Boxer troubles, and who point to occasional threats and riots as evidence thereof. The calmer judgment, however, agrees with the opinion that I have held for a long time—that incipient troubles are inevitable for some years to come, that the Imperial government recognizes the folly of entering a second time on the pathway of four years ago, that no movement of the kind can become formidable without patronage from above, and that the foreign ministers in Peking will be ever on the alert to head off such trouble. This leaves room for the cherished hope that a period of quiet will allow time for the dissemination of Christian literature, for the broad scat-tering of the seed of the kingdom, for the planting and culture of that new life which shall usher in the new China.

[1]The Legation Quarter had been greatly enlarged by the terms of the Boxer Protocol. It had become a walled and fortified enclave stretching for more than a mile in length and six-tenths of a mile in width. In addition, legation guards were permanently stationed there to protect the diplomats and others. By 1913, over two thousand marines and soldiers from ten nations were living in the Legation Quarter.

[2]Chinese Bible women visited Chinese women in their homes and spoke about Christianity and social reforms advocated by the missionaries, such as anti-footbinding and opposition to female infanticide. At this time the Bible women received only limited training.

Charles to the Ewing Family, November 19, 1904, Lin Ching, Shantung

Dear Ewing Family:

I am visiting our two Mission stations in the Shantung province. I am trav-eling with Charles Stanley, Jr. and his wife, who are going to their station in Pang Chuan. We came by house boat on the Grand Canal,[1] taking eight days for the four hundred miles, though we stopped over Sunday at a station of the London Mission and delivered to them fifteen boxes of books.

As I remained with Dr. Arthur Smith[2] in Pang Chuan for almost a week I learned a great deal about the work there. The hospital is an important part, attracting patients from great distances. From Pang Chuan to this station of Lin Ching is 75 miles and I came by cart in three days, visiting two out-stations on the way.

One afternoon I took a walk with Mr. [F. M.] Chapin and climbed the two hundred steps to the top of the [nine storey] Lin Ching pagoda. From this lofty place we gained an extensive view of the landscape. It was a beautiful sight—the river, the fields, the villages (someone had counted two hundred), the city. If I have ever expressed the opinion that this vast plain is dull, dreary, or uninteresting, I was thoroughly cured of that illusion during my trip up the river. To one who loves the mountains, the plain becomes monotonous, nevertheless, one only needs a good point of vantage in order to see the real beauty of the fertile fields, the villages far enough away to look picturesque instead of dirty, the clumps of trees that mark the private cemeteries, the occasional orchards of fruit trees, and the grey city walls and towers.

Inside the city are interesting sights. On the busiest streets there are mattings from roof to roof, making them appear like arcades, with open shop fronts. One of these might well be called Bamboo Street, as it is lined on both sides for a long distance with shops dealing in all sorts of articles made out of bamboo strips. . . .

I started for home at ten o'clock on Monday aiming to reach there for Thanksgiving on Thursday, though ordinarily it would take five days. How did I manage? I hired a cart with two fast mules, making forty miles that day. To do this, the animals traveled without food on the road and with only so much rest as they could get while they were being watered two or three times, at a rate of more than four miles an hour. The mules go tandem and seldom out of a walk as rough roads and no springs would make a faster gait unbearable. . . . On Wednesday I went by train to Peking and stayed over that night with Mr. Ament. . . . He had just returned from a month's trip in the country. . . .

On Thursday I left Peking on the seven o'clock train, reaching Tientsin at 10:30. We had Thanksgiving dinner at the [James H. and Netta A.] McCanns and at four went to the consulate for the annual American gathering.

[1]The Grand or Imperial Canal (Yun Ho in Chinese, i.e., Transit River) in 1904 extended from Hangchow to Tientsin, a distance of about 850 miles. Although portions of the canal dated to before the Christian era, the major work between the Yangtze and Yellow rivers was

completed during the reign of the Emperor Yang Ti (A.D. 605–617). However, the section of the canal extending to Tientsin and Peking was only constructed during the Yuan dynasty (A.D. 1260–1368) in order that the imperial city would safely obtain rice tributes from the south of China.

[2]Arthur H. Smith, an American Board missionary whom the Ewings had known in their earlier years in China, had published his account of the Boxer Uprising during their absence (*China in Convulsion* [New York: Fleming H. Revell, 1901]).

Charles to Judson Smith, November 26, 1904, Tientsin

Dear Dr. Smith:

[T]here are certain expenses that are necessary at such a station [as Pang Chuan], where much of the work is away from the home center, that I might never have understood if I had not been there to see for myself. For instance, at other stations we can hire carts for touring whenever we want them. At Pang Chuan it is next to impossible to hire, and yet the work is very largely touring and carts are a daily necessity. This explains why the station must own its own carts and own and feed the animals. . . .

The matter of self-support for the native church is probably as hard to push in the Pang Chuan field as in any part of the Mission. It is becoming harder, year by year, for the people to make both ends meet in their own living expenses, and there is little prospect of an immediate improvement in self support by the church. Dr. Smith has suggested to the people at Hsia Ching, however, that the time has arrived when they ought to pay the salary of the preacher—in which case he would probably be ordained. I fear that this will not come to pass just now, but we may hope for it soon.

[T]his movement [to the American Board mission in Lin Ching] began as a protest against the Roman Catholics, and thus may properly be called a *protestant* affair. Some of the Roman Church members in that region, as elsewhere, relying on the protection of the powerful church behind them and on the awe that it inspired in people and officials alike, had been carrying things with a high hand, imposing on their neighbors, among others, and on some of those who were already inquirers in connection with our work, tho not yet church members. It was evident that, if any work was to be done in those districts, justice must be secured. . . . The people in all of that region were impressed with two things—first, that the Protestant Church had influence as well as the Catholic; secondly, that the Protestant influence was to be preferred as being in accord with the common desire for justice and peace. The natural result has been that many people want to join the church.

[O]ther questions for the [proposed] deputation to consider are those that have arisen largely as a result of the disturbances of 1900. I merely mention some of these. How far should missionaries go in taking up law cases? should they limit themselves to cases of persecution and protection of property? or may they properly take up cases for church members or outsiders, in order to see to it that the corrupt courts give just judgment? How far is it wise now to reverse mistakes that may have been made in indemnity settlements? Is it wise to retain temples that were turned over to the Church for indemnity? or should they, even now, be returned? Should regulations be made about renting to tenants some of the real estate not used for Mission purposes? or should it be possible to rent such property to shopkeepers who open their shops for business on Sundays? or who sell alcoholic drinks? How much of the funds secured from rental should be reported back to the Board? or shall they be used entirely, as was doubtless intended in the first place, for the benefit of the local station or out-station? Should a teacher be retained in Mission employ, of whom it is reported (I have not verified the report) that he received proof of the execution of the Boxers who killed his relatives by having their ears brought to him?

Then there is the whole question of the style in which the mission property should be rebuilt. Some of this is done, and cannot be undone anyway. Some is not yet done. Some mistakes that have been made may still be remedied. These things are largely a matter of individual opinion, and my opinion may not be that of others. I think that the houses at Peking are, for the most part, about as modest as they could well be and meet the requirements, and that it is an excellent thing to have in the capital city a church building that is imposing, but I doubt not there may be others who think the church building too fine. At Tungchow, my opinion is that the whole property is many times as large as it ought to be, that it would very likely be wise, even at this late date, to dispose of some of it, and that the houses are too large and pretentious. My wife, after a week's visit there, reports that most of the ladies wish they might be back in the midst of more modest surroundings, and that they regret the expenditure of so much money, and I know that some of the men agree with this. The Tungchow people may not have written thus themselves, and very likely they would not thank me for doing so, for the simple reason that the work is done and cannot be undone. But other work of the same kind is yet to be done, as at Tientsin and Lin Ching.

Charles to the Ewing Family, December 27, 1904, Tientsin

Dear Ewing Family:

Besides the Stanleys and the McCanns of our [American Board] Mission, we have in our compound an English lady working independently and the Harvey family of the Y.M.C.A. The mother of Mr. McCann is also with them. . . .

[A]fter the children were in bed, we had Christmas dinner here, inviting all the Americans in our compound and also Dr. [Albert C.] and Mrs. [Celia] Peck and their son [Myron], who is a professor in the Chinese University here. Dr. and Mrs. Peck were formerly members of our Mission in Pang Chuan, he is now in private practice here and is our family physician.

Charles to Editor, New Haven Shoreline Times, December 28, 1904, Tientsin

To the Editor:

We find many changes in China [since our departure in 1900]. . . . In Peking, where we lived from 1895 to 1900, the changes are very marked. The property belonging to the legations of the various nations represented in Peking is all in one section of the city separated from the native population by a broad open space, and fortified and garrisoned. There are many new buildings, some of them very fine. The missionary societies laboring in the city are all of them outside this exclusive section, but all have acquired enlarged grounds and have put up new buildings better than the old. Macadam roads are being put in place of the rough and rutty thoroughfares of former days. Street lamps are now in use that dispense light instead of darkness. Two railways land passengers near the front gate of the palace. . . .

In Tientsin, where we are now living, the foreign concessions have been largely extended, so that a large area is under the control of several European governments.[1] The native city itself shows many changes, the walls have been demolished and in their place are broad and busy streets, filtered river water may be bought at hydrants located in convenient places, and other innovations are evident everywhere.

Out in the country, where I spend much of my time, I find that silver dollars are coming into use, railways are surveyed or already built, and a foreigner is not the strange phenomenon that he used to be. Here and there I find army blankets left on the way by soldiers of some foreign nation in 1900, and cigarettes from North Carolina are every where in evidence.

The attitude of the people toward foreigners is a matter of no little interest. On the surface everything looks favorable. The Empress Dowager delights to receive the legation ladies in imperial audience. Officials of all ranks treat foreigners with respect and often receive them cordially. . . .

Of course, however, much of this popularity must be discounted, since for one thing it is the fashion now to ape foreigners. Fashions change, even in China, and at present one finds many men, especially in places like Peking and Tientsin, following the example of Shanghai, close-fitting sleeves taking the place of the loose Oriental style, straw hats very generally worn in warm weather, and the inevitable cigarette. Furthermore, the Chinese being a very practical people, are making the best of an undesirable but unavoidable situation; the foreigner can not be got rid of and the better they treat him the better they can get along with him and endure his presence. Again, it pays to give attention to him and his wants, his wants are many and often not easy to supply, but if he can be made to pay a good price for what he gets, those who follow in his wake are likely to come out ahead financially. Most certainly should one not deceive himself with the idea that all this apparent popularity is real.

After the Boxer infatuation had passed, the people in many regions hastened to pay the required indemnity. It was mere justice that they should do so, and it is literally true that force was not used to compel them to do so, but it is doubtlessly equally true that in many instances they did what they were required to do and did it because they did not dare to refuse. The erection of memorials to martyrs or others by the Chinese indicated that they recognized either the propriety or the necessity of so doing and it meant little or nothing more.

At bottom then what is the real attitude toward foreigners on the part of the Chinese? I give three answers. First, there is an underlying hatred that has probably not diminished, but rather increased in the last five years. Many of the people forget the suffering of the foreigners and of the native Christians and remember only the injuries inflicted by the European [American and Japanese] armies; the enforced demands of the European [and other] governments; and the heavy indemnity that is even now being paid by increased taxation. Secondly, however, at the same time there is an evident recognition of the superiority of the foreigner in very many ways and a consequent eagerness to learn from him and discover the secret of his success. This does not interfere with the dislike of the foreigner, but helps to explain his apparent popularity. Thirdly, this dislike or hatred is by no means universal. With large and increasing numbers of people, and in many places there is great and genuine openness of mind and a readiness to respond kindly to the approach of foreigners. The Chinese know us better than they did, not only our bad points, but our good points. They are approachable, more so than ever in the past. While we must not deceive ourselves with the vain hope that the anti-foreign feeling is a thing of the past, neither should we be so suspicious as to discredit the real and widespread kindliness of feeling toward us that exists among the people.

And what of the prospects? Is the future likely to bring further trouble? Or is something better in store? These questions are asked, and some definite answer should be possible. Still, the true answer is somewhat complicated.

There are likely to be occasional outbreaks, more or less anti-foreign in character, for some years to come. Some incipient eruptions of this kind have already occurred. Others may take place and it is well to be watchful at all times.

On the other hand it is quite clear that such troubles will be infrequent and easily managed if dealt with immediately. They are local and will not spread unless given opportunity. Furthermore, it is equally evident that such opportunity will not be given. On the one hand the foreigners are and will continue to be, on the watch, and everything that threatens a recurrence of the conditions of 1900 will be immediately reported to the proper authorities. On the other hand, the Chinese government is disposed to act promptly and summarily in all such cases. These contentions are abundantly warranted by what has taken place in several districts where recent Boxer trouble was threatened. The foreigners concerned reported these facts to their minister in Peking and the result was a strong imperial edict promptly showing the spirit and purpose of the government.

Meanwhile, everything is peaceful. I had apprehended that country touring would be somewhat embarrassed by the need for extra watchfulness in the midst of disturbed conditions, but just the opposite is true, conditions are not disturbed, extra watchfulness is not required, country touring was never more free from embarrassment and one is as quiet and safe as in America. There is every indication that these favorable conditions will continue indefinitely.

It naturally follows that now is the time when missionary effort should be pushed. There is such an opportunity as never before, every door is standing ajar and all that is needed is an adequate working force. On the other hand if the present opportunity is let slip there may be nothing again.

[1]In 1904 the foreign concessions (i.e., settlements) in Tientsin numbered eight. All eight together totaled more than five square miles. In the concessions area there were churches, lodges, national associations, a library, and recreation clubs (tennis, riding, cricket, and racing). To protect those concessions, there were by 1913 over 6,200 marines, sailors, and soldiers.

Charles to Judson Smith, December 31, 1904, Tientsin

Dear Dr. Smith:

The past month I have largely devoted to acquainting myself with my own station, having visited the various districts in which our work is located. From November 29 to December 5, I was in the villages to the northwest, in the neighborhood of the railway station at Laofa. . . . For most of the time I made my headquarters at the village of Chien Ying, where we have a goodly company of Christians who meet every evening for worship to the number of thirty or forty. After the Boxer troubles, this village turned over to us all of its temples. In one of these, we have our local chapel and an attractive day school for boys. In another building that was once a temple, I had my room, and there we had meetings each morning. . . .

From December 5 to December 10, I was at home, and was able to visit the street chapel in the native city and take some part in the work there.

The daily attendance is excellent, . . . I find from forty to sixty present, which number increases to over a hundred when the foreigner speaks.

From December 10 to December 23, I was again in the country. . . . At the village of Tu Ling Hua [over 100 miles southwest of Tientsin] I spent four days in the family home of helper Chiang. Mr. Chiang himself, who is located at Laofa in charge of the country work in the northern villages, accompanied me on all this trip, and I had some opportunity to become acquainted with him. He is, on the whole, the most efficient of our helpers, but unfortunately he seems to have the idea that the principal business of the native helper is to take up law cases and settle troubles and disputes. The church members come to depend on him for such things.

. . . In my last letter to you, I wrote something about the future of the Tientsin station. The more that I study the whole situation the less clear I am as to the wisest policy. The rest of the [North China] Mission needs strengthening, and no other station can possibly be dropped without leaving a distinct gap in the fighting line. . . . I state briefly my reasons for hesitating about giving up the Tientsin work.

(1) Being conservative in temperament, giving up this old station would seem to me something like taking a backward step.

(2) Being an optimist, I can scarcely bring myself to believe that the Board will continue to withhold the supply of men and money that is needed.

(3) Even with the present working force, I believe that a fairly effective work can be done, altho not what it ought to be.

(4) Certain parts of the field are left for us to work, and there is no indication that others will work them if we do not.

(a) The Pao Ti Hsien district, a large district immediately north of Tientsin, on the east side of the [Pei Ho] river that comes down from Tungchow, a district that has been almost untouched.

(b) The north side of the city of Tientsin itself, running all the way out to our new premises at Hsiku.

If this station continues to exist, we ought to make the move to the new premises . . . the planning and building can be wisely done only as we know what to expect. The decision of this matter does not rest with the station, nor even with the Mission, but ultimately with the Prudential Committee, for it involves the financial prospect, which we out here do not know. . . . [However] so long as Dr. and Mrs. Stanley are in the work, it is doubtful whether anyone in the Mission would favor an entire abandonment of the Tientsin station. Their lives for so many years [nearly forty] have been wrapped up in this work that, entirely apart from other considerations, it would seem cruel to divorce them from it.

3

The Rising Storm
1905–1908

JAPAN'S overwhelming defeat of Russia in their 1904–5 war had a considerable impact upon the Chinese, both in China and abroad. China in 1905 was not the same as it had been a decade earlier, when the Sino-Japanese War had had little impact upon Chinese students and the urban elite. But newspapers, periodicals, and magazines printed in the Chinese language had flourished during the decade, and hence many more Chinese were aware of outside events than before. Cities such as Shanghai, Tientsin, and Canton had become printing centers for wall posters and pamphlets of nearly every political persuasion. The number of high school students had more than doubled. Chinese students in Japan had gone from a handful in 1896 (one authority[1] gives the figure as nine) to several thousand in less than a decade. Most of the students and urban elite saw in the Japanese victory a racial success story: the revitalized and modernized oriental over the imperialist occidental. It was a vision that caused them to believe that Japan's route to modernization was what China could duplicate. Chinese nationalism and racial pride had been stimulated.

An event that was immediately effected by the resurgence of Chinese nationalism and racial pride was the Chinese boycott of American goods. The boycott was supported mainly by students and the Chinese business community in the treaty ports. It took place during a six-month period in 1905 and stemmed mainly from the discriminatory immigration laws of the United States that affected Chinese migration and travel not only to America but also to Hawaii and the Philippines. Because of the laws and the often unfair administration of them, as many as one out of four Chinese arriving in the United States was turned away.[2] The boycott of American goods started in Shanghai and spread to most ports as a protest against these

[1]Frederic Wakeman, Jr., *The Fall of Imperial China* (New York: Free Press, 1975), 239.
[2]Edward J. M. Rhoads, *China's Republican Revolution: The Case of Kwangtung, 1895–1913* (Cambridge, Mass.: Harvard University Press, 1975), 84.

laws. The boycott, the first of its kind, demonstrated a common purpose not recently witnessed in China.

Many of the Chinese students in Japan began a new revolutionary phase after the Russo-Japanese War by forming themselves into a kind of secret society. About 1,300 students and others, led by Dr. Sun Yat-sen, founded the Alliance Society, or Tung Meng Hui. The society's primary goals were simple and hence appealing: overthrow the Manchus and abolish the monarchy. Although the Alliance lasted only a few years, it provided Sun with an additional means of advancing his revolutionary activities. Sun, from Kwang-tung, who had received his medical training in Hong Kong and had been educated in the English language in mission schools in Hawaii, recognized the latent power of the Chinese students in Japan. Mainly children of the lower-gentry class and merchant families, they were to be of use in the ouster of the Manchu dynasty. Many of the students who returned to army units in China became the nucleus of revolutionary cells. Such cells, although not necessarily associated with the Alliance Society, would eventually create the situation that would help bring about the end of the Manchus in Peking.

While student revolutionaries in Japan and in China were plotting the end of the dynasty, that beleaguered entity continued under Tzu Hsi to determine how best to preserve its power through reforms. In July 1905 an edict was issued that opened the door to constitutionalism in China. That edict, which called for a commission to study foreign institutions, set in motion a series of government revisions that, the Manchus hoped, would allow modification within their administration without a sacrifice of the throne's ultimate power. Tzu Hsi had opened the bottle; the genie was out and could not be controlled by the dynasty.

While Japan's success pushed the Manchu court along the path of speeding up its program of reform and to use the Japanese model, the rulers of China were equally aware of Japan's threat to China via her deep involvement in southern Manchuria. With tens of thousands of Japanese soldiers only a few hundred miles from Peking, China's rulers concluded that a modernized Chinese army must be quickly developed. Viceroy Yuan Shih-kai's modern army, the Peiyang, held large-scale maneuvers in Chihli in October 1905. Since his army had been partially financed from funds provided by other provinces, Yuan held the maneuvers to show his critics that great progress had been made. Yuan's army, admittedly with the assistance of Japanese advisers, showed the foreign audience in 1905 and again in 1906 that indeed the Peiyang was a force to be reckoned with. However, the dynasty was truly on the horns of a dilemma. On the one hand, Yuan's troops could probably prevent foreign aggression against China, but at the same time they presented a threat to the throne. Newly trained and better-educated troops were not as politically reliable as the old-style Bannermen and militia who were incapable of preventing foreign aggression. In addition, the Peking-Hankow railway, opened in the summer of 1905, meant that troops from Central China could be quickly moved north and that the Peiyang could just as easily travel by rail to the Yangtze River. Progress and modernization were proving to be a mixed bag for the elderly lady in the Forbidden City.

Although the missionary schools had been excluded from the education reforms of 1904, the expansion of those schools following the end of the Boxer Uprising was truly remarkable. By the end of 1905, the 2,585 schools directed by the Protestant missionaries had enrolled more than 57,000 students, of whom nearly 20 percent were female.[3] Fourteen of those schools offered college-level curricula. The American minister W. W. Rockhill[4] attempted unsuccessfully in 1905 to obtain Chinese registration of the mission schools and recognition of their graduates. Although anti-Christian bias may have been the motive for the nonrecognition, the reason was more likely the desire to exclude the foreigner from control of the education of Chinese and the central authorities' wish to regulate curriculum.

Besides the foreigners and revolutionaries, China had another significant problem from within and without. Opium was certainly China's curse during much of the nineteenth and early-twentieth century. Millions of people, at all social levels, were addicted to its use. It had been legalized by treaty and as late as 1900 remained China's chief import. Much of the drug had originally come from India, via a British monopoly and on British ships. By 1906, however, even with Britain's shipments of 7 million pounds sterling–worth of opium into Chinese ports, the greater share of the drug used by the Chinese was homegrown. In the spring of that year Peking issued a decree calling for the reduction of the drug through heavy taxation. Because of its import value, it was a great source of revenue for the throne; in addition, it provided many provincial officials with incomes that enhanced their official salaries. By September the government took even more forceful action by issuing a proclamation calling for the stamping out of both the use of opium and the growing of the opium poppy. For many years missionaries had made efforts to stop the use of opium, but to little avail. Chinese students returning from Japan had argued strenuously against the drug, and the officers of the modernized Chinese armies would not recruit young men if they were known users of opium. Finally, the British government agreed to stop the legal flow of Indian opium to China if the Chinese government took steps to eliminate the use of the drug. Perhaps Japan's occupation of

---

[3]Hosea Ballow Morse, *The Period of Subjection, 1894–1911*, vol. 3 of *The International Relations of the Chinese Empire* (London: Paragon Book Gallery, 1918), 413.

[4]William W. Rockhill, a noted Orientalist and longtime diplomat, succeeded Clement Conger as the American minister to China in 1905. In 1899, while serving in the Department of State, he helped to draft the Open Door policy of Secretary Hay.

southern Manchuria and the loss of the poppy fields located there may also have influenced the throne to take its action against opium. Within a ten-year period opium in China was expected to be eliminated. Between 1906 and 1911 the Manchu dynasty took its most aggressive reform action in the suppression of opium use and the cultivation of the poppy.

The Manchu dynasty's successful efforts to eliminate opium smoking and poppy growing had their negative effects. Because of the size of the opium-using population and the profits to be made from the drug, many farmers and provincial middlemen opposed the elimination of poppy production. Armed conflicts often were the result of the suppression, and a group emerged that considered the Peking authorities responsible for their loss of legal activities and of revenue. As one scholar has put it, the poppy growers "became one of the elements in that general chorus of dissatisfaction which culminated in the Revolution."[5]

As required by the treaty between the powers and China following the Boxer Uprising, the Imperial Maritime Customs, under the indefatigable Sir Robert Hart, was required to carry out the collection of revenues (except the likin tax)[6] at and near the treaty ports. For this purpose Hart had under his control at the beginning of 1906 some 1,324 foreigners and 9,465 Chinese scattered throughout most of China.[7] Of the foreigners, there were 713 British, 156 Germans, 102 Americans, and a remaining 353 representing fifteen nationalities. This staff not only collected taxes and looked after all sorts of other matters involving shipping and ports but continued to handle the Chinese postal service.

By the end of 1907, it had become evident to some in Peking that through additional duties placed upon goods moving into the towns, the provincial Chinese gentry were being forced to obtain funds for China's modern army and to pay for the new schools. These same gentry, who were educated in the Confucianist system and who acted as intermediaries between government authorities and the farmer-peasants, were concerned about the need to put more squeeze on China's land tillers in order to meet the dynasty's centralization programs. They feared their loss of authority and income. Yet another element of the Chinese society was being disturbed by the actions of the Manchu court.

In April 1907, a viceroy for Manchuria was appointed by the Dowager empress in the hope the reestablishment of the imperial presence in the

[5]Meribeth E. Cameron, *The Reform Movement in China* (Palo Alto, Calif.: Stanford University Press, 1931), 152.

[6]The likin tax was levied upon goods that were in transit from one province to another, or from one district to another within the same province.

[7]Stanley F. Wright, *Hart and the Chinese Customs* (Belfast: Queens University-W. Mullan, 1950), 902.

Manchu homeland would allow the Open Door policy to function there. The hope of the court was that countries other than Japan and Russia would invest in the development of Manchuria. The involvement of Britain and the United States would offset the well-established footholds already carved out by the Japanese and Russians. One foreign dignitary who visited Shanghai and Vladivostok and learned about the potential for American investment in Manchuria from the American consul general in Mukden, Willard Straight, was William Howard Taft, then the American Secretary of War. For the next several years, Straight and other Americans attempted to force the door open in Manchuria. Because of Russian and Japanese opposition, their efforts were without success.

While the throne, through the constitutional reform program, was preparing to have provincial assemblies established, the Chinese municipality of Tientsin had held elections in July 1907. Viceroy Yuan, who was disliked and feared by many Manchu officials, had prepared for the elections and after some persuasion, 8,763 men voted, out of a total of 13,567 registered.[8] At the time of the elections, Tientsin had an estimated population of over a million.

The following September, Viceroy Yuan was promoted up and out of his position of power. Tzu Hsi brought him to Peking and promoted him to the Grand Council, where he served as minister of foreign affairs. The result of his new position in Peking was that he no longer had troops under his control. Another powerful viceroy who was relieved of his post and ordered to Peking to become a member of the Grand Council was Chang Chih-tung, from Central China.

On August 27, 1908, an edict was issued in the name of the emperor that outlined the steps to be taken in order to establish a constitutional monarchy. The steps were to require a long educational and preparatory period that, after nine years, would eventually have seen elected bodies at provincial and national levels and a constitutional monarchy instead of an absolute rule. The plan to be followed and the steps to be taken looked reasonable on paper, but on the whole they were a fantasy. The amount of power the throne proposed to give up was not great, the time frame was overly long and impractical, and it is doubtful that the administrative machinery and revenue required for implementation could ever have been put into place and made to work. More and more, the throne passed the responsibility for raising revenue for its reforms to the provinces. Only time would tell whether the constitutional edict was meant to be a Manchu shadow show or a reform of substance.

The edict of August 1908 was the last reform act presided over by the Dowager Empress Tzu Hsi. On November 15 of that year she died in her

[8]Jerome Chen, *Yuan Shih-kai* (Palo Alto, Calif.: Stanford University Press, 1972), 73.

Palace of Tranquil Old Age within the Forbidden City. Whether by coincidence or by murder, the emperor, Kuang Hsu, had died the day before, at only thirty-eight years of age. Tzu Hsi, the Old Buddha to many, had gotten her way right to the very end. Her tormented and captive nephew was dead, and she had selected his successor, the child Pu Yi. Pu Yi's reign title was Hsuan Tung; and he not only sat on the Dragon Throne and was the Son of Heaven but was also He Who Is Above, the Enthroned One, the Lord of Ten Thousand Years, the Lord of Myriad Years, the One Who Faces South, the Celestial Emperor, and finally the predestined Last Emperor of Cathay, of the Middle Kingdom and of China.[9] The new emperor was a child of almost three when he ascended the throne and proceeded to ruin the pageant by crying. His father, Prince Chun, who had been named regent by Tzu Hsi, was the brother of the deceased emperor.

The funeral for Tzu Hsi, who had ruled China for more than forty years, was described by one Western observer as "a gorgeous spectacle" that because of the "red robes of bearers, yellow robes of Lamaist priests, silver and gold rich embroideries . . . [had] the colors of a sunset."[10] Tzu Hsi's mausoleum was a treasure trove, one of whose riches was a single strand of matched pearls wrapped around her body nine times.

While the old empress was exiting this world in ornate and exotic style, the new regent inherited the reins of a government with a myriad of unfulfilled reforms and far beyond his ambitions or talents to control. Prince Chun proved quickly to be inexperienced, disinterested, unimaginative, and lacking in inner strength. Worst of all, he looked for advice and direction to fellow Manchu princes who were as poorly equipped as he to administer the government in times of great change. One opinionated British citizen who knew Chun wrote: "During several years of fairly intimate contact with Prince Chun, I came to be . . . deeply impressed by his fatal tendency to do the wrong thing or choose the wrong course in matters affecting the imperial house or the interests of the young emperor, his son."[11]

Although greatly overshadowed by the deaths of Tzu Hsi and the emperor, an event took place during the second half of 1908 that was intended to assist China and to appease the Chinese students. The United States agreed that a portion of the Boxer indemnity would be returned to China for support of Chinese students sent to American schools. No other power had used its indemnity for the purpose of developing China.

[9]Arnold C. Brackman, *The Prisoner of Peking* (New York: Scribner, 1980), xii.
[10]Ibid., 46.
[11]Reginald F. Johnston, *Twilight in the Forbidden City* (New York: D. Appleton-Century, 1934), 61.

Ewing Papers,
January 1905 to December 1908

Charles to Ellen Ewing, January 13, 1905, Tientsin

My Dear Mother:

The children all seem to be very happy. They enjoy China. The girls [Marion, aged nine, and Ellen, six] say it is better than they expected. They have children to play with. Ellen plays with the younger ones in our own compound with content, but Marion wants older company some of the time and has found two girls her own age in the English Mission next door to us.

. . . Bessie teaches a Sunday school class of nine Chinese girls from the school, attends or leads two prayer meetings for Chinese women and directs the calling for a Chinese Bible woman. There are some people who need to be urged to Christian work, but Bessie is one who needs to be restricted from doing too much.

For myself, I am enjoying the Chinese preaching this winter more than any work I have done in China before. I have written about the custom of having a chapel opening on a main street besides the one for members meetings, which is in an inner court [yard]. Whenever I am in the city [of Tientsin] I go to this street chapel about four each afternoon and after a few of us have sung two or three hymns in order to attract attention, I speak for nearly an hour. They [the Chinese] come and go quite informally but recently there have been at least a hundred at a time. Many of them sit quietly listening for some time, also certain persons appear day after day, . . . a few have the courage to come to the inner chapel and meet the Christians at worship.

While there are three Missions with chapels in the city there are none on the north side and our Mission has purchased premises in that section [Hsiku] bordering on the open country. We have over fifteen acres, with the river [Pei Ho] on the south side and plan to build there and move next year. This will be a better location for work and much better for health.

Charles to Judson Smith, February 1, 1905, Tientsin

Dear Dr. Smith:

These [revival] meetings, beginning on Sunday, Jan. 8, continued until Thursday evening, Jan. 19, with afternoon services in our chapel in the native city and evening services in the Wesley M. E. [Methodist Episcopal] Church at the foreign settlement. The purpose of these meetings was exactly what the name indicates, not to reach the non-Christian population through evangelistic efforts, but to arouse and quicken the native church membership. The meetings, which had been planned by a committee appointed by the Missionary Association, were under the charge of Drs. Pyke and [W. T.] Hobart of the M. E. Mission, others of us helping as we were able. The method of the leaders was to present, emphasize, and re-emphasize the necessity of being rid of sin, to urge self-examination, confession, and reconsecration, and to give much of the time in each meeting to prayer. The results, while not as deep and radical as some had hoped, were quite soul searching in several individuals, while not a few others were much helped and strengthened.

. . . I must tell you about a fine man who has recently joined the church, Mr. Chang. He has won his first literary degree, and has a small official position in one of the yamens [government offices]. His home is in a village not far from Tungchow, where one of the Tungchow out-stations is located. He has been for some years a member of the Greek Church. Recently, however, he has discovered the superiority of Protestant Christianity, and two or three months ago he was received into church membership. His business requires his attention for only a small part of each day, and he spends nearly every afternoon at the city chapel. . . . Mr. Chang hopes that, after he has had further instruction and becomes more thoroughly familiar with Christian truth, he may give up his present business and devote himself to the work of the church, depending for his income on his own property. This is encouraging and may some time prove to be a partial response to our eager desire for well qualified workers. . . .

The building at Hsiku has been delayed for several reasons. Dr. Stanley's health was one. My own unwillingness to take the lead in this work . . . has perhaps been another. . . . I see no reason why we cannot go on this year, in case some satisfactory disposition of our present property can be made. Yes, I do see one reason: the cost of building material is so high that building this year is expensive. Lumber is twenty per cent (at least) above normal, on account of the war, which has shut off the imports from Manchuria [where Japan and Russia were fighting]. Bricks are probably at a fairly high rate, on account of the large amount of building that is going on, especially in the Japanese Concession.

. . . The limited appropriation made by the Prudential Committee, as you will learn from other letters than mine, is further cut by the present ruinous rate of exchange, which is likely to continue indefinitely unless the war comes to an end. The same difference in exchange will make the missionaries less than ever able to help the work from their own pockets.

Bessie to Ellen Ewing, February 1905, Tientsin

My Dear Mother Ewing:

Each morning I have school with the girls. Mrs. McCann tries to give an hour of kindergarten work to the three little ones [Frances and Robert McCann and Edward Ewing, aged four] . . . but she has had many interruptions. She has had to help her husband in his office work because his eyes are troubling him.

Andrew [aged two and a half] has developed a great deal lately. His shyness has been more prolonged and more pronounced than that of any of the other children. He clung to me for everything, even seemed afraid of his father after he was in the country [side] for three weeks. But since Christmas he has changed. Now he lets Charles romp with him, plays with the other children, even letting Ellen and Edward boss him. He is quite a little king over the nurse[1] and she has amused him a great deal while school was going on. . . . The children have all picked up the Chinese language very quickly. That is, they know many words, though they cannot string them together in the proper way. The idiom will come naturally to Andrew, but the others try to translate the English idiom which is never the right way to learn. One has to become accustomed to thinking in a different language, before the idiom is acquired.

[1] A Chinese servant was normally referred to by the Chinese word, amah.

Charles to Judson Smith, March 6, 1905, Tientsin

Dear Dr. Smith:

Your letter of Jan. 19 reached me two days ago. . . .[1]

[I]t appears that a peculiar problem is already emerging at Paoting, and is likely to call for very wise and careful handling. In that station, if I am rightly informed, there is, more than elsewhere in our Mission, a spirit of independence among the native Christian community, that may perhaps be compared with what was found in Japan a few years ago. If this presages continued similarity to Japan, it may well call for the careful consideration and care of the wisest men. There have, in the past, been so many changes in the personnel of the missionary force at Paoting that there has been opportunity for the growth of the self-managing spirit. It is not in my heart to regret the presence of such a spirit, for in it lies the hope of the future, but it does mean that the whole situation at Paoting is likely to demand most careful and tactful handling for many years to come. What I have just written comes not at all from personal observation (for Paoting is one of the places that I have been unable to visit since my return to the field), but from remarks made by others, taken in connection with what I knew of the station formerly.

[I]n this region [Laofa], numerous temples were turned over to our church at the time of [the Boxer] indemnity settlement. In two of the villages where this was done, we agreed to open schools for the benefit of the village. At Chien Ying, we have done so, and have a prosperous school. At Laofa, we at one time opened a school, but there were no pupils. Now, however, there is promise of pupils, and, if I can find the money I hope to open a school there. Indeed, even tho we have given no promise in the other villages, I feel that we ought to make the converted temples a public benefit. Accordingly, I hope that before long I may be able to report that in several of these places there are either schools or resident helpers or church members qualified to lead meetings and instruct inquirers. Already there is call for schools in some villages. Thirty dollars a year will support such a school: that is, it will enable me to say to the Christians of the village, "Here is $2.50 for each month of the year, take it, use it, add what is needed, and see that the school is kept up."

[I]n the city [Tientsin], we have been obliged to dismiss the chapel-keeper, who has been in Mission work for many years, it being discovered that he has the opium habit.

[1]All things considered, forty-four days for a letter to travel from Boston to Tientsin was good for the year 1905.

Charles to Judson Smith, April 6, 1905, Tientsin

Dear Dr. Smith:

Most of the month of March I spent away from home. From the ninth to the thirty-first, I was absent on a trip to the southwest, . . . I made the outward trip on bicycle, the return by river boat.

. . . I had two delightful days at the London Mission station at Tsang Chow. It still appears to me, as I think I suggested to you after my visit there last November, that their work is in advance of that which I have seen elsewhere. . . . Mr. Murray [of the London Mission] feels that the large country field, with its insistent demands, can not wait for men to take the full college and theological course, and that the men who can do this will be too few at best, and accordingly he is putting about thirty men through a "short-cut" course of two years, after which they may be used as second-grade helpers and teachers of village schools. This is not in any way a depreciation of the more thorough and scholarly work of the few, who will without question be the leaders in the churches, but it is an appreciation of the need for more men as soon as possible. I visited the class, and I heartily endorse the plan. Dr. Peill [also of the London Mission] has similar ideas about the medical work. He feels that he must have men to relieve him of many of the less important cases that overcrowd the hospital, and that it will be a great help to have some of these men at the various out-stations, and he is undertaking two classes, one for the training of men who will be, not thoroughly equipped physicians, but capable of doing the important work I have already referred to, and another class in which he is preparing a few men for efficient service as nurses.

Charles to Henry Ewing, April 27, 1905, Tientsin

Dear Henry:

There are some intimate Mission matters of which I wish to write to you in particular. The first concerns the increasing number of law cases, one of the vexations of the missionary today, of which we formerly knew little. The whole matter is thoroughly distasteful to me, and I sometimes threaten to cut loose from the whole business—in which case I should incur the unanimous disfavor of the native church members, who think it is the business of the pastor to take care of their affairs.

Because of the losses suffered in 1900 because of the Boxers, the Chinese government (on request from our government) gave an indemnity to all the churches in the way of real estate and money. But one thing that seems hard to understand is that this indemnity which we have received has been enough to replace our losses many times over. For instance, in one section we had before, one chapel, but now we have, after funeral expenses and indemnity for native Christians have been amply paid, several hundred acres of land, yielding $250 a year, one temple in each of six villages, and all the temples in another village. The London Mission, working in this same region, was similarly indemnified, but has now turned back nearly all the property. Most of the missionaries of our Mission consider it questionable wisdom to keep temples, tho I hear little criticism as to land. My own opinion is just the opposite: I think we ought to keep the temples, which were public property before, and consider ourselves as trustees, under obligation to use them for the real benefit of the several villages. This we are really doing in some places, where the temples now serve as schools or chapels. On the other hand, the land that we hold was formerly private property. We rent it to private persons, we have already received more than adequate refund, and I am coming to believe that it will be well to turn back this property if we find that it can be done without too much friction. But again I would have the whole native [Chinese] church down on me. I have sometimes thought that since they want to keep the land, I might turn it over to them to manage, giving them no right of appeal to foreign authority if they have trouble about it.

I will write you of two examples of requests that have come to me for decision. A false charge was brought against one of our members by the widow of a murdered man who had owed money to him. I felt it necessary to refuse him as this was not a case of persecution on account of religion, the only type of cases that we are privileged to take up according to international treaty. The other case seemed to me different. A man was connected with the Boxers and was obliged to help materially in the payment of indemnity has taken every opportunity since then to pick on a church member in the next village, a man who is exceptionally meek and mild. Last autumn he brought against this man a false charge of stealing crops from the fields, and had the church member and his witnesses locked up until they had been fleeced out of $200, the official being a young reprobate considerably worse than the average. Mr. Stanley and then I took the matter up, a higher official was sent from Tientsin, and it was settled that the church member and his witnesses should be released and the persecutors should pay them $100. The money was brought to the man's house to be turned over to him in the presence of our helper. There proved to be only $80, but they [the helper and church member] agreed to accept it, but were informed that, as there were men waiting outside with guns they [the helper and church member] would have to return the money—which they did. We wrote to the official to take the persecutor into custody. Since then there has been a change of officials. I have seen the new man and he is pushing the case, and I have let him know that I shall not ask for the release of the persecutor until the full $100 is paid, not a cash [cent] less, nor until he has signed a document agreeing to make no trouble in the future. My position on such matters is complicated by the fact that in other places some of our Mission leaders take the extreme opposite view from mine, and as the Chinese say "So-and-so likes to manage our affairs." . . .

In your [former] station of Paoting there are also conflicting policies, but they [the Americans] agree to differ, working separately and each of the two missionaries presenting his individual report at annual mission meeting. One leaves his field almost entirely to native oversight, turning the money over to them and giving them entire freedom. The other missionary is so prodigal of both his time and his money that his [Chinese] helpers lean heavily on him. . . .

There is one more subject which I wish to let you know and that is the criticism about the use of funds in rebuilding. Some of us who are younger in the [North China] Mission think the new Peking Church is too showy and too foreign in style, and that the houses for the missionaries are too large and that they look too fine, even though ours are much more modest than those in some of the other missions. Criticism is also heard from outside sources, who do not know that missionaries are able to make their money go further than others and think we have spent too much on buildings. For ourselves in planning our new house, we are trying to make expense under the appropriation rather than over, as has been the case elsewhere.

Charles to Judson Smith, May 4, 1905, Tientsin

Dear Dr. Smith:

I have now seen all of our converted temples in that region [Laofa], tho some of them are not thoroughly converted as yet. Some however, we are using. . . . It is a busy time in the country. The people are planting, also smearing their roofs with mud against the expected heavy summer rains.

One of the disagreeable things is that we find ourselves constantly importuned to take up law-suits. When they are that pure and simple, we can refuse. When they are cases of persecution, we feel under some obligation to take them up—tho I personally believe that it would have been a good thing if, from the first, no missionary had received the legal privilege of defending the native converts, even in cases of persecution. That would have been in accord with the spirit of our Master (I think), who depended not on power for protection; and it would have made possible a Chinese church with little if any taint of the foreign about it. However, that matter was settled, right or wrong, long ago. The best we can do now is to exhort the brethren to long-suffering and do what we can to prevent the recurrence of persecution in all places. But there is a third class of cases where persecution and law-suits are mixed together so inextricably that one cannot tell whether to meddle with the matter or not. I have about made up my mind to refuse to take up cases where church members have presented (at the yamen)[1] charges against any one else, to try to settle out of court all cases of persecution, in such a way as to guard against their repetition, to go to the official only as a last resort, and in cases where outsiders have accused church members at the yamen, to request the official to see that justice is done and go no further.

In the region where I have just been visiting, we have had considerable legal and financial trouble, on account of holding so much property, 150 acres beside temple lands. To this we have clear legal title; . . . I dislike to see the church as a landlord: it appears to outsiders that here is a rich (!) corporation collecting rents from poor people, in direct contradiction to the gospel of Christ. It must make it necessary for us to set aside something of the spirit of our Master's gospel. Such a course is ruinous policy at any price.

Yesterday I went to a village within ten miles of here, where one of our Tientsin church members lives, . . . In twenty-four villages, this one man is the only Christian, and all within a half day's ride of Tientsin! In all the years that foreigners have lived in Tientsin, this man tells me that none has ever before been to his village except the soldiers in 1900. Thus, at our very doors, people do not know what we are here for, and there is plenty of room for misunderstanding and opposition. But I find the people very kindly disposed. I went on my bicycle, and of course it was easy to attract a crowd.

[1] A yamen was a Chinese government office.

Charles to Edward C. Ewing, May 4, 1905, Tientsin

Dear Father:

Last month, after my trip into the country, I wrote and made hectograph copies to 150 churches in America where I had spoken during my furlough. This is my part in trying to influence them to greater liberality, by giving them first-hand information. . . . The year 1900, when the Boxer cataclysm swept over the country is the dividing line between the old and the new. The Empress Dowager is still in power but she treats the foreigners in a new way. Immediate attention is given to any signs of anti-foreign sentiment, leaving little room for doubt in the minds of the people as to the proper treatment expected.

Another sign of the new day is in the national system of education.[1] The requirements for civil service examinations now include many subjects besides the Chinese classics. Among them are mathematics and elementary science. I am told that last year it was required that the candidates for the first literary degree should study the gospel of John and be prepared to write a thesis on the study.[2] The general oversight of all the government schools in the province [Chihli], including the two university centers in Paoting and Tientsin, is intrusted to Mr. C. D. Tenney,[3] an American, a graduate of Oberlin College, and after leaving our Mission, being the official interpreter at the American consulate here in Tientsin, then instructor for the grandchildren of Li Hung-chang, and principal of a private school. Later [he was] the first president of Tientsin University, now decorated as a Chinese mandarin and in charge of both the university and of all the secondary schools of this province. The Chinese idea is that higher educational schools will give the impetus to elementary schools and that those will be started when there is the demand. This condition puts on the missionaries a special responsibility, i.e. to provide that education which the government will not be ready to give for some years yet, education for little children, for girls, and for a large number of youth and adults who will never be taught otherwise. Also to give all this on a basis that is Christian, reminding ourselves that the best education in all lands has been the natural fruitage of the Christ-spirit in the world.

. . . More and more do I feel that what I want to do is to get [Chinese] people, not to join the church at my persuasion, but to accept the truth and live by it. The thought has been borne in upon me forceibly [*sic*] during some recent reading—the utter disregard of Jesus for forms and ceremonies, his single emphasis on true service of the heart and life. How un-Christ like for us to set ourselves up as being above other people on account of any distinction, either professional, intellectual, national or personal. What people [here] want is the spirit of Christ, not ecclesiasticism. The primary interest of the church [in China] should be in a full life for all people, "abundant," for body, mind, and spirit.

[1]See chapter 3.
[2]Just where Charles Ewing obtained this information he does not say.
[3]Charles D. Tenney came to China in 1882 as an American Board missionary. In 1896 he left the Board and took the position of head of the government university at Tientsin. From 1908 until 1919 he was the Chinese secretary at the American legation in Peking.

Bessie to Home Folks, May 24, 1905, Tientsin

Dear Folks at Home:
This month brings us three birthdays. Andrew's [third birthday] came on Saturday and we all went out into the country for a picnic. Charles went on his bicycle, which he uses a great deal now. Marion and Ellen rode in one riksha, Edward and the Chinese nurse in another and Andrew and I in a third. Our ride took us outside the city for three miles. We went along a beautifully paved road, bordered by willow trees, to the race course in the British concession. As no one was there we rested on the hotel piazza for awhile before returning. The Tientsin Race Club races came off last week. This is the event of the year for the Tientsin community and post offices,[1] general offices, and nearly all foreign stores shut up for three afternoons in the week. Some say there is less gambling here at this time than at similar affairs in England. . . .

Now I want to tell you some very new experiences that some have had in connection with the Empress Dowager. To show her friendliness and good intentions to foreigners she invited the ladies from various legations to her palace for a meal. As these ladies could not speak or understand Chinese, she invited some missionaries as interpreters and Mrs. Ament was one of these. The Empress Dowager did not appear herself, but of her ladies-in-waiting, whom [*sic*] do you suppose was next to Mrs. Ament? None other than Princess Der Ling,[2] a devoted friend and companion of the Empress Dowager. The entire meal was all in Chinese style, served on beautiful lacquered tables, delicate Chinese porcelain bowls, silver tipped chop sticks, but also foreign forks. Later in the year the Chinese official ladies were invited to the American Legation and were served a meal in our style, Mrs. Ament again being an interpreter. She reported that there was not a single social error in table manners, as each Chinese lady watched every move of the hostess [Sarah Conger] and took up the right utensil at the right time. Later still a third party was given, again at the Empress Dowager's [palace]. On this occasion the tables were set with damask and cut glass, full quotas of silver, beautiful bouquets and there were twenty-four courses, alternating Chinese and Western dishes. How is that for keeping up with the foreigners?

[1]At this time Tientsin had British, French, German, Italian, Japanese, and Russian post offices in addition to the Chinese.
[2]See Der Ling, *Two Years in the Forbidden City* (New York: Moffat, Yard Co., 1917). Princess Der Ling, daughter of a Manchu nobleman, attended a convent school in France, was first lady-in-waiting to the Empress Tzu Hsi, and in May 1907 married Thaddeus White, an American.

Charles to Judson Smith, June 3, 1905, Tientsin

Dear Dr. Smith:

[T]his spring has been in marked contrast with that of 1898, when you were here. As I remember you did not use your umbrella once in North China, tho that season was unusually dry, but this year we have had more rain than in any spring of which I have even heard in this part of the world.

. . . About the middle of the month I took a trip to Peking and Tungchow. At Peking I met with the joint committee—Messrs Meech, Bryson and Howard Smith of the L. M. S. [London Missionary Society] and [Howard] Galt, [William] Stelle, and myself of our Mission—to settle the limits of our field in the region between here and Peking. The result was necessarily a compromise, in which we had to yield more than we intended; but as I went into the meeting with the feeling that almost any decision would be better than none, I felt that we were to be congratulated on coming to a unanimous conclusion, at any rate.

According to the new agreement, we exchange our work in the market town of Laofa for their work in the market town of Huang How Tien, the property being turned over without expense to either party. . . . [Our Mission has] the large market town of Yangtsun, where there is a station on the railroad [and an important bridge], and I hope that before long we may open work there. . . .

You will receive information also of the intercollegiate debate between Peking University and of North China Union College [of Tungchow]. It was a good beginning. I was reminded of the first Yale-Princeton debate at New Haven. Another new thing is intercollegiate athletics. North China Union College went to Peking and won from Peking University by 104 to 46. Here in Tientsin last Saturday, the various colleges contested at the University grounds. Today the Anglo-Chinese College[1] has its field sports. . . . The outward semblance of Occidental school and college life is being taken on out here in the Far East. And it is not too much to say that education is really making rapid strides. The schools do not all do first class work, but they do good work and are improving all the time. Tientsin is a great educational center. Several schools for girls are already in running order. When we move to our new premises [at Hsiku], we shall be not far from Tientsin University, and we may be able to come into some touch with the faculty and students. . . .

The Rockefeller agitation, while it has made you much trouble, and while it may damage the treasury for a time, will be a good thing, as it seems to me, both in clearing the atmosphere and in bringing out clearly the deep conscientiousness of Congregationalism. Of course the Prudential Committee could not reject the gift [from Rockefeller] without instructions from the corporate members, and I think the discussion has made it clear that the Board is justified in receiving all gifts, but not in showing distinguished honor to the givers, simply because of their gifts.[2] I respect the conscience and feeling of the protestants, with whom I strongly sympathize, but the progress of the discussion has led me to believe their judgment at fault.

The real indictment is not against Rockefeller alone; for it is only inability (not scrupulousness) that prevents many businessmen from doing as he has done. Men are naturally cruel oppressors, if they can line their pockets at the expense of their fellow men. The real indictment is against our economic system, which makes trusts, monopolies, oppression, poverty, excessive wealth, and all attendant evils possible. *When the Christian Church accepts the principles of Jesus, and when Christians begin to live in accordance therewith, the new day of the Lord will come.*

[1]The Anglo-Chinese College at Tientsin was founded by Dr. Lavington Hart of the London Missionary Society in 1902.

[2]John D. Rockefeller had for some years had an interest in China because of his Standard Oil, railroad, and shipping investments there. In February 1905, Rockefeller offered the American Board $100,000 for specific educational projects in China. After considerable debate about the ethics of accepting the offer due to Rockefeller's reputation for unethical business practices, the Board agreed to take the Rockefeller grant.

Charles to the Ewing Family, June 1905, Tientsin

Dear Ewing Family:
[W]hile there [in Peking] I attended a meeting of the Union Committee, whom [*sic*] I found were planning large things, even the federation of all Christians in China, with an outlook toward the breaking down of all denominational lines. Included was a representative of the high-church

Episcopals. It was Mr. Norris with whom I was associated on the fortification staff in the Peking siege.

While in Peking I was invited to two social affairs which show the growing fellowship between Chinese and Westerners. Miss [Nellie] Russell was the hostess. Her other guests were two missionary ladies, two Chinese pastors and two Chinese teachers from our boys school, all of whom I had known in earlier years. It was a delightful occasion and I was much pleased that none of the Americans spoke English at the table.

Charles to Judson Smith, July 4, 1905, Tientsin

Dear Dr. Smith:

. . . My second June visit to the country took me to Laofa. I went on June 23, returning on the 26th. The time was brief, largely because the farming people were very busy getting in their wheat crop. By taking my bicycle on the train to Laofa, I was able from that point as a center to reach all the places that I particularly wished to visit in one day. . . .

The affair [a church member is owed money by a recently widowed woman who counter-sues the man for murdering her husband] has been settled in a thoroughly Oriental fashion. The official neither condemned nor acquitted our man. Instead, he told the two parties to make use of middlemen and settle up in some way or other. This they have done, with the result that this man has had to pay nearly three hundred dollars, and as that was the total value of his land, he has turned the deed over to the official, and after reaping his autumn crops will have nothing left but his house. This case is like many here in China!

. . . I went to Peitaiho on June 20 with my family, leaving them there and returning here on June 22. This seashore resort is a beautiful place, and I have no doubt it has saved and will save many furloughs. Both Mrs. Ewing and I have protested against going, only yielding to the advice of others. And even so, we should probably not have gone if it were not for our annual Mission meeting being held there this year. As it is our going will probably keep me in debt to the Board for some time yet. Prices here in Tientsin are so high that it is only by close economy that we can afford to live here. If we put our girls in the new public school (which is not free), we shall have to cut somewhere, or else ask for a special provision to be made. As for the seashore resort, I presume that we shall want to go there every summer, having once tasted its delights.

. . . The news of the death of Secretary [of State John] Hay comes as a personal loss to all Americans who have rejoiced in him as the Golden Rule statesman, combining straightforward honesty with the highest diplomatic acumen. But I believe he has held his high position long enough to set a standard from which his successors will not venture to depart.

The war [Russo-Japanese] has not really kept things stirred up here, altho every one is alive to its importance. The peace toward which we look with hope will mean much to China. Meanwhile, I hope that Russia is sufficiently stirred up to make sure of a brighter better day throughout all her population.

The anti-American boycott has hardly been wise in all particulars, but I hope it will help to bring about very speedily a more equitable treatment for Chinese who go to our country. So far as I see, the boycott does not interfere with us and our work at all.

Charles to the Ewing Family, July 4, 1905, Tientsin

Dear Ewing Family:

Tientsin is about as usual today, with no celebration that I know of. The French are preparing for July 14, when they celebrate the fall of the Bastille (1789), and the capture of Tientsin (1900). There is a street in the French Concession called "Rue de 14 de Juillet."

[T]he anti-American boycott has been quite a topic of conversation here. It seems to be destined to collapse. . . . it is a sign that the Chinese are capable of being aroused, not only to violence as in 1900, but to effective action, and even if this outburst (entirely peaceable by the way) has not been very well considered, it gives some evidence of national spirit.

Charles to Judson Smith, August 1, 1905, Rocky Point, Peitaiho

My Dear Dr. Smith:

I came [here] to the shore on July 29. . . . during the month [of July], I did not stir from Tientsin [except to deal with a persecution case in a village thirteen miles northeast of Tientsin]. Li Shih I [the alleged persecuted] is a man who has been a member of our Tientsin church for many years. . . . One of these [fellow villagers] in particular seems to have a special spite against him, and it is not unlikely that in this case, as in many such, a personal quarrel is mixed up with the persecution. However . . . we have become quite satisfied that this is a genuine case of religious persecution, and as China has agreed that all Christian converts shall have religious freedom, it was necessary either to persuade Mr. Li to endure hardship patiently or appeal to the authorities to guarantee protection. For a long time past, the former method has been practiced, and much patience has been shown, . . . [Following additional trouble] I consulted the American Consul-general at Tientsin, and he gave me a letter of introduction to the county magistrate. I called on this man twice, found that he did not treat me with proper courtesy, and could get from him no assurance that the case would be fairly managed. He refused to guarantee peace in the village, repeatedly affirming that such a guarantee was impossible, altho I knew that such settlement had been made in various cases heretofore. At last I gave up trying to do anything through him, and before leaving Tientsin last week, I put the affair in the hands of the Consul-general. I hope that he will push it effectively, as a fair settlement . . . may save much trouble for us, for the native Christians, and for the Chinese officials.

. . . I never want to ask to have a man beaten, imprisoned, or otherwise harshly treated [for persecuting a convert]. Such a course seems unChristlike, would be bad policy for the Church, and would misrepresent Christianity before the people.

Charles to the Ewing Family, August 2, 1905, Rocky Point, Peitaiho

Dear Ewing Family:

I brought the family here to the seashore more than a month ago, but myself returned to Tientsin for the month of July. The weather there was not excessively hot, so I was quite comfortable. I did some reading, writing, playing games: Flinch and Patience by myself and chess with others, some street chapel preaching and considerable work with my teacher in preparation for the part I have to take in the Conference for Christian Workers which is to be held here at the shore the end of August. Each Tuesday evening I had some of the British soldiers at the house; on Tuesday seven of them took supper with me at a Chinese restaurant, coming to the house afterwards. . . .

About 1898 a large tract of land was bought here [Peitaiho] on the coast by a group of foreigners who formed an association. The location is about 150 miles from Peking and not far from the place where the Great Wall comes down to the sea. There are three colonies of residents. The central section is called "Rocky Point" and that is where we are living, in Miss [Elizabeth] Porter's house, quite near the beach. The ground here rises easily to a hill two hundred feet high, so that even the houses further back get a fine expansive view. Our house is one of the best. We have a large porch, a large dining-room, and two good sized bedrooms. . . . The Ament's house is very near with two fine tennis courts in front, made of ashes and lime pounded hard and smooth. . . . behind us is the ladies' house built as a memorial for Miss [Mary] Morrill and Miss [Annie] Gould, who were killed by the Boxers in 1900 at Paoting. Many missionaries of other Boards have houses here and some business people. Three miles from us is the section called "West End," occupied almost entirely by people from the various foreign legations. In the opposite direction about two miles, is "East Cliff," where there are at present only seven houses, all owned by missionaries.

Now I want to emphasize the greatest attraction of this place, which is the beach. It is of hard sand. There is a bar about a hundred feet out, on which the water is shallow, with deeper water between there and the beach, and also further out, so that the place is admirably adapted for those who can swim and for those who cannot. . . . The children find the beach a paradise.

Charles and Bessie to Jessie E. Payne,[1] September 1, 1905, Rocky Point, Peitaiho

A little light was kindled in a prairie home.
Was kindled there, intended far away to shine
From there to distant places on across the brine
Where China's million children live beneath the dome
Of that same sky which arches o'er the gleam and gloam
Of freedom's newest Western land, your land and mine—
Where China's million women live and die and pine
Away for want of light. The prairie light has come.
The winds of many leagues, the storms of many years,
Have not put out that light, which shines but brighter now,
Fed not by oil of earth, but purer oil of heaven.
Kept clear through all the winds and storms and foolish fears.
O life, and lighting up the eyes and face and brow
Of one who now has reached the age of twenty-seven.

[1]This birthday poem was given to Jessie E. Payne, who had traveled with the Ewings from Chicago to China in 1904.

Charles to the Ewing Family, September 5, 1905, Rocky Point, Peitaiho

Dear Ewing Family:

[A]n acute attack of lumbago . . . prevented my appearance on the Conference for Christian Workers [at Peitaiho]. My absence there was not a loss to the program, for Bishop [James Whitford] Bashford, being on hand, was drafted to take my place. He is the Methodist bishop for China and it was a fine thing that the native leaders could hear him. At the evening sessions of our meeting we heard several addresses on conditions in various parts of the Empire, presented by men from these various sections who are spending the summer here. This general summer gathering of missionaries is invaluable in its opportunity.

Men from several Missions have met informally to do what we can to bring about a better delimitation of field work, to prevent overlapping. Arrangements were planned for exchange of fields and properties among the

American Methodists, the English Methodists, the London Mission (English Congregational) and our own, in the district around Tientsin. This promises good things for the future, but in our endeavors to systematize the country work, we shall have to work against the inertia of some of the older missionaries, who look upon the past quite as much as they do at the present and the future. Others are inclined to go ahead on their own without much consultation.

Our local situation will undoubtedly be influenced by an important meeting to be held in Peking the end of this month. This is the first national conference on the federation of all [Protestant] missions and churches in China. This first meeting may not accomplish much, but it may stand, in relation to the future meetings of the same kind, much as it is hoped that the first Hague Conference[1] stands to its successors. I have written before about the formation of the Educational Union of North China, with Women's College in Peking (to be opened after the Chinese New Year) as Union institutions. The Union Theological Seminary at the Presbyterian Mission in Peking will open in the autumn, with our Dr. [Chauncey] Goodrich as the dean; and the Union Medical College is also expected to open in the autumn at the London Mission in Peking. In addition, plans are well started toward the establishment of a Medical College for Women at the Methodist Mission in Peking, with other Missions joining.

One day at Mission Meeting, I made something of a stir by announcing that I had been converted on three subjects in three days—whereupon some one remarked that I ought to be ready for baptism. The first of these subjects was Church Endowment and it was the Chinese argument that won me. They have been accustomed to the endowment of temples, and it seems most natural for them, when they have any money for the church, instead of using it at once, to invest it, preferably in land for rent, using the proceeds for the church from year to year. As no one proposes this method for the entire support of any church, and because of Chinese customs, I withdrew my objections.

The second subject was on the matter of teaching English in our Mission schools including the College. While I have not been a vehement opponent of such teaching, it has seemed to me that missionaries could spend their time to better advantage, limiting our education to the preparation of Christian workers. I was won by Bishop Bashford's argument. He said that we will surely and speedily lose our leadership in the intellectual uplift of new China, if we do not teach English. The best students will not come to us and we shall be unable to prepare the best Christian workers or to influence towards Christianity the best minds among the youth of this land.

The third subject on which I experienced a change was in the matter of sharing by many Missions in the support of a General Secretary for the

North China Tract Society, who will be primarily a business man, editor of a magazine, a publisher, printer and distributing agent for Christian books. At first it seemed unwise when our Board is not able to finance our present work. But Dr. Arthur Smith showed that it was very unwise and short-sighted not to make such a plan and provision for the future.

Eventually, of course, the Chinese themselves must take up and carry on this work, but if we wait until they have come to the point of being able to do so, we have lost the present incomparable opportunity and handicapped the future of China.

[1]Charles here refers to the International Peace Conference of 1899 at The Hague. That conference was followed by a second in 1907 that resulted in the founding of the Permanent Court of Arbitration at The Hague.

Charles to the Ewing Family, October 10, 1905, Tientsin

Dear Ewing Family:

The middle of September was a time of great excitement here and in Peking because of the visit of the Congressional party from America. While it was distinctly understood that this visit had no official significance, it was impossible that its importance should be overlooked. As might be expected in an Oriental and monarchical country (whose attitude seems to be quite in accord with that of our American press) "Princess Alice" [Roosevelt] was the central figure.[1] She appears to have won the respect and esteem of all who met her. The whole party was treated with unprecedented cordiality by the Empress Dowager, who received the visitors in her private apartments, and by the Viceroy Yuan Shih Kai at Tientsin. He gave the first reception he has ever given, his wife and other Chinese ladies receiving, and he [Yuan] paid all the bills for the party at the best foreign hotel, the Astor House. The inference to be drawn from this marked hospitality is that, at this time of the anti-American boycott,[2] the government wishes to emphasize the cordial official relations between the two nations. It is to be hoped, also, that the Congressional delegation will be disposed to favor [American] legislation that will be more considerate of both justice and humanity as regards the admission of Chinese, especially merchants, students, and travelers, to the privileges of temporary residence in the U.S.A.

The last week in September I went to Peking to attend the Conference of Federation. Representatives were present from nearly all [Protestant] denominations and the task was to find enough common ground to agree on points of cooperation. . . . the Southern Baptists, the Episcopalians, and some delegates from the China Inland Mission held back. . . . What we actually accomplished was small, but it is much to have got together and done anything. We approved a unified hymnbook, the use of some common

Christian terms for our chapels, the disuse of all denominational names, and we authorized a committee to bring about the formation of a National Council, by the election of representatives, both missionary and Chinese, from all parts of the Empire—to be presented to the great Centenary Conference at Shanghai in 1907.

Returning to Tientsin I was busy with . . . a deputation bringing us the spirit of the Peking Conference, especially the idea of Christian union. This deputation was entirely of Chinese pastors and is evidence of the self-consciousness of the Chinese Christian Church, for the initiative, which has previously been taken by the foreign missionaries, is now taken by the Chinese leaders. Thus, there is a movement already inaugurated for exhibiting Christian patriotism by contributing as much as possible to help the government pay the Boxer indemnities.

[1]In addition to the twenty-one-year-old daughter of President Theodore Roosevelt, the American delegation included her future husband, Congressman Nicholas Longworth of Cincinnati, Senator and Mrs. Francis Newlands, Congressman Frederick Gillett, and Congressman Bourke Cockran. Included in the party were Mabel Boardman and Amy McMillan, who were friends of Alice Roosevelt. This was the first time that members of the American Congress had visited China.

[2]See chapter 3.

Charles to Judson Smith, October 14, 1905, Tientsin

Dear Dr. Smith:

[Y]ou will remember the decision of a joint committee of our Mission and the London Mission [English Congregationalists] concerning the work near the railway between here and Peking. . . . You know that the decision was approved by the Mission and also by the London Mission. You write that you are "not altogether satisfied to have our field pared down anywhere." I appreciate your feeling, and therefore I am glad to report that this particular case of delimitation involved no real "paring down," but only a defining of our field and that of the London Mission.[1] Technically, they claimed the whole region, while we claimed what we were working. . . . We now know the field for which we are responsible and shall try to work it as vigorously as possible. . . .

The exchange of chapels that was involved in the settlement with the London Mission was concluded this week. I met with Mr. Meech at Laofa,[2] examined the property both there and at Huang How Tien (literally translated, Empress Dowager Shop), exchanged what furniture we conveniently could, and arranged concerning exchange of deeds. . . . In the present situation neither party to the agreement is a strict constructionist, [Chinese] helpers of each Mission are assured that they will be warmly welcomed everywhere. We understand that there are no boundaries in the preaching of the gospel. . . .

We [the delegates meeting to discuss the eventual unification of a Chinese Protestant church] disapproved of all divisive and sectarian terminology, such as the regular use of denominational names, except where absolutely necessary, and even refused to take any action concerning a term for Protestantism. We favored the general use of common terms for street chapels (Gospel Hall) and domestic chapels (Worship Hall). We urged the use of the "compromise terms" for God and the Holy Spirit in Christian literature. We favored an attempt to provide a basis for common hymnology. And we took action favorable to other special proposals. But, as we claimed no authority, our actions have weight principally in that they vice a very general agreement of opinion. The really most important action that we took was that which looked toward permanent federation. . . .

The Y.M.C.A. has taken a fine position of leadership here in Tientsin, is much appreciated by the missionaries, and exerts a very considerable influence throughout the city.

. . . The best thing that can happen, or one of the best things, is for the Chinese Church to arise, shake itself, and say: I am not a child; I am of age; I have ideas and ideals of my own; I shake myself free from denominational control; I am one body, the body of Christ in China, with no schisms and divisions; I welcome help and counsel from the experience and strength of the Church in other lands; but I acknowledge the authority of Christ alone, working through His Holy Spirit in His Church in China. I believe that when this is done, it will be done in the right spirit, and I hope that we need not wait many years for it.

[1]Although Charles uses the word *delimitation*, it appears that Judson Smith's "paring down" was more correct in explaining the exchange between the American Board and the London Mission.

[2]It was near Laofa on the Tientsin-Peking railway that the Seymour Expedition was turned back by the Boxers and Chinese soldiers in July 1900.

Charles to the Ewing Family, November 6, 1905, Tientsin

Dear Ewing Family:

On October 19 Bessie went with me for a country trip. Mrs. Chang, the Bible woman, went with us. . . . We traveled by train, by mule cart and I, part way by bicycle. We went to seven villages, visiting in Christian homes and holding meetings at three chapels. At one place the great annual [Buddhist] temple fair was in progress, with the attendant theatricals and historical plays. Besides enjoying the plays, which are free (being provided by someone in payment of a vow) the crowds buy incense and burn it as they bow down before the image of Buddha. Many get their fortunes told by a peculiar method. The worshipper, after paying his money, takes a bamboo vase (really one hollow joint of the bamboo tree) filled with long thin sticks, shakes the vase until a stick falls out, reads the number on the stick, goes to a line of pegs at the side of the room, where he finds a peg bearing his number, takes from this peg a printed sheet hanging there, and thereon reads his future. . . .

We saw fields of cotton ready to gather, but in trying to take a picture we scared the women, who ignorantly believe that the picture is themselves and that they therefore will be carried off. . . .[1]

By going to Peking . . . I was able to take a seven o'clock train for Paoting the next morning . . . and reached there before eleven o'clock. In the second class compartment with me was a Chinese boy of sixteen years who had just had his queue cut off and was wearing European clothes for the first time. He was on his way to Hankow, thence to Shanghai, and then in company with fourteen others going to study in Europe. These fifteen young men have all been students at the Imperial University in Peking; five are going to London, five to Paris, three to Berlin, and two to St. Petersburg. This boy . . . had studied German for two years, and judging from the acquaintance he showed with English, after what he said was only a month's study, he must be very bright. He plans to remain in Germany five years, making a speciality of the study of law, especially with reference to government methods.

[1]This fear by the women of a picture of themselves is based upon an animistic belief and is still common in many parts of the world today.

Charles to Judson Smith, November 7, 1905, Tientsin

Dear Dr. Smith:

Mrs. Ewing accompanied me [on a country trip], taking the Bible woman [Mrs. Chang] with her. The peculiar value of this trip was not in my going, but in the opportunity afforded to the country women to have some special interest shown in them. It is evident that if a missionary lady, or even a Bible woman, could devote herself to the country work, results would be most encouraging. As no one of the ladies of the station can do much work of this kind, we wait the more eagerly for the coming of our new lady workers. We have only one Bible woman, and she cannot leave Tientsin for country work more than for a few days at a time, occasionally. But we shall hope that other women may be discovered and made ready for such work.

Charles to Edward and Ellen Ewing, November 26, 1905, Tientsin

My Dear Father and Mother:

Foreign troops from many nations are still in China and it is doubted as wise to withdraw them all at once. We anticipate no trouble, but one can never tell what may inflame an ignorant and superstitious populace when they are not our cordial lovers. Here in the north, Yuan Shih Kai repressed the threatened anti-American boycott, but in Kwangtung there was serious trouble. China is still a problem, an unsettled problem for America and the rest of the world. The final answer is not the "mailed fist," though temporary force be necessary, but recognition of the authority of Love, as exemplified by Jesus. . . .

Another view of the required method of renewing China is that expressed by the Customs official, Mr. Liang. He was one of the students who went to America in 1875 (?), was in the class of '82 at Yale, and speaks English perfectly. He said that China ought to send, not a few hundred students to Japan, but ten or twenty thousand to Europe and America. I asked him whether the new educational system in China would not accomplish this, to which he answered most emphatically: "No, what is needed cannot be learned from books." And then he said repeatedly that the real value of his life in America consisted, more than anything else in the privilege of living in an American home and observing and learning to appreciate the "Homelife." He is eager to visit America again, and he wishes he could send his children there to be educated.

Charles to Judson Smith, December 6, 1905, Tientsin

Dear Dr. Smith:

One trip I did take to our northern field [October and November being the best time for country visiting]. It was almost entirely devoted to collecting rents from our land in that region. We have come, more and more, to feel that the holding of this land was hindering the spiritual life of the Church, that the minds of the church members were being set on material things, and that it would be wise to get rid of the land at the first favorable opportunity. I am happy to report that we have just made arrangements to sell most of this land in lump to one man, at a price that is not all that we desired, but in a way that will save all the trouble of detailed selling, as well as the future collecting of rents. The man who is buying the land is unwilling to take the land at one of the villages because it is very poor. But I have just discovered that a new station on the railway is to be opened at that village, and this may enhance the value of the land. This new station will also be a convenience to us in reaching our field.

In the matter of the sale of our present compound here at Tientsin and the building of our new premises, we have made little progress as yet. We have torn down some old buildings that we shall not want to sell with the land [and] . . . have plotted the ground into lots. . . .

The whole of the general situation in China is in such a volatile condition that almost anything may happen at any time. My own impression, however, is that there is enough of steadiness and good sense among those in high places so that any serious and widespread outbreak will be averted, both now and permanently. China is evidently coming to a new self-consciousness, a new self-assertion, and I hope, in the course of time, a new self-respect that will be healthy and not haughty. The Japanese are, without doubt, having a widespread influence, but I am afraid that its spirit, its methods, and its effects will prove to be rather superficial.

Charles to the Ewing Family, December 6, 1905, Tientsin

Dear Ewing Family:

Since my last letter I have taken only one short trip into the country. That was by railway and for the purpose of collecting rents. This land business is a great disadvantage to the church. The only benefit is financial. This financial element has tended to impoverish the spiritual life of the church in that region. Dr. Stanley and I have become fairly well convinced that it would be better if we did not have the land. In other years we have hired a man to collect the rents, but this year I tried doing it myself, but I am sure that this tends still more to degrade the church in the eyes of observant people to the level of a financial corporation. Now, however, the way has opened to sell most of this land, and as a down payment has been made, the deal probably will be closed soon and my next trip to that place will be given in part to explanations how and why we have taken this step without consulting the church members there.

[M]uch of my [recent] work seems to be in the nature of getting ready to work instead of doing that for which I came [to China]. Some of this is removing obstacles, as in ridding ourselves of the land in the country. Some has been the management of cases of persecution which I conceive to be distinctly aside from the main purpose of our work. Some has been, and will be for some months yet, in the preparing of buildings at the new location. Work of this nature may continue to be necessary for a long time, certainly for the immediate future. But one sometimes feels that it ought not to be necessary, and that one's time and energies are being frittered away. While it is sometimes disheartening it is nothing peculiar to the Mission field. Indeed, we here have the cheering thought that we are engaged in a work that must make its impress on a nation. Every great end is accomplished by means of many littles. It may even be doubted whether anyone ever did a great deed and knew at the time, that it was great. Many have done little things, thinking they were great; some have done great things, thinking they were small. But for the most part, many small efforts are required for one large accomplishment. This is no new thought, but it has been borne in upon me repeatedly and forcefully since my return to China.

We are conscious that our individual efforts are very meager, but we are also well assured that we are engaged in an undertaking of large import. . . .

[On Thanksgiving] a goodly company of Americans met at the American Consulate, where by invitation I had charge of the religious service. Choosing the text, "Be ye thankful," I recounted a large number of reasons for thankfulness but laid especial emphasis on two. One was in the political field, the meeting in Brussels of the Interparliamentary Union. This as it seems to me, presages "the parliament of man, the federation of the world,"[1] and one who considers it sympathetically can scarcely fail to look forward to the glad day when, proud as each may still be of his own nationality, we shall rejoice yet more in that we are world citizens, members of a common human family. The other cause for thankfulness is that there is ground for the same hope in religion; for religion, as men are coming to see, goes deeper than forms and is quite independent of them. I agree with Tolstoy when he claims that all religions are at bottom one, and that within five hundred years humanity will discover that that one is Christianity, not "church Christianity" but the essence of Christ's teaching. . . . While a formal union of religions may not occur I look forward to the religious reunion of men under the control of the spirit of Jesus Christ. And now goodbye for 1905 and best wishes for 1906.

[1]The Interparliamentary Union met in Brussels to strengthen the already established Permanent Court of Arbitration at The Hague.

Charles to the Ewing Family, January 1906, Tientsin

Dear Ewing Family:
I find that the training of chess is a good thing for me, as it shows up some of my weak points and helps me, I think, to overcome them. Miss Winterbotham is an English lady who has been in China a long time; works independently, principally teaching English to Chinese young men. She lives in a small house in our compound. Some two years ago she met with an accident which makes it necessary for her to use a crutch. At chess she invariably beats me.

Charles to Edward C. Ewing, January 1906, Tientsin

Dear Father:
I see that you have misunderstood something that I wrote to Henry [in a letter dated April 27, 1905] about affairs in Paoting, quite likely for anyone not familiar with the conditions. I did not intend to intimate that there is friction between the missionaries. The two men are so different in temperament, theology, views of life and methods of work that they go on with

their work independently, the result being, so far as I can judge, friction is the very thing that is eliminated. You are not mistaken, however, in your inference that . . . [one] is exhibiting an excess of theological individuality. He is so extremely "liberal" that, if he were now applying for appointment, I have no idea he would receive it. Even I cannot approve of some of his radical statements (at least in the form in which he makes them); and I suppose I am broader in my views than almost anyone else in the [North China] Mission. I have been growing more so during the past year, and I account this one of the great privileges that God has been granting me since my return to China. Narrowness is not divine, but human—and a fault.

Charles to Judson Smith, January 9, 1906, Tientsin

Dear Dr. Smith:

This is a rather discouraging time in our missionary work. Others beside myself note this fact. Dr. Ament went so far as to say that we do well if we hold our own for the present, and, while that may be an over-statement, it is close to the truth.

This depression in our work is partly due to general causes. A very marked change is appearing in the general character of Chinese thought. I mean something quite different from the tendency toward progress that has been marked ever since 1900. Now there is something newer still, that has arisen almost entirely within a year. I scarcely feel competent to describe it—the Chinese are taking many people by surprise in these days, tho perhaps the only cause for surprise in this case is the early date of this movement and its speedy development,—but I am inclined to define it by the word *independence*. We expected it sooner or later, but mostly later. The anti-American boycott is only one manifestation of this feeling among the people. On the part of the government, the same is evident in various ways. For one thing, it appears that there is to be a stricter insistence that foreigners in China keep within their treaty rights. . . . foreign firms doing business in the interior without special permission are receiving notice that they must retire; railway and other concessions are not to be extended indefinitely or too leniently.

The same attitude is being exhibited, on occasion, in the diplomatic dealings of China with other nations. A recent disagreement between Chinese and foreign officials over Shanghai police court affairs, while the immediate cause was other than this, may perhaps be traced back in part to this new realization of national independence. Of course, it is natural that the first effect on mission work shall be prejudicial to any show of speedy success, but the ultimate result cannot be other than healthy.

Another cause for depression in our work is the increasing activity and questionable conduct of the Roman Church through its agents in many places. . . . One of these [cases of misconduct] was that of a man in the village of Chien Ying who, having given offence to a Catholic family, was obliged to join the church to make peace. . . . The district official . . . told me that nearly a quarter of the law cases are those in which Catholics are concerned. . . . we are somewhat involved in their reputation, and it behooves us to take especial pains to be above reproach in all such matters. . . .

Other reasons for depression in mission work at present are merely local or temporary. With us, the most serious obstacle is our ownership of real estate in the region where our most prosperous work is situated. As long as we own the property, the income of which the church members of that region understand is to be used in that part of the field, a damper is put on their self-support. . . . so fully are we persuaded that the holding of this land is not a blessing, but a hindrance to the best things, that we are eager to rid ourselves of the burden, even if we cut our annual funds thereby.

Bessie to the Ewing Family, February 1906, Tientsin

Dear Ewing Family:

Mrs. [Louise] Stanley heard me say I wanted some [ice] skates, and gave me a pair that belonged to some of her children. There is a fine rink in the British Concession, kept up by private subscriptions by the gentlemen. Altho Charles has not subscribed, I was invited to go as much as I pleased and take the children. An older girl gave Marion a pair of skates and I have been down with her twice.

There is a Literary and Social Guild which is in connection with the Union Church (for foreign residents). This month we had a lecture on "Wireless Telegraphy" [radio] by Dr. [Lavington] Hart of the London Mission. He had many pieces of apparatus to illustrate the progress of discovery and invention leading up to the successful instruments in practical use today. In his experiments he was assisted by Mr. Taylor, a young man who was studying with Sir Oliver Lodge[1] when he was making his successful experiments leading to the present "wireless" instruments. Mr. Taylor is a new member of the staff of the College. . . .

We have become acquainted with a number of the British soldiers stationed here belonging to the Royal West Kent Regiment, and most of them from London. These are Christian men, converted by the Salvation Army in Ceylon. They are good jovial company, but their solid sober interest is in their religion. . . . Some of them are proposing to leave the army and enter mission work—which we do not encourage—and are studying the Chinese language. One man is a sergeant of the King's Hussars, and is in charge of the Sikhs at the field hospital. He speaks Hindustani, and as another interest he has encouraged his Chinese cook, two sweepers and a carpenter in Christianity.

[1]Sir Oliver Lodge taught at University College, Liverpool, and at the University of Birmingham. His experiments with electrons, ether, and lightning contributed to the early development of radio.

Charles to the Ewing Family, February 7, 1906, Tientsin

Dear Ewing Family:

During the [Chinese] New Year vacation, nearly everything is quiet, including national politics. There is every reason that the progress already begun will continue. The progressive spirit is in the van. So many new things are imagined and proposed that it is hard to predict what will be next. Just now, suggestions are being made for the establishment of colleges to meet the needs of the students who are returning dissatisfied from Japan.[1] Whether or not this is done, we may be sure that China is committed to the new education. Within a few days, the Woman's College at Peking will enter on its first term. It is an outgrowth of the Bridgman School, and will be under the same [American Board] oversight. The Union Medical College at Peking begins work next week, February 14.

Dr. [Charles D.] Tenney has resigned the presidency of the [Chihli] provincial university. The reason appears to be the obstructive spirit of the Chinese managers. While China is in truth committed to the new learning, the best methods do not always find the way smooth. It is probable that the Japanese will have increasing influence in education, as well as in other affairs. The place of the missionary schools and colleges will be of no secondary importance.

[1]See chapter 3.

Charles to Judson Smith, February 8, 1906, Tientsin

Dear Dr. Smith:

Living in the foreign settlement[1] at Tientsin we find ourselves responding to some outside demands that seem quite legitimate. Our two girls are in the newly established school, which promises to be quite successful. I am a member of the School Committee, it does not take much time but recently we have been pushing for subscriptions for a school building, with dormitory and boarding accommodation and rooms for the teachers and principal to cost approximately $35,000. . . .

While I record these facts [quarrels between Catholic converts and nonconverts], I do it with no inclination whatever to boast that we are holier than they. No one is more desirous than I of being able to emphasize the kinship of Christians of every name or sect, and my recognition of the Roman Church as an acknowledged representative of Christianity makes me sorrow over anything either unwise or unChristlike in its presentment of religion. Furthermore, there is great temptation to Protestant missionaries to take essentially the same position as the Roman priests, tho not going to the same extent. It is so easy to persuade oneself to appeal to civil authority to defend the church members. It is so easy to do things that will make a fair show from the Chinese point of view. It is so easy to seek the alliance of the "respectable" people in any place where we go, instead of trying to get at the hearts of the sinsick, to ask the commendation of Pharisees instead of giving sympathy to publicans and sinners. It is so easy to expend our energy and effort in recurring evidences of outward prosperity, in establishing a visible organization, which may be a hindrance sometimes to the normal growth of the spiritual assembly of disciples. The Chinese take very naturally to showy forms, and our church members are very glad when we can put up buildings and exhibit a prestige and an ecclesiastical and civil power that will bear comparison with the Catholics. I consider it extremely fortunate that we can honestly assure them that such is impossible. And we do well out here to be especially on our guard against the supremacy of the ecclesiastical temper, which, even in the home land [America], sometimes interferes with the Church giving its best service to humanity. . . .

I have [recently] taken what time I could from the special planning for house and compound to help in the work at the city chapel. . . . I find [very enjoyable] this work of speaking to the people the message of life. The problem is, even when one knows the language, how to speak so as to make the gospel intelligible to the hearers, not merely words for their ears, but the reality for their hearts.

In the present juncture of affairs, the gospel is just what is needed, bringing Christ to the people and the people to Christ. But minds are so occupied with the new life that is coming in with marvelous rapidity that few are prepared to settle their acceptance of Christ. It seems as if what is settled today may be unsettled tomorrow. . . .

In spite of all this, and in spite of the recent missionary martyrdoms [of 1900], I see no evidence of any probable anti-foreign outbreak. It is not the anti-foreign sentiment that is in the ascendant, but a national sentiment that concerns foreigners only secondarily. There is not that atmospheric condition that preceded the outbreak of 1900, a realization that we were on the crater of an active volcano. Instead, the sensation is that which would naturally be expected to accompany such rapid transformation as is now in progress, a sense of expectancy, of waiting for the unknown, but withal more hopeful than fearful. That a great change, amounting to a revolution, should take place soon would not be strange. If such an occurrence takes place, there is considerable reason for believing that it will not involve a bloody conflict. During the crisis—whatever it may prove to be—it will be wise for foreigners in China to "lie low," attracting as little attention as possible. When the new China is really ushered in, it will very likely be found that the special privileges heretofore accorded to aliens will be at an end, but that on the other hand, all may expect such treatment and such a popular attitude as might be expected toward foreigners in any land, with of course a necessary Chinese fashion in it all. There! I have ventured much further in the way of prediction than I intended.

[1]From 1904 to 1906 the Ewings lived in the American Board compound, which was located in the French Concession.

Charles to Ellen Ewing, March 1906, Tientsin

My Dear Mother:

You sent me ten dollars [U.S.] last June and twenty dollars in August. The ten changed for $20.78 Mexican,[1] and the twenty for $41.56. The total just about covered the expense for [the Chinese] helper at Ching Hai Hsien, for six months, and to that I devoted it. I have kept you informed of the progress of the work in that place, which is our only city center outside of Tientsin. . . . Our work [there] is handicapped for the lack of men thoroly fitted. We have only one [Chinese] man in our whole area who has been through college. . . . We now have three men from Tientsin taking this [new "short cut"] course; while they will not have college training we hope to find them usable men. . . . Of these three [one] is a man who has been at Ching Hai Hsien for six months, a little over fifty, energetic and rather excessively efficient. . . . your money is now supporting a different type, a young man who never studied until he was over fifteen, then entered our school and worked persistently until he had gone half way through college, when his health broke down. Until now, tho never strong, and easily feeling the nervous burden of the work (for Chinese do have nerves) he has worked at country churches.

[1]Silver Mexican dollars were used extensively in the Chinese port cities.

Charles to the Ewing Family, April 1906, Tientsin

Dear Ewing Family:

We have intimate contacts with several of the Y.M.C.A. families. That organization has an advantage here, as everywhere, in getting hold of a certain class of men whom the church finds it hard to reach. I attribute this to the obstacle of ecclesiasticism, from which they are free. To the church, as to individual Christians, there is great temptation to exercise lordship, instead of remembering that the Master's law of greatness in service is a universal principle. Churches that devote themselves to the service of humanity, like the Master himself, gain for themselves an enviable place in the community where they are—as St. George's in New York, the Chicago Avenue Church, the Fourth Church in Hartford, and others that might be noted.

Charles to Judson Smith, April 7, 1906, Tientsin

Dear Dr. Smith:

It should be no cause for surprise that the American people are being aroused to a fresh interest in China. Something occurs to produce such a result every year—usually something unexpected. This year there is more than oridinarily. If the visit of the Chinese Commissioners[1] does not succeed in its original purpose, I hope that it may have helped the West to a more sympathetic appreciation of the real position of Chinese leaders. If America can understand that China has not only an outward form of etiquette, but a certain real dignity and honest self-respect, that it is right for her to insist on her proper privileges among the nations, and that the present outburst of national feeling means that she will no longer submit to domineering interference from outside, something will have been accomplished. If the Occident can learn that courtesy is a prime virtue in the Orient, and can appropriate the teaching, better relations between East and West will be the result.

[1]The Chinese Commissioners went to the United States and Europe in an effort to ameliorate the terms of the Boxer treaties and to study Western methods of government.

Charles to Edward and Ellen Ewing, May 1906, Tientsin

Dear Father and Mother:

I was able [last month] to take a little run in the country. I traveled on foot (23 miles), by boat (10 miles), by train (15 miles), and by riksha (possibly 2 miles). I visited three villages, where there are Christians, and a new place where there was a large fair. This fair, like most of its kind, is held in connection with a temple; its principle [*sic*] attraction is a theatrical company that gives exhibitions daily for several days, and of course all sorts of buyers and sellers avail themselves of the opportunity to do business among the crowds that gather. A wealthy man pays the theatrical company as a work of religious merit and then everything is free. Sunday was the regular market day in the village, and the helper, attracting a crowd by the use of an accordion, the bookseller with his gospels spread out, and myself, preached our three ways on the street. There were many interested listeners, no opposition, but no inquirers as yet.

Charles to Dr. J. L. Barton, May 12, 1906, Tientsin

Dear Dr. Barton:

Let me thank you for your kind letters in response to my recent letters to Secretary [Judson] Smith. I write this personal note to you, and it may be that to you will still fall the burdensome duty of perusing my too-lengthy monthly reports. The reports from Dr. Smith are so discouraging that we have begun to question whether he will ever again be able to take up full work. My heart goes out in sympathy to him. We in China have not been unappreciative of the special interest he has taken in the work here during all these years.[1]

[1]Charles sent with this letter to Dr. James Levi Barton, the acting secretary of the American Board in Boston, a short letter to Judson Smith. It was to be the last letter to be exchanged between them and ended their thirteen years of correspondence. Dr. Smith had been the secretary of the American Board for twenty-two years and was aged sixty-nine at the time of his death.

Charles to Edward and Ellen Ewing, June 1906, Tungchow

Dear Mother and Father:

[Annual] Mission meeting is on and therefore I am here [in Tungchow]. I wish you might drop down into this garden spot. There are seven houses, in a long, curving line. Each one has a pretty yard in front, reaching to the driveway. To the west is REVIVAL VILLAGE, an entirely Christian village since it was taken over in the [Boxer] settlement after 1900. To the east are the College buildings and beyond is the railway station. If you could sit on one of the porches and look off thru the lines of trees and across the green fields and the sunken highway, a public road that passes through the Mission property, after the manner of Chinese roads, at a level of some fifteen feet below the surrounding land, and watch a train start for Peking, you might think you were in America.

This is indeed a delightful place. It must be something of an education for the College students to do their studying in such a place as this, quite apart from what they learn. . . . When the number and capacity of Chinese pastors, teachers, Bible women, reaches or even begins to approach the ideal and hope that we set before ourselves, then we can gradually lessen the number of missionaries, but it is easy to judge, by comparing with Japan and other fields, that this hoped for time can come only slowly. . . . Our greatest and most pressing needs are spiritual. Our next need, which is not so very different after all, is for Chinese leaders of real power and efficiency. . . .

It looks as if people in America have been rather scared about the situation in China [the anti-American boycott]. It is quite true that affairs are not in a settled condition here, and probably will not be for some years to come. But this is on account of the radical changes that are taking place among the Chinese themselves. It is not primarily an international affair at all, but all such disturbances are likely to involve foreigners. Furthermore, the new national self-consciousness—"China for the Chinese" is very apt to break out in anti-foreign riots in different places, as such a spirit does in any country. The anti-American boycott has produced quite an agitation in some parts of the country, but is held in check here. In fact, Yuan Shih Kai has public affairs well in hand in this metropolitan province [of Chihli]. In Tientsin, where the viceroy lives, where many foreign soldiers are stationed, and where large commercial interests, both foreign and Chinese, would be involved in any trouble that might arise, such trouble is unlikely.

Bessie to the Ewing Family, July 1906, Tientsin

Dear Ewing Family:

I have bought white shoes and stockings for Ellen as all children of her age [seven] here wear them. A Chinese shoemaker made the low canvas style for $1.25 (U.S. currency) and they are very good. . . . A Japanese shoemaker will make a pair for Marion for $2.50 (U.S.) while the English stores here charge $3.50 or $4.00. White stockings are sixty or seventy-five cents a pair.

. . . I must tell of a bad accident that Andrew [aged four] had in June. He had gone with the sewing woman to her room to watch her get her breakfast. While she was making the fire he picked up her shears and began cutting paper. He often does this with his dull end scissors but has never used mine. The first thing the woman knew, Andrew screamed, saying he had stuck the shears in his eye. She brought him right home and the doctor answered my phone call[1] and was here in a very little while. He has been here twice a day since. The cornea was cut through and at first it seemed as though the iris was not injured but later we found that it also was cut and our little boy will have sight in only one eye.[2]

[1]This is the Ewings' first reference to the use of a telephone in China.
[2]Andrew Ewing never regained full sight in his eye.

Charles to Edward C. Ewing, July 1906, Tientsin

Dear Father:

[There are a number of]. . . . reasons for moving our Mission plant [to Hsiku]. First we will have a larger plant. Second we will have new buildings more adequate for present and future needs, and the expense of the change will be met by the sale of part of our present plant, as the French

Concession will buy land for a street and also two of our houses. With the funds thus promised we can buy fifteen acres to take the place of our present four acres, build three houses, move our schools and have some [space] towards a new church. The third reason is the most important of all, a better location. When the present plant was chosen it was wise to be in or near the foreign concessions for health reasons. Now we and other Missions find ourselves too far removed from Chinese residence sections and are four Missions close together. At the new place we shall be several miles from other Missions, two large villages at our doors, on the bank of the river going to Tungchow, and a public highway on one border, and just off the great road to Peking. While the new location will cut us off somewhat from other foreigners, it will thereby relieve us from many demands on our time, energy, and attention. As to depriving the girls of a good school, we have found that the expense is beyond our means while we live in the Settlement [the foreign concessions]. Living expenses outside the city are sure to be much less. As to English-speaking neighbors, the Tientsin Government University is also on the river, only a mile from us, with three American professors and their families and other foreign professors and English-speaking Chinese professors.

Our whole family has been out to see the new house several times. Once we left by riksha at 6:20 [a.m.], arrived shortly after seven, ate the lunch we had carried and returned by rowboat, arriving at about ten. The house ought to be ready next month. The plan is better than its execution, as our Chinese workmen have not the slightest conception of absolute accuracy of workmanship.

Bessie to Myra Smith, August 1906, Tientsin

My Dear Aunt Myra:

We have a visitor, a lady from a special Mission. I will explain their "speciality" that you may see that even in the mission field there are hindrances from our own countrymen. One man, Mr. Houlding, gets people to come out [to China] and they all trust that support will be provided, mostly by personal friends, as a result of his printed reports and public meetings in America. He accepts applicants without regard to education or training or experience. He puts a great deal of stress on outward forms of holiness and claims that he and his mission are the only ones who are doing real self-sacrificing work. . . . He requires that his missionaries put all their money into the mission and all live in common and to take nothing out if they leave, but men say he is legally bound to send them back to America if he dismisses them. . . . the missionaries are forced into work before they have had enough study to even be able to speak the language. Again, the leader does not believe in treating the Chinese as equals, but always acting as tho they were servants and inferiors. In these matters, the few who control, antagonize many of the members. Some who object are dismissed and others who have means leave of their own accord. I think one third of the force has left within the twelve years since Mr. Houlding first came out and there are now about sixty members. Our visitor is one type. She was married at seventeen, widowed two years later. Worked in a department store for ten years, heard Mr. Houlding speak and ask for volunteers, offered herself and came out here two years ago. She has now been dismissed but would like to stay in China and do mission work if any Board would take her. I like her personality and her attitude towards the Chinese, and her general intelligence, but with very little background of formal schooling, I feel that our Board would not think it wise to engage her. Mr. Houlding would only give her money enough to get to Shanghai. . . . Many have found work in other Missions and we have two families who have proved their worth [and]. . . . came to us from the "Houlding Mission."[1]

[1]Mr. Houlding eventually provided funds for the American woman to return to the United States.

Charles to J. L. Barton, August 8, 1906, Tientsin

Dear Dr. Barton:

The recent news of Dr. [Judson] Smith's death has come to me, as to many out here, not merely as affecting the Mission and the Board, but as a personal matter. But I cannot feel grieved, nevertheless; his suffering is over and joy is now his share. He has kept at the work that he loved, almost to the end. It will be long before his successor can hope to become as familiar with the field, the work and the workers as Dr. Smith was, but the Lord doubtless has a man for the place.

Charles to the Ewing Family, September 1906, Tientsin

Dear Ewing Family:

On the day that I reached Peitaiho [for a conference of the North China Union Colleges], a most interesting event had occurred, the conclusion of sixteen years of work by the committee which has been translating the New Testament into the classical Chinese. The committee consisted of four foreigners and four Chinese. After the work was finished and the Chinese teachers gone, the three reverend gentlemen left celebrated the occasion. The method of this celebration should be preserved as a valuable record. It was suggested by our member, Dr. [Devello] Sheffield, who remembered his youthful athletic feats, that they all stand on their heads. He tried, but his arms were not strong enough to raise his feet. Mr. Pierce of the London Mission put his head on the floor and wriggled. Only Mr. Lloyd, the worthy representative of the Church of England, actually succeeded in the gleeful attempt. The translators completed their work with First and Second Peter, which gave occasion for Dr. Sheffield's remark, that they "Petered out" at the end.

This month I attended the autumn opening of the Settlement Y.M.C.A. The president, a Chinese, read a carefully prepared paper in English, emphasizing the importance of education in these days. Prefect Lo, in charge of the Imperial railways, spoke on the value of becoming familiar with the new, without throwing away the old. Then Mr. Ting, editor of the most influential Chinese daily in this part of the country, a man of wide experience and large ability, (but knowing no language but his own) spoke in Chinese about the new constitution,[1] reading to us his leading editorial for the next morning's paper. At interludes the German army band played. The whole occasion was very enjoyable.

One day Tientsin was elaborately decorated in celebration of the Imperial edict announcing the intention to promulgate a constitution. This culminates the report of the High Commissioners. Other sovereigns have granted constitutions and summoned parliaments only in response to the insistent demands of the people. The Chinese government is acting voluntarily, after investigation and before the demand. May it not be that, after all our Occidental disapproval and scorn of China, her people are really wiser than ours?

[1] See chapter 3.

Charles to J. L. Barton, October 19, 1906, Hsiku, Tientsin

Dear Dr. Barton:

There is no question that the work of moving our plant [from the French concession to Hsiku] is well worth while, but it is equally true that the country field has suffered temporarily. During my first year back in China (1904–1905), I was away from my family about two-thirds of the time, most of it in the country. During the year ending with September 30 [1906]. . . . hardly more than a month have I been able to devote to this field work. Now that the move is made, I can go at it again. . . .

On account of the workmen still busy in our [Hsiku] compound, it has not seemed wise to give any general invitations [to visit], except for Sundays. On Sundays, however, the place is thronged. As we have no gate yet hung, it is impossible to keep people out if we would, and with fifteen acres of land and almost no one to help, it is next to impossible to hold in bound the crowds of boys who come. These defects will be remedied soon, and without alienating any of the people, I hope. We are pleased to find that they are not suspicious of us, even the women come freely to meetings and to call on Mrs. Ewing, and earnestly inviting her to their homes.

Bessie to the Ewing Family, October 1906, Hsiku, Tientsin

Dear Ewing Family:

We moved [to Hsiku] the end of September and do enjoy the house. We have double doors between the rooms but with moving panels in the center of each so that we can throw the whole downstairs of three rooms into one large room in order to accommodate large gatherings. The Stanleys moved in October. It is of course very hard for them as they had lived in their home thirty-nine years [i.e., since 1867]. But they are cheerful for they know it is best for the work.

. . . I am having a Chinese upper garment made to wear at home with old skirts, I shall like it better than tight foreign waists, now that we live more among the Chinese. The children want Chinese garments. . . .

Sergeant Morel of the British army has a boat on a small pond near his house and the girls were invited to go out with him several times, which they were delighted to do. Thru these Britishers we have also met a German soldier a Mr. Simon . . . they [the children] like him very much. He has taken some pictures which I will send with this letter. . . .

The girls set and clear the table and change the courses, as we had a serving entrance built between the dining room and the pantry. We do not want them to be ignorant of simple household tasks as are some missionary children when they return to America. Sometimes Edward [aged five] helps. . . . The girls keep upstairs on Sundays when the Chinese women come, as they dislike being questioned and hearing remarks about their looks. Andrew [aged four] does not like to be petted by strangers. But Edward pays no attention. When a crowd of [Chinese] children surround him he acts as tho no one was there unless they get in his way, then beware. Once I caught him throwing sand at boys who teased him, again it was bricks and a third time I discovered about a dozen big boys admiring him from a safe distance while he brandished the ax at them. "Well" he said, "they didn't go away when Papa told them to."

Bessie to Myra Smith, October 28, 1906, Hsiku, Tientsin

My Dear Aunt Myra:

The first Sunday [in the new house at Hsiku] we went thru the village on all sides inviting the [Chinese] neighbors to come to the Christian service when they heard the bell ring. We put no limits at first. As a result, 120 were present at the service and we estimated three hundred probably came during the day. The next Sunday we asked the boys and men to go to another place. Today only women and girls were allowed in our house and I kept count of all arrivals. At the close of the service there were 34 women and 38 children. By four o'clock the count stood 107 and 134. Now that the people know they are welcome we have to begin some restrictions. . . .

Another encouraging sign is that I was invited to call at several [Chinese] homes, which I did after the [first] Sunday. At such neighborhood calls the first polite questions are "have you eaten?", "how old are you?", "how many children have you?" All this getting acquainted is done while we drink our first cups of tea. Near neighbors crowd the small room and as soon as the formalities are over the hostess says, "Now begin," when we say "begin what?" she answers, "Tell us about your religion." This curiosity is . . . friendly.

Charles to the Ewing Family,, November 1906, Hsiku, Tientsin

Dear Ewing Family:
A rather new experience on this trip is the many invitations to meals, averaging more than one a day. Among those who invited me was a Buddhist priest connected with a temple in a market town some thirty miles south of where I was staying. He was here taking medical treatments at a dispensary which has recently been established by a young Chinese trained at the London Mission in Peking. . . . This young man invited me with the priest, to a meal served in the dispensary. Then the priest invited us. Then I invited them. These various social meetings gave me opportunity for conversation with the priest. I found him to be intelligent, educated, and fairly well informed. It appears that he knows that his own religion is a sham, still, if he gave it up he would give up his support which comes from land belonging to his temple.

Another dinner invitation was from a man who was formerly a member of our church, but went off to the Catholics and has been their most efficient manager. He served a fine meal, consisting of twenty-four separate dishes in three sets of eight each, all but three or four being meat. I ate enough meat in those ten days to confirm me still further in my vegetarianism, and next time I come I will have it to be understood that I eat no meat. . . . [At this time Charles Ewing weighed 214 pounds.]

There is a totally new attitude of mind on the part of educated Chinese toward foreigners and foreign affairs. It is more healthy and hopeful than anything heretofore. It recognizes and desires the good that maybe gotten, but not in any fawning way. It is self-respecting, adopting the new things where usable, but modifying them to accord with the national genius. The Japanese are accepted for what can be got out of them, admired for what they have accomplished, but not liked by the Chinese. Mr. St. John, of the

Methodist Mission in Tientsin, who spent some months in Tokyo, establishing Y.M.C.A. work among the thousands of Chinese students there, reports that these students cordially hate the Japanese.

Christianity in China is getting a hearing, as one of the many things from abroad, but not the hearing that it ought to have. Perhaps the fault is our own. We have so far yielded to the temptation of building up an admirable institution, under foreign supervision and protection, that it is practicably impossible to preach the simple gospel without the immediate conclusion of the hearer that this is an ecclesiastical affair, and foreign at that.

Charles to the Ewing Family, November 25, 1906, Hsiku, Tientsin

Dear Ewing Family:

[H]e [Henry Ewing] asks how seriously reports of new laws in China, such as that against foot-binding,[1] are to be taken. In general, they indicate tendencies, not achievements. In China, laws are seldom made with the intention of enforcing them absolutely. But the tendencies are really for reform, only with a care not to move too rapidly. Even when really radically progressive the government will retain a certain prestige by apearing conservative. Just after a radical measure has been promulgated, look for some apparently retrograde ruling. For example, after insisting on the cutting off of all queues now the word is that queues must not be cut off. Another tendency is to keep from allowing too much foreign influence. Thus there is the new edict, forbidding the issuing of permits for schools to be established by foreigners or foreign missions. This is probably only an indirect way of saying that, if there is any trouble about such schools, the government assumes no responsibility.

[1]See Chapter 3.

Bessie to the Ewing Family, December 1906, Hsiku, Tientsin

Dear Ewing Family:

Most of the adults and also Marion [aged eleven] went to the American Consulate for a half past three [Thanksgiving Day] service, followed by an hour of social chat amidst substantial refreshments—chicken salad, biscuits, cakes, candies, ice cream, tea and coffee. . . . We all stayed overnight with Mrs. [Netta] McCann and the next morning I took the children to see the foreign stores decorated for Christmas.

Charles to Enoch Bell, December 18, 1906, Hsiku, Tientsin

Dear Mr. Bell:

Dr. Barton writes that during his absence from Boston (and later also, I presume), correspondence from the Missions may be addressed to you. . . .

It has been my custom since my return to the North China Mission in the autumn of 1904, to write to the Secretary in charge of our work every month. Last month, I failed for the first time. . . . With my family, I moved to our new home at our new station site [at Hsiku] on September 27. . . . Both the English and American Methodist Missions expect, sometime, to move from their present places in the French concession so as to be nearer to the Chinese resident part of the city [of Tientsin]. Only our Mission has yet made a move. . . . We are at the point where city and country meet, and extension of the north suburb of the Chinese city, with a constantly growing population and a long busy street reaches almost to our gate. On all other sides are villages, with their less shifting, less hurried, less sophisticated class of people. Four villages are within a stone's throw, beyond these are others, and others, and others, reaching on and on and helping to swell the teeming millions of China. What a field for work!

Charles to the Ewing Family, December 31, 1906, Hsiku, Tientsin

Dear Ewing Family:

[I]n speaking of new acquaintances I think I left out one very interesting man. He is the older brother of one of our theological students. He is a teacher with a literary degree of the old classical school. He has been an opium smoker, but in repose I judge, to the solicitations of his Christian brother, has just stopped using the drug. He came to the country chapel to see me on two evenings. It was a privilege to talk with an intelligent educated man like him, but it makes me realize more my lack of familiarity with the Chinese classics, especially the "four books."[1] As part of our required study I read them once, last autumn I reread them in preparation for two addresses that I was asked to give in connection with the "Bible Institute" conducted by the Y.M.C.A. The topics assigned to me were taken from the classics "The Great Learning," but discussed from the Christian point of view. First "What is the will of heaven?" and second, "The perfect nature of matter." Those in attendance were mostly familiar with the classical passages but quite unaware of the rich meaning with which Christianity could fill them.

[1]The four books of the Chinese classics are the *Analects of Confucius,* the *Great Learning, Doctrine of the Mean,* and the *Book of Mencius.*

Charles to Edward and Ellen Ewing, January 14, 1907, Hsiku, Tientsin

Dear Father and Mother:

In looking over your recent letters I find several things to which I have not replied. Father writes of getting in coal, 6 or 8 tons at $7.50 per ton, and hopes that we get off more cheaply. As I did not have ready money to buy coal for the season, I decided to use soft coal, which we can buy at the railway terminus just across the river, as we require it. We have it delivered here for $7.00 (Mexican) a ton, but a ton means 2240 pounds (English long ton), and $7.00 means about $3.90 U.S. gold. . . . we burn a ton in about ten days, which may mean fifteen tons for the season, at an approximate cost of $60.00 U.S. money. This is coal dust, which makes a good furnace fire—so good that we may take a similar course next year. In the kitchen stove, a ton of soft coal, in small pieces, lasts about six weeks and costs about $6.00 U.S. money. While there is no coal "trust" in China, the number of competitors is limited, and here in Tientsin the soft coal market is practically controlled by the Chinese Engineering and Mining Company. Most of the smaller dealers buying from them and selling at a higher price. Father is quite right in supposing that Standard Oil sets the price for lights in North China.

[H]ave I written about the variety of currency that we use?[1] We do most of our spending in silver, Mexican dollars and fractional coins with Chinese copper cents. This is somewhat simpler than the old time method of lump silver by weight and brass cash with a hole in the middle, a hundred on a string. Still it is not as simple as it sounds, because the relative value of the different coins varies. A 20 cent piece is always worth just two 10 cent pieces, but a dollar generally changes for eleven dimes, sometimes less, but just now five or six cents more. And there are at least three kinds of dollars—the Hong Kong dollar, the Peiyang or government dollar and the Mexican. When we came back to China a dollar would buy eighty copper cents (the Chinese coins) more or less; the number has gradually risen until now we get about 105. Each cent is stamped and coined as worth ten pieces of brass cash, but is really worth only eight. Approximately 800 cash equal one dollar.

You ask concerning our drinking water. We have neither well nor cistern, but drink river water, settled by use of alum, not too much. After that, we treat it exactly as we should cistern water—and well water too, unless the well were driven deep and really tapped a pure stream—that is we boil, cool and filter before drinking. It seems quite satisfactory, and we are well.

[1]See chapter 4.

Charles to Enoch Bell, January 27, 1907, Hsiku, Tientsin

My Dear Mr. Bell:

As I am on a country trip, I will not head this letter with the name of the place. The place is likely to vary from day to day until the letter is ready to mail. Just at present I am writing from Pai Chow Szu (pronounced

By Jo Ss), a very small village of just over forty families. It is in the Chiao Ho district [of Chihli province], one hundred miles from Tientsin in a southwesterly direction. Our field [of work] reaches still west from here, possibly twenty miles further. Our Tientsin station has had work in two counties here for many years. Formerly there were not a few church members, tho scattered in many different villages. Now, however, some have died, others have moved away, several had to be dropped from fellowship and some have gone to the Roman Catholics. . . . This part of our field is so far from Tientsin, and there are so many things to demand our attention urgently nearer home, that the work and the Christians in this region have suffered from neglect.

Charles to the Ewing Family, January 30, 1907, Hsien Hsien, Chihli

Dear Ewing Family:

To give you a word picture of country living in winter, I will describe my room in an inn in this city. My room is about twelve feet square, with only a passage way in front of the brick platform which is the bed. I am sitting on a box marked "65 pounds of oil," but the Standard Oil which it once contained has been used elsewhere and for my purpose the box brought a charcoal stove and pipe. This stove is now set up on the same brick platform in front of me and its fire considerably moderates the temperature. It would be quite impossible to make the room really warm, as there is a crack from one to two inches wide at each side of the door, but as I can sit close by the stove without my overcoat, and can see my breath only with the closest attention, this little corner of the room may be said to be fairly comfortable. On the platform also is my army cot bed made up for the night. Another article is a regular low table, also on the platform, about a foot high and 20 by 24 inches across. This is my dining-table or desk as needed. On the table is a Chinese candlestick whose wick gives a better light than the ordinary Chinese lamp, even better than the small foreign lamp that is becoming common. The Chinese candle is also better than the foreign candle tho not as pleasant to smell and handle. I am pinching the wick about once in ten minutes between a knife blade and a key. The Chinese use chopsticks or even their fingers. . . .

One discouraging thing occurred at one of the villages we visited. The woman who had given us a chapel and whom we had considered most faithful, announced her intention, which nothing could shake, of going over to the Roman Catholics. And why? Because she wants to escape paying the new indemnity taxes, which the Catholics of the region are refusing to pay, while we tell the Christians connected with us that they, as loyal subjects, should pay their taxes without hesitation.

Charles to J. L. Barton, February 13, 1907, Hsiku, Tientsin

Dear Dr. Barton:

When you were here, you asked me if our station has any "problems," I answered No, and I think you understood me—that is, there is nothing of an acute nature demanding summary treatment.

In another sense, it can never be true of any station that there are really no problems. Certainly this could not be true here, where we are just entering on an entirely new period of our experience. There is one problem, thus set before us by the new conditions. . . . even tho I see no way at present of dealing with it.

All about us here, at our very doors, is a large population. It has been our hope and expectation to reach these people. We are not reaching them, we are scarcely making an impression on them, beyond the impression of a great institution at whose buildings they can look.

Bessie to Myra Smith, March 1, 1907, Hsiku, Tientsin

Dear Aunt Myra:

Last month I went to Peking to attend the girls' high school graduation as one of our Tientsin girls was finishing her course. . . . She is the one we expect to be the teacher here next year. We have not been able to open our girl's school this winter. The dormitories were not ready, the new worker that we expected did not come, Mrs. Stanley has not felt equal to the work, and the former teacher was ill. And now comes the astounding word from the Woman's Board in Chicago, who gave the money for the ladies' house and some for the school, that they will not give any further support and want the price of the old buildings returned when they are sold. The work of the two Woman's Boards (. . . Chicago and Boston) has been mixed, one supplying buildings or the missionary and the other granting the yearly expenses of the school. We have had no woman missionary for three years and now just when we are moving [forward], the Chicago Board wants to withdraw all together. We cannot understand why exchanges [of views] were not made in America.

The [graduating] class numbered six and they had had two years of college work. Three will continue the other two years. Our girl is not well enough to go on and the other two are to be married. One feature of the program was the singing of a farewell song by the three who were [leaving], and the singing of a reply by the other three. Each three composed their own song and insisted on using the most mournful of minor tunes. It was almost enough to make the hardest heart melt, but the weeping was restrained. Only girls and ladies and a very few special gentlemen were admitted. Chinese girls' schools must still entertain only select audiences.

. . . Andrew [aged four] and I went to Tungchow, three quarters of an hour train ride. I could not help contrasting this with the old time travel over the same road, four lonely hours in a sedan chair with little chance of changing one's position.

Charles to Myra Smith, March 19, 1907, Hsiku, Tientsin

Dear Aunt Myra:

I have been very grateful to you for the Christmas present you sent. Everybody knows that a minister values books. Most people think that he wants scholarly books of solid worth—which is equally true, and I was glad to receive several such at Christmas time. But you seemed to have the happy intuition, quite as true as the other, that light reading is not out of place in a missionary's library. You have no idea how delighted I was to find the most popular novel of the year (Coniston) "in my [Christmas] stocking." I thank you very much. Of all the new books that was the first one read. Then Bessie read it and it has been loaned to several other story-hungry persons.

You are probably often asked the question, "How are those people getting on over in China?" and "What success are they having in their work?" It [*sic*] is an entirely natural and proper question. It is impossible to give a complete answer because so much and so important a part of what is being done can not be reported in figures, nor even estimated intelligently. It is that unseen influence which consists in permeating an old civilization with new ideas, partly intellectual and ethical, but largely spiritual and intangible. That effects of this kind are being produced there is good evidence. Educated men are reading the Bible with interest, approval and intelligence. For the present we see only one or two men of this type making open confession, but while as yet there are not many joining the church who come from the ranks of the highest Chinese literary attainments there are many men of ability and of excellent standing in their communities who have been courageous enough to take such a stand. Some of these are here in Tientsin, but I will tell of those in our country field. On March 10 at Chien Ying,[1] we received six persons in to full church membership after several years of probation. One was a woman from one of the best families; two were young men, sons of Christians; one was a busy physician, perhaps the best in the whole region; another has been for some years a school teacher and has just taken charge of our village school; and the last of the six is a man past middle life, of good education and ability and held in esteem by all who know him.

China is in the midst of a radical transformation and various schemes proposed are haphazard and disconnected. Yet as has occurred before, when one looks backwards, the separate parts have fitted together so well we see evidence of a higher intelligence, a divinity that shapes our ends rough-hew them tho we may. This has been true in American history in the past, and our own nation is even now in the midst of such a radical transformation, without being quite sure where we shall come out. That I believe to be no less true of China. I hope to live here long enough to see the outcome made clear, and meanwhile perhaps have a humble part in deciding that future.

[1]Chien Ying is twenty miles north of Tientsin. Charles has described it (December 31, 1904) as a village of particular kindness during the Boxer Uprising.

Bessie to Myra Smith, May 1907, Hsiku, Tientsin

My Dear Aunt Myra:

This year the [annual] Mission meeting was in April because of the deputation that was here from the American Board. Our whole family went to Tungchow this time, going on a houseboat, taking all of one night and a day. . . . We were there a week. The children had a wonderful time with so many playmates. . . .

The meetings were disheartening because the deputation [from Boston] had to tell us of decreasing funds, making it necessary for us to curtail work. We found it hard to understand, to believe, or to accept.

Charles to the Ewing Family, May 24, 1907, Hsiku, Tientsin

Dear Ewing Family:

I have reported the Shanghai Conference[1] to four groups here, but now I want to give you all some of my impressions. This conference was one of the most important religious gatherings ever held anywhere. I have listed at least five [sic] remarkable aspects: personnel, chairman, what is represented, what is planned, its spirit of unity and its setting of prayer.

The first conference of this body was held in 1877, with an attendance of 100. The second one had 400 and this time there were almost 1100 present. Of these latter there were 180 from abroad, and they were evidently greatly surprised at the character and ability of the deliberations and decisions. Probably of higher grade than would be found in most religious gatherings in the home land.

Of the two chairmen, our Arthur H. Smith was the American member and Rev. J. C. Gibson[2] the English. Both of these men were outstanding in the rich humor with which they enlived the days and Dr. Gibson was especially able in preserving order and harmony.

In representing the history and progress of one hundred years of Protestant Missions in China the contrast was an evidence of the force and forces which have already made the return of old China impossible and are even now making the new China a certainty. One hundred years [ago] there was one missionary, Dr. Robert Morrison, and not even one Chinese Protestant Christian. A later missionary reckoned that after a century, they might hope for one thousand. Instead what do we find today? Over 3800 missionaries, more than 175,000 baptized church members and at least 500,000 adherents. Plus hundreds of Christian institutions, schools, hospitals, social centers, and printing houses with an annual sale of millions of pieces of literature.

The first subject discussed was the Chinese Christian Church. We decided that we desire only one church and that this certainly is to be a Chinese Church, free at the earliest possible day from foreign control, and that a beginning should be made immediately by combining denominations instead of, for instance, having several Methodist Boards and at least six Presbyterian Boards. We Congregationalists are working under four Boards, not in conflict but as I have written, not always in consultation. We also adopted a plan for federation of all existing churches in China, with provincial councils and a national council.[3] In all of this planning it was kept in mind that none of these plans can be carried out by foreigners, but must be accomplished by the Chinese Church in its own way. . . .

I have now been home for ten days and find our climate trying, much wind with dust. I found the climate in the Yangtze valley very damp, but that was harder for me to bear with heat.

During the Conference the great famine claimed our attention every day, and appeals kept coming in for missionaries to go and help in the distribution of relief. Many responded but I felt that I should not stay away any longer. This famine was caused, not by drouth, but by too much water. Supplies of grain and money, especially from the U.S., promise to be more adequate than the organization for distributing them. Relief works are in progress, such as the digging of canals to carry off the excessive water. There is danger that the people will eat the seed they need for planting, for why plant if you are to die of hunger before the harvest? The best we can do in this impossible task is to save a few now and build dikes for future floods.

[1]Charles attended the China Centenary Missionary Conference held in Shanghai as an American Board delegate from North China.

[2]John Campbell Gibson had written "Mission Problems and Mission Methods in South China" in 1901.

[3]Ecumenicism proved to be a slow process in China, and only in 1922 was a national council finally formed.

Charles to Enoch Bell, June 4, 1907, Hsiku, Tientsin

Dear Mr. Bell:

[There are] numerous indications that the Chinese Church is "finding itself." I am glad to be able to believe that the missionaries are quite as ready for the new conditions as the Chinese Christians. I think this is true in Tientsin in all the Missions, certainly in ours. . . . At the [Centennial] Conference at Shanghai, I was pleased, not to say surprised, to find the same conditions manifest in remarks from our missionaries representing all parts of China and all denominations. It is evident that no one wants to get caught as some have been in Japan.

It may have seemed to you at home that the Chinese Christians have not been doing all that they could and should do to put the Church on a self-supporting basis. Dr. Barton raised the question [during his trip to China] why this is so. We missionaries admitted the fact, altho we see the poverty of many of the Christians, but we were inclined to put the responsibility for this condition on ourselves more than on the Chinese. I am of opinion that one further word of explanation should be added. Heretofore the churches have been largely under foreign control, either in name or in reality, and it would be quite natural, and I think has been true, that there is less ambition or desire to support an institution that is foreign in appearance, and that can if necessary fall back on the wealthy (!) foreigner for support, than would be shown in case the Church were evidently and thoroly Chinese. I prophesy that, when the Chinese Church "finds itself," as it is now in process of doing, you will note an immediate and striking assumption of self-support, as well as self-control. The advance toward this has not been rapid under foreign supervision: it may come all at once and very soon.

Situated at a port as we are here in Tientsin, we are subjected to surveillance and criticism, both by Chinese officials and by foreign residents and travelers, much more than our fellow-workers in the interior. Some of this criticism is doubtless just, more is not. You will have noticed one recent sample, in the article by Mr. W. T. Ellis[1] on Tientsin. When he was here, we all got the idea that he would be fair and sympathetic in his attitude. We made too little effort, perhaps, to show him our work, but the fact was, he did not see it, and apparently did not care to see it. Instead, he made a point to consult Chinese officials and non-missionary foreigners. Who gave him the information on which he based his criticisms, I do not know. I shall try to send you copies of the *China Times* for May 16 and 18, with comments by the editor.

This paper is controlled by two brothers, of Jewish extraction. One of them was converted and joined the Union Church last year, under the ministry of Rev. J. Miller Graham, formerly a missionary in Manchuria. This man, Mr. John Cowen, has devoted himself since his new life began, to fighting vice in the foreign concessions in Tientsin. He has met with very great success in closing places where gambling and other disreputable business was [sic] conducted, but has had to defend himself in at least one libel suit, brought by the French Catholic priests, in which he was legally beaten but morally vindicated; and has lost not a little patronage from those who object to his wholesale condemnation of gambling in a community where the "best people," at the very least, bet on horse races. . . .

In Tientsin the missionaries—at least, those of our own Board—seldom see the Chinese officials except when we need to do so on business—which is very seldom—or to attend an occasional public reception given by Viceroy Yuan [Shih-Kai]. We should enjoy cultivating social relations with many such officials, but they are busy men, and it often seems as if any call on their time would be almost an impertinence. In smaller cities in the interior, we feel quite differently. Even there, the officials have plenty to do to keep them busy, but foreign visitors are not frequent, and they are nearly always received courteously, often cordially when they call at the yamen. Missionaries living away from the ports often take pains to maintain the most friendly intercourse with the officials in the city where they reside, and such intercourse is evidently a pleasure to both parties. On our country trips . . . [we] sometimes call on district officials, even when we have no business.

Here in Tientsin, the one official with whom foreigners are supposed to consult when necessary is the Customs Taotai. The man appointed to this position is always one who speaks English, and generally (perhaps always) has studied in England or America. Mr. Liang, who has held this position for some time past (over two years) has just been appointed minister to the United States. In appearance, he is very different from his predecessor, but he is a quiet man of good quality and ability, and will doubtless approve himself at Washington. . . . his study and residence in America made a great impression on him with regard to the type and quality of American family life. For this reason in particular, he wants Chinese youth to study in America.

[1]William T. Ellis was an American writer who wrote on a variety of religious topics.

Charles to the Ewing Family, July 10, 1907, Hsiku, Tientsin

Dear Ewing Family:

I have written about Mrs. Li,[1] our former nurse, [who was] working for the church. . . . The last three months she has not been well and while Bessie was away [to Peitaiho] her disease (T.B.) took a sudden turn for the worse and she died on July first. Toward the end she asked repeatedly for Bessie. Principally through her efforts some thirty homes in the village of Hsiku are open to us and these friends of hers have been much impressed by the quiet and peaceful way in which she faced death. We never knew until too late that she had this disease. She probably never recovered from the exposure and fear of the summer of 1900 [during the Boxer Uprising], when she wandered from place to place, no one daring to harbor her for long. She thought often of jumping into a well, but her faith kept her from such a deed. Her younger sister now sews for us and she has a little girl about Edward's age [six]. Playing with our children she has picked up a good deal of English, so we are teaching her to read with Edward and in the afternoon she goes to the Chinese school. We have given her the name Lucy Lee.

[1]Neither Charles nor Bessie wrote if Mrs. Li was related to Mr. Li Shih I (see letter dated August 1, 1905).

Charles to J. L. Barton, July 25, 1907, Hsiku, Tientsin

Dear Dr. Barton:
You will have noted increasing signs of ferment in China. The revolutionary society is making itself felt. Frequent letters are received by students in schools here from friends studying in Japan, showing that the seeds of revolution are being sown broadcast. The most fearless act has been the murder of the governor of Anhwei. It is not strange, it is most prudent, that the government should take the greatest precautions. There have been suggestions of suspicion of the Christian Church, but it is evident, not only that the church will have nothing to do with revolution, but that the revolutionaries do not consider the Church their friend. Mr. Chung, a member of the faculty of the Canton Christian College, was arrested while visiting Paoting, evidently under suspicion of being connected with the anti-dynastic movement. He has now been released with the express recognition that there was absolutely no ground for his arrest and detention.

One can hardly tell how much of an uprising might take place if opportunity offered, but it is probable that the amount of sympathy with such a move is, in this part of the country, extremely small. The movement is avowedly anti-dynastic, wherever it shows itself, it will not be likely to affect foreigners or Chinese Christians, except incidentally to the disturbed conditions that would be attendant on any revolutionary uprising. There may be such occurrences in other parts of China—of that I cannot predict—but here we see no signs whatever of that sort.

Charles to the Ewing Family, July 26, 1907, Hsiku, Tientsin

Dear Ewing Family:
A recent letter from father notes reports from China indicating troublous times ahead. The lack of rain [in North China] and the consequent failure of crops always tends to upset the people and one can hardly venture to predict what a bad year might mean. The most dangerous tendency at present is the stirring up of anti-foreign feeling by revolutionaries. I think

that nearly all the Chinese in America are in sympathy with the movement. It is strong among the students now in Japan and they frequently write to their friends here, urging their cooperation. There has been some feeling that revolutionists were likely to be found among the Christians. But the missionaries have put themselves on record so unequivocally, the church has held aloof so consistently and the Christians have given it such scanty courtesy, that the revolutionaries look on Christianity as hostile to them and their plans.

The revolutionary movement is avowedly anti-dynastic. Without question such sentiment is widespread in the South,[1] but here in the North,[2] while the Chinese waste no affection on the Manchus, there is very little disposition to break the peace. In the midst of these many changing conditions, we are peaceful and very hopeful. As far as I can judge, riots in San Francisco and other American cities are more likely than in the large cities of China. Possibly the anti-foreign feeling in China is stronger, probably it is more widespread, than the anti-Chinese feeling in America. Of course we flatter ourselves that our American government is more just and more efficient that that of China. But how much more efficient is it really, when a mob takes things into its own hands. You may credit actual facts reported on good authority about China, but always question the authority if the report sounds scarey [sic]. Discount 90% of any scarey deductions from the facts—holding the other 10% as also uncertain.

[1]As used here, the South could mean either the southernmost province of Kwangtung, or all of China south of the Yangtze River.

[2]By the North, Charles most likely meant the province of Chihli and the city of Peking, although the phrase could also mean the entire region north of the Yangtze.

Charles to J. L. Barton, September 4, 1907, Hsiku, Tientsin

Dear Dr. Barton:

I reluctantly accept the conclusion that it may become necessary to cut some station from our list. But I still think that the decision can be more wisely rendered by sympathetic and critical friends from outside of the Mission, for they are more independent and unprejudiced in their conclusions than it is possible for us to be. . . .

Dr. [Charles] Stanley [Sr.] and I both spoke strongly to the [recent] Deputation [from Boston] of the need of medical work at the new Tientsin station [at Hsiku]. Our opinion is strengthened as time goes on. We have had considerable sickness in the compound this year—due to the unusual heat of the summer and to other causes, apparently not at all to any thing unfavorable in our location—and there is no physician on whom we can call nearer than the Settlement, except for Chinese assistant women physicians near the Viceroy's yamen. Our regular attendant, Dr. [Albert] Peck, is five miles away. All this, however, would not be sufficient to justify the demand for medical work of our own. The real reason why we urgently desire this is just the argument that weighs in favor of any medical missionary work—a double argument: first, the service that we may render to the people all around us; second, the evangelistic effectiveness of medical work.

Charles to the Ewing Family, September 15, 1907, Hsiku, Tientsin

Dear Ewing Family:

Bessie has not written much because the summer has been a very hard one for her. We were all well the first part and were glad we could stay together at home, but the last weeks have been very oppressive and Bessie has kept up a low fever and more recently a cough. She would go to the shore [Peitaiho] now except that all our friends have gone home. Therefore we have another plan. I have hired a houseboat and four of us are going down river while I visit some of the churches. The girls entered the English boarding school[1] two weeks ago. . . . The regular rule is for boarders to be allowed away only one "week-end" (as the English call it) but the matron says that does not apply to going to your own home. The new building is attractive. There are fifty-two pupils, seventeen of them being boarders.

During the year there has been increased growth of the power of the revolutionary party. It is unquestionably true that they are determined on the overthrow of the Manchu dynasty. In view of this the government proposes now to do away with all special Manchu privileges, such as a stipend for all Manchu men.[2] Rumors have been plenty about the possible abdication of the Empress Dowager, or the proclamation of an heir to the throne. Some changes have really been made. Yuan Shih Kai has been summoned from Tientsin, has nominated his own successor as viceroy of this province, and has been given a high place at the capital comparable to that of prime minister in other lands.[3] The apparent setback of last year is just as I predicted only a measure of caution. Chinese wisdom is largely opportunist in character, and the growth of the revolutionary movement has decided the first step in compromise. With national conditions as they are it is particularly advisable that the Christians be prudent, lest anything that is said or done be interpreted as having political significance. At the same time, it can hardly be doubted that many intelligent observers of Christianity are becoming persuaded that it is what it claims to be and are recognizing it as desirable for China, and even as a religion that they may soon be willing to accept as their own. How much this may mean I do not know, nor whether the spirit of Jesus Christ has really touched and vitalized such persons. But at least we may look forward with large hope for toleration of Christianity.

[1]Here Charles does not indicate where the school is, but it was located in the British Concession in Tientsin.

[2]One of the privileges the Manchus were granted by the dynasty was an annual rice or cash stipend. The justification for the stipend was that all Manchu men were soldiers and therefore eligible for payment as a kind of military reservist. The stipend was a bone of contention to many Chinese.

[3]See chapter 3.

Charles to the Ewing Family, October 27, 1907, Chihli Province

Dear Ewing Family:

Our boat trip lasted from Monday thru Friday instead of the two weeks [we planned]. Bessie's fever returned—also indigestion, so we shortened the trip. [However] . . . during the trip I was able to visit five villages, in one of which I concluded the purchase of a chapel site. One day while the boat went its leisurely way up the winding river[1] I walked my longest stretch, 32 miles, seeing members in three villages. The next day I rested on the boat. . . .

At a session [of the Y.M.C.A. Bible Institute] I did what I have never attempted before. As there were southern Chinese present who did not understand Mandarin, and northerners who did not understand English, I gave my whole address [on the subject of "Man's Duty Toward God"] section by section, first in English and then in Chinese. . . . I judge that it was effective and appreciated [in spite of the time it took].

After that meeting, I had the first opportunity that I have had for conversation with a Chinese "esoteric Buddhist." I was too tired to get the full benefit of all that he had to say, but it was interesting to find that he disavows the corruptions of present-day Buddhism, and goes back to the pure uncorrupted doctrine of a former age.[2] I apply to him the term "esoteric" for this reason: when I asked him where he got his interesting and suggestive views, whether from other men or books, he replied that neither way is possible, except as one already has the root idea in his own soul. That reminded me of the "esoteric" quality of Christianity as expressed in I Corinthians, 1 and 2, where Paul says that God has revealed the hidden things to us by his spirit, that to man's wisdom these hidden things seem foolishness and that he cannot know them, because they are spiritually discerned. This priest is not an infrequent attendant at special meetings in connection with the Y.M.C.A.

[1]To go upstream the boat used a sail and eight to ten men who pulled it by a rope.

[2]This priest or monk may have followed Theravedic Buddhism.

Charles to the Ewing Family, November 30, 1907, Hsiku, Tientsin

Dear Ewing Family:

I had hoped to be relieved from some of the responsibilities at the foreign settlement[1] as the going and coming takes so much time besides the late evening gatherings. . . . [However] much to my surprise I was elected to a larger place and did not feel that I could refuse as after all it is part of one's missionary work to keep in touch with foreigners outside the Mission circle. This new position is the president of the Tientsin Temperance Society. Their main work has been with British soldiers, keeping open house with library, game room, light refreshments, billiard table, besides religious meetings. Now they are to add fortnightly programs when I must preside. . . . a modest building has been erected with equipment for a clubhouse for young men who would like to keep away from special temptations. This will open on January first [1908] and the club idea has met with such response that there is likely to be a full membership from the start, ladies as well as men being admitted. The main provisions are that membership pay all current expenses and that alcoholic liquors and gambling are not allowed. . . .

We are instituting two new plans in our church work. You will remember that land was given to the church to repay for losses during the Boxer attacks. The use of the rents from such land has delayed self-support. At last we have sold some [land] to buy other chapel sites, and our proposal to one church has been accepted. This church has formed a society for self-management, we promise them the remaining rental money (about two-thirds enough to pay expenses) and they have agreed to contribute the rest. This may seem a small matter to you, but it marks a big step in Chinese church affairs, where everything has been provided from abroad all these years.

During the coming week we hope to have the helpers and deacons in from city and country to organize our first Tientsin Congregational Association. This will be the first step towards general self-management of all our churches. Up to this time all decisions have been made by the missionaries, not even have we had any Chinese on committees. We have only a very few [Chinese] even yet that have had sufficient training, but . . . [we] hope to accomplish some independence before the Chinese demand it, as happened in the churches in Japan.

[1]In 1907 the foreign settlement at Tientsin consisted of eight concessions: Austrian, Belgian, British, French, German, Italian, Japanese, and Russian.

Charles to Edward C. Ewing, December 1907, Hsiku, Tientsin

Dear Father:

You often write as tho you must think I am very busy all the time. Altho I am busy I do not accomplish as much as many missionaries in definite literary and educational work. My aim in our work in Tientsin is to act upon others so that they shall be real laborers, and to organize them for service and systematize the methods in use so that I may, as time goes on, need to do less myself.

Charles to the Ewing Family, January 17, 1908, Hsien Hsien, Chihli

Dear Ewing Family:

Ever since I have been in China I have needed a first-class teacher. Now I have such a man. For some time I have thought he was the one that I wanted, but not until the recent death of his mother could he leave his home. Even then he was not willing to come to me until he had first quit his habit of opium smoking. After taking the treatment at an official opium refuge in Tientsin he came to me. Reading the Chinese books with him, getting his explanation of the deep meanings beneath the surface, and conversing with him all give great pleasure.

The Missionary Association plans the Week of Prayer schedule for our united Chinese meetings. I had to manoever [*sic*] to get their special committee to turn these arrangements over to the Chinese, and then allow myself to be commissioned to put it before them—partly because last year, when it was turned over to the Chinese entirely there were some infelicities and partly because missionaries who theoretically want the Chinese Church to come into its own are very much afraid when the time comes to put theory into practice, fearing that the Chinese will make mistakes. Of course they will, that's the way to learn.

Charles to Edward and Ellen Ewing, February 25, 1908, Hsiku, Tientsin

Dear Father and Mother:

My last letter [to you] was written at Hsien Hsien, where I had just completed the purchase of new chapel premises. Here a "chapel" means not merely one building for meeting. There are included on the premises a residence for the preacher's family, an inquiry room, and if possible accommodations for schools. The chapel just purchased has all these, and also a large yard, surrounded by a wall.

Charles to the Ewing Family, March 27, 1908, Enroute to Hsien Hsien

Dear Ewing Family:

Another popular week-day game [at the girls' boarding school] is "Boxers and Missionaries." They play this in the British Recreation Ground which is across the street from the school. Each corner represents a station where missionaries were besieged or took refuge in 1900. The pavilion is Shanghai and if the missionaries can reach there, they are safe. But the [pretend] Boxers are entrenched in front of the pavilion, where there are two long trenches, and they try to capture the [pretend] missionaries before they can reach Shanghai. If captured, the missionaries are imprisoned under a flight of steps leading up to the pavilion, while their tormentors poke at them with sticks thru the cracks. This is very real to many of the pupils as both among the boarders and the day pupils are a number who were in either Peking or Tientsin during the siege in those cities.

When recovering . . . [from chicken-pox] Ellen [aged nine] wrote . . . "When we were down at school we saw the Scotch soldiers. We saw them get off the boat. They had on brown coats and plaid skirts with little kind of brushes hanging from their belts. Mama thinks there were more than three hundred. They came to take the place of the Sikhs from India. I like my school but of course I like to be at home the most."

On special parade days the Recreation Grounds are very colorful, with the British red-coats, the Scotch plaids, the Sikh headdress and uniforms of the Irish Inniskillens. In school the girls have pupils from England, Canada, Switzerland, and Russia. No wonder Marion [aged twelve] wrote "Living in Tientsin is like living in all the world."

Charles in the Tientsin Station Report, April 1908, Hsiku, Tientsin

There is no city in this empire where changes have been more rapid and complete than here in Tientsin. The world has been slow to realize that Tientsin is anything more than the gateway and port of Peking. The railway to Peking and the new line to the south [to Hankow], with connections with Shanghai, make this the port of entry and the shipping center for a greatly increased commerce. Six rivers, from three directions, meet here and being navigable [for small vessels] one hundred or more miles inland make this a distributing center.

The construction of the railway to Peking and Manchuria makes Tientsin the shipping center for the enlarged traffic. The newer railway to the south going on to Shanghai is to have its terminal at Tientsin within a few minutes walk of our own mission premises. The political importance is shown by the fact that the official residence of the viceroy of this province has been moved from Paoting to Tientsin. The worthy successor of Li Hung-chang is Yuan Shih Kai, who is now living here, making our city next to Peking in political importance in the North.[1] Under the fostering care of these two [Chinese], and following the far reaching plan laid down by the American, Dr. C. [Charles] D. Tenney, there has grown up a network of schools and colleges, some supported by officials, others by private funds but with official recognition. These include primary, intermediate and high schools; police, telegraph and industrial institutes; colleges of technology, international law, and medicine; schools where special attention is given to the study of European languages; normal training schools, kindergartens; and day and boarding schools for girls.

Similar manifestations of the progressive spirit are seen in other public institutions such as popular lecture halls which are really popular; free reading rooms; public hospitals and dispensaries; opium refuges where applicants [addicts] wait to be admitted. There is a home for widows and an infant asylum, with a Christian woman physician as medical and sanitary overseer. There is a model industrial prison, on the lines of the best similar work at home. All of the foregoing are entirely Chinese. The Christian forces at work are in two distinct sections, those among the foreign residents and those for the benefit of the Chinese. Among the foreign residents there are three Protestant churches, an Episcopal, one Union and one Japanese. There is also considerable work by the Church of Rome.

[T]he *China Times* is worthy of mention, and especially its managing editor, Mr. John Cowen. Ever since he experienced a change of heart and joined the Union church, he has been a militant Christian, using his daily paper to combat vice, instrumental in closing vile resorts, throwing light on corrupt practices, and even stirring up some sentiment against gambling.

[1]At the time this report was published Yuan Shih-kai had already been transferred to Peking.

Charles to the Ewing Family, June 30, 1908, Rocky Point, Peitaiho

Dear Ewing Family:

Following our [annual] Mission meeting . . . we all went to the shore [Peitaiho] and are pleasantly settled in our own [beach] house. We thought we might be crowded in only two rooms, but we live mostly on the porch, always eating on the south end, and leaving plenty of room for chairs and a small table for writing on the west side. The children have fine playmates. We are about four minutes walk from the bathing beach and near to everything central—Assembly Hall, ball field, store, post office, yet with an open sweep of the country before us. This view takes in the sea to the southwest, the nearby Lotus Hills and the more distant Chang Li Hills to the west, and ranges of mountains to the north with a glimpse of the Great Wall on the highest ridge, twenty or thirty miles away. . . .

[O]ur house is half of a "German Barrack,"[1] the other half owned by Mr. [Howard] Galt and this year occupied by a drug store. We are really resting this summer. The family will remain almost three months. I will return home [Hsiku] in one month, . . . I am not even reading heavy books, I play tennis and chess and some days baseball, this sport being quite a feature of our life here. We have frequent picnics [and a vegetable garden].

[1]Charles does not explain just what he meant by a "German Barrack."

Charles to the Ewing Family, August 26, 1908, Rocky Point, Peitaiho

Dear Ewing Family:

An important event for Tientsin is the recent decision of Mr. Chang Po Ling to be a Christian. He is one of the leading educators of Tientsin, a man of most attractive personality, sincerely devoted to the welfare of the people, a true philanthropist. He has become intimate with some of the Y.M.C.A. workers thru fellowship in educational affairs. One of these men, Mr. [C. H.] Robertson, invited Mr. Chang to spend a week as his guest here at the shore. Mr. Chang had long been a reader of the Bible, had appreciated, but had failed to comprehend the deep realities of Christian truth. He said to Mr. Robinson [sic], "My friends say that I am a Christian but you say I am not. What is the reason?" This week of converse resulted in a true understanding of the spirit of Christ, and a conviction of the power of that spirit to give meaning to all of life. Mr. Chang returned to Tientsin and told his associates and superiors of his new decision and experience and even went so far as to resign his positions of trust. Finally, when it was understood that this decision was deliberate, rational and irrevocable, his friends accepted the situation and urged him to retain his offices, which he was glad to do if he was still wanted. He had been appointed as one of China's commissioners to the Fisheries Conference in Washington—after which he and an associate are to study educational methods in the United States and several European countries, reporting at Peking late in the winter.[1]

[1]Mr. Chang Po Ling was to become one of North China's leading educators. He was a strong believer in the Y.M.C.A. movement and founded Nankai University in Tientsin. Although not originally a member of the Kuomintang, he was a member of the Peoples Political Council in Chunking from 1938 to 1945.

Charles to the Ewing Family, October 21, 1908, Hsiku, Tientsin

Dear Ewing Family:

I am inclosing the program of the [sixth annual] athletic contest which we all attended. As it was on a Saturday the girls were home [from school], as they are for each weekend this term. The day was perfect and it is estimated that 7,000 people were present. There were competitors from about a dozen schools, government and missionary. The majority of the prizes were won by the pupils of the Y.M.C.A. school, evidently because they had enjoyed more thoro training under foreign instruction. The best athlete of all will probably go to America to fit himself as athletic director in connection with the Y.M.C.A. The prizes are to be presented this evening when there will also be a discussion on the question, "When will China take part in an Olympic Contest?"[1] If you could have heard the school "yell" as given by the Y.M.C.A. pupils, you would have thought that this was NEW China with a vengeance. . . .

Bessie had had heavy responsibilities since her return from the shore, working right up to the limit of her strength, which had happily been recuperated during the summer [at Peitaiho]. . . . It was while she was alone here with the children, before I came home, that she had the greatest strain. She had to get our two girls off to school; then the Chinese school-girls off by boat to Tungchow (our school being closed until Miss Marian MacGowan is ready to take charge); had to take precautionary measures against the flood when the river rose so high as to invade our premises; had the grief of Mrs. [Louise] Stanley's death and funeral; and in the midst of all that had to get the household wheels running again. . . .

[1]As the Olympic Games had been held in London in 1908, this was an appropriate topic.

Charles to the Ewing Family, December 7, 1908, Hsiku, Tientsin

Dear Ewing Family:

The heavy rains of last summer, flooding the land before harvest has left much suffering [but] still not severe enough to warrant asking for famine relief funds. When such funds are given there must be constant oversight by a missionary, careful investigation of all applicants, distribution to the most needy, [and] without regard to Christian or non-Christian. We cannot under-take such a task until it becomes imperative. I have visited one of the villages where there are 70 families, with over a third of them in our church. Several of these families have not enough food to carry them through the winter, or any winter clothing or bedding. While there are no funds available for simply "Christians," there are some sources on which I can count. One such is the Christmas offering at the Union Church,[1] which will be divided [among] the four Missions. A new source is from the voluntary decision of our own church members, when those Chinese voted that, instead of follow-ing the former custom of eating a big Christmas feast together at the chapel, the members will contribute what they can, clothing, food, or money, for the poor, contenting themselves with a tea-meeting instead of a feast.

You know that the Emperor [Kuang Hsu] and the Empress Dowager [Tzu Hsi] had both died. The orders for mourning are quite strict. No Chi-nese can have his head shaved for a hundred days. All red signs have been covered over with blue or white. Even gilded signs are in many places painted over. No red clothing is worn except by little children or by an occasional bride who probably has nothing else. No weddings are allowed for three months, Manchus are forbidden to marry for three years. Manchus and officials have to dress in white, the latter wearing sheepskin robes with the fur outside. No music is allowed for 27 days, except in temples. In Peking the Mission churches have given up singing, but elsewhere we in-terpret the temple clause as permitting religious music. Here in Tientsin we had no Thanksgiving service at the consulate on account of the Imperial mourning. Mourning was suspended for one day, when the infant Emperor [Pu Yi] ascended the dragon throne carried by the Prince Regent [Chun].

[1]The Union Church in Tientsin was primarily attended by the foreign community.

Charles to J. L. Barton, December 17, 1908, Ching Hai, Chihli Province

Dear Dr. Barton:

The death of the Emperor Kuang Hsu, followed immediately by the death of the Empress Dowager, produced a profound impression, not only in China, but all over the world. Neither event by itself would have been surprising, but it is not strange that the close concurrence of the two should have given rise to various rumors, some of them disquieting. So far as can be judged, none of the more threatening rumors were in the least justified by the facts. Indeed, the effect proved to be sobering, rather than disturbing. The minds of men at the present time are thoughtful, not turbulent. The progress of events at the capital, and the smoothness which the necessary changes at the Imperial Court have been made, won the admiration of the ministers of the foreign nations, who were close enough to the center of affairs to see for themselves. All of this, however, is history already to you, who get your news by cable. We are not always *quite* sure of things ourselves, until they are cabled back from London as having appeared in the [London] *Times*.

4

The End of a Dynasty
1909–1913

ONE of Prince Chun's first actions as regent for the child emperor was to deal with his late brother's wish to have Viceroy Yuan Shih-kai beheaded. Emperor Kuang Hsu's will had made such a request as he believed, with reason, that it was Yuan's information to Prince Jung Lu that caused Tzu Hsi to end his rule and hold him in captivity for the remaining ten years of his life. Prince Chun did not cause Yuan to lose his head, but on January 2, 1909, he issued an imperial edict dismissing the viceroy from his offices and ordering him to return to his home province of Honan.

Shortly after Yuan's dismissal, the regent authorized as part of the throne's reform program the election of provincial assemblies. The elections were held from February to June and followed the pattern established in Chihli for the Tientsin municipality. Less than one percent of the provinces' adult male population was authorized to vote. Even with such a limited electorate, the results were disappointing to the throne, as the men elected, rather than debating abstract constitutional principles, voiced criticism of Peking. It was obvious to foreign observers that the assemblymen were interested in curtailing the powers of the throne and in sharing some of its authority.

Even before an unofficial Shanghai meeting by fifty-one members of sixteen provincial assemblies met and unsuccessfully petitioned the throne for a parliament, Peking issued another questionable reform decree. It dealt with the finances of the nation and called for the preparation of a national budget. No such budget had ever been undertaken before, and the Manchu dynasty was soon to learn the truth about China's finances and its reform program. The decree not only called for the preparation of budgets but also the collection of revenues, which would go to Peking, by provincial treasurers. The result was that all of the newly prepared provincial budgets showed deficits and, thus, no new money for local reforms or for additional revenues for Peking. By the end of 1909, the dynasty was fast approaching bankruptcy and the failure of its reform program. The only remaining source of new money for the dynasty was from the banks of Europe and America. Such foreign loans were usually secured by a pledge to allow either further rail and mineral exploitation, or the increase of an existing tax, or by permission to foreigners to collect additional taxes via the Imperial Maritime Customs. The Manchus were never able to resolve their fiscal dilemma.

Part of the problem in tax collection and budget preparation was the matter of currency. China in 1909 had no common currency except the copper cash that was used in small-scale endeavors or for local transactions. At the treaty ports the most common form of money was the Mexican or Spanish silver dollar and silver bars called *sycee*. There was no paper currency except that which local bankers and money changers issued. Provincial payments and other large transactions were calculated in taels of silver. However taels were a unit of measure and were not in coined units. Furthermore, there were almost as many different forms of taels as there were provinces in China. As one scholar of the period has written, "China was a money-changers' paradise."[1] But foreign or domestic, the snags over the form of the repayment, various exchange rates, and the fluctuation in the price of silver turned it into a nightmare when it came to arranging a loan.

The regent, sitting within the walls of the Forbidden City, was slow to grasp the fact that in order to continue with the planned reforms, including building an army that could protect China, his government must go to the foreign bankers for money. Early in 1910 those bankers, responding to the throne's request, asked China's government to pledge the railways as loan security. But in order to pledge the railways, the throne would first find it necessary to nationalize them. Although the needs of national defense, famine relief, and internal migration made a nationalized rail system sensible, such action would mean a further centralization of power; and provincial and regional forces were already agitated against additional control from Peking. This conflict was particularly accentuated when Chinese financiers demanded to fund the building of both provincial and interprovincial railways because of the profits to be gained from railroad construction. They were opposed not only to foreign loans but particularly to the nationalization of China's railroads. Peking, however, was determined to secure foreign loans because of the need to obtain foreign currencies and the lower interest rates offered by foreign banks. The throne specifically wanted to nationalize and therefore control the Hankow-Canton line that, together with the Peking-Hankow line, would link the north with the south of China. A French-British-German consortium proposed to finance the line, and the dynasty agreed. But when America's President Taft insisted on an American share of the loan, undoubtedly provoked by the rebuff of American banks'

[1]Cameron, *Reform Movement in China*, 165.

offers to provide loans for the expansion of Manchurian railways, a four-power banking arrangement was eventually worked out. The loan, totaling $19 million, was finally concluded on May 20, 1911.

Meanwhile, the Chinese political scene was approaching a distinct change. On October 3, 1910, the National Assembly met in Peking for the first time. The Assembly's membership (consisting of 200, of whom half were chosen by the elected provincial assemblies and the other 100 chosen by the throne) was made up largely of high-level gentry who were representatives of privilege and were expected to discuss only those issues the court had sent them. The throne quickly learned, though, that the assemblymen were not going to play the game according to the prearranged rules. In November members of the Assembly formally rejected the government's action approving the foreign railway loan. The assembly not only had voted against the consortium's loan but, indirectly, against the throne's plan to nationalize China's railways. By early December the members of the appointed Grand Council had resigned, and the regent had proclaimed that the Assembly had exceeded its powers. Later he appeared to change his mind, as on December 25 orders were issued for the acceleration of the constitutional government, including formation of a cabinet. On January 11, 1911, the first session of the National Assembly was completed; it had demonstrated resolve, but the throne had shown indecision and weakness.

While the dynasty in Peking was continuing its efforts to finance a modern army, members of the army were being organized into secret revolutionary cells. Many of the organizing members of the cells had been students in Japan who realized upon their return to China that their goal of overthrowing the Manchus could best be achieved by military action. Most revolutionary cells were hidden behind such innocuous names as the Literary Society, the Common Advancement Society, and the Science Study Group. By the end of 1910, most army units at the viceregal seat of Wuchang had revolutionary cells. Wuchang, located across the Yangtze from the Central China treaty port of Hankow, was to prove to be the ideal place for anti-Manchu activities in the army.[2]

When the fateful year of 1911 opened, the Chinese numbered approximately 440 million, making China far and away the world's most populous country. Of that number only 1.7 million were students. Yet many of those students played an inordinately important role in the antidynasty activities. They were involved in organizing revolutionary cells in the army, in promoting a demand for a constitution and a parliament, in boycotts of foreign goods, and in demonstrating opposition to foreign loans for railways. Students had become one of the new forces in China.

[2]Wuchang, Hankow, and the nearby city of Hanyang are collectively known as Wuhan.

Instead of allying himself with the constitutional cause and promoting Chinese who were sincere reformers, Prince Chun had taken the path of accepting the advice of his Manchu cronies and creating a smoke-screen reform program. At about the same time the foreign loan agreement was signed in May 1911, an imperial edict announced that all trunk railway lines, the bailiwick of provincial authorities, were to be nationalized. In the following month, Peking announced a plan in which all provincial interests in railways would be bought out by the central government—this in spite of the warning that had come from the National Assembly. Although the provincial companies in Hupeh, Hunan, and Kwangtung were to receive payment in full, not so for Szechwan, where, because of provincial mismanagement, only a third was to be repaid. The Szechwanese resented the proposed arrangement and under the leadership of powerful gentry and merchant investors instigated resistance through a general strike and rioting. In September the Manchu governor ordered the arrest of the leaders of Szechwan's Railway Protective Association. Armed rebellion followed, as the leaders of the railway movement were determined to resist. The governor fled the provincial capital, and other parts of Szechwan were in open revolt.

In early October 1911, Wuchang, together with its sister cities of Hankow and Hanyang, contained an estimated 7,000 army troops. About half of those troops were in revolutionary cells. In addition, about 1,500 police and 1,000 Manchu Patrol and Defense Force personnel watched the area, nearly all of them loyal to the Manchus. One brigade of the army had already been sent to Szechwan to quell the disturbances there, and more were expected. If the members of the revolutionary cells were to act against the dynasty and in conjunction with Szechwan turmoil, the time was ripe. On October 9 an accidental explosion occurred in the Russian Concession of Hankow that was to lead to the overthrow of the Manchu dynasty and the establishment of the Chinese Republic. The explosion was in the residence of members of a revolutionary organization with ties to the anti-Manchu cells in the army units in Wuchang. The explosion quickly led the police to the cells and on October 10 (Double Ten) to a revolt by the compromised army units. The following day Wuchang was in the hands of the revolutionary army units and the Hupeh Provincial Assembly became their headquarters. A republic was quickly proclaimed under the unlikely name of the Central Florescent Republic. Within a few days time the army had also occupied Hankow and Hanyang on the northern bank of the Yangtze, had taken the viceregal and provincial treasuries, seized the largest arsenal in China at Hanyang, and assured the consuls in Hankow's concessions that foreign property and lives would be protected.

Peking soon came to realize that the events in Wuhan and in Szechwan were serious and that retaliatory action had to be taken quickly. In an act of self-humiliation, the regent called Yuan Shih-kai out of retirement and made him viceroy of Hupeh and Hunan. He was ordered, perhaps naively, to put down the revolt. The viceroy did not immediately take up those duties but instead began a protracted negotiation with Prince Chun. Yuan did order elements of the Peiyang Army to move by rail to Hankow to subdue the mutinous troops of the "republic." By November 1 the units loyal to Peking had attacked the revolutionary army and in doing so, had destroyed with artillery fire most of the Chinese city of Hankow. Neither side moved into the foreign concessions that stretched for almost four miles along the Yangtze. For much of the month of November the battle for Hankow and Hanyang raged between the two armies. Both sides were ready to negotiate after sustaining heavy casualties.

While severe fighting was taking place in Central China, a number of actions had happened in Peking that would affect both armies. Late in October a unit of the Peiyang Army located at Lanchow, in Chihli, demonstrated against being sent to Hankow. That demonstration, coupled with the Wuhan revolt, resulted in the regent's issue of a decree termed the Manchu Renunciation. It was an act of atonement designed to placate the nation. The Renunciation dated October 31, 1911, recognized freedom of thought, granted amnesty to political offenders, excluded Manchu princes from the cabinet, and ordered the constitution to be given to the National Assembly for consideration. The following day Yuan Shih-kai was named premier. On November 13, Yuan entered Peking with a regiment of Peiyang troops. Shortly thereafter, the regent swore to uphold a constitution and obey the advice of the National Assembly which had been in session since October 24. For practical purposes Price Chun had resigned his regency, even though his son, the child emperor Pu Yi, remained on the throne.

While Peking was quietly collapsing into Yuan's hands, the battle for the Wuhan cities raged, and the flight away from the faltering Manchu dynasty took over in the provinces. By mid-November fourteen provinces had declared against the Manchu dynasty. Only Chihli and Honan remained uncommitted, while Szechwan, the last of the non-Manchurian provinces to act, already was in a state of revolt but had not declared its intent. In nine provinces the rich gentry and merchants, together with the members of the provincial assemblies, had declared their independence from Peking. In the other provinces it was essentially soldiers of the revolutionary cells in the army units that initiated the revolt from the Manchu control.

On the same day that Yuan had entered Peking, the governor of Shanghai cabled fourteen revolutionary governors to send representatives to a meeting in his city to discuss cooperation and a new central government. Just before the delegates were able to gather at Shanghai, the revolutionary army had captured the old capital city of Nanking, and so the delegates agreed to go there instead. Nanking, just 200 miles up the Yangtze from Shanghai, and a symbol of Chinese nationalism, was where the delegates met on December 14. They proceeded to consider for provisional president none other than Yuan Shih-kai. Before he could be selected, however, he had to announce his support of the revolution. Since he had not yet indicated a willingness to do so, the delegates had a problem to resolve.

The resolution came a few days later. The revolutionary organizer, Sun Yat-sen, reached Shanghai on Christmas day. At the time of the outbreak of the revolution he had been in Denver, Colorado, raising money for the anticipated revolt. After a lengthy trip through the United States and Europe, he had at last reached China, where the revolution that he had long hoped for had erupted. Dr. Sun was elected provisional president of the republic and was formally sworn in at Nanking on January 1, 1912.

While the provincial politicians were shifting to Nanking and selecting Sun Yat-sen as the provisional president, a cease-fire' and truce had gone into effect in Central China. In effect, the Yangtze River had become the truce line, as the provinces north of it supported Premier Yuan, while those to the south recognized Sun Yat-sen as president of the republic.

While China struggled with her incomplete revolution, the foreign powers were equally at sea. They greatly feared a reappearance of Boxerism and so were relieved when both Chinese sides pointed out their desire not to change the status of the treaties and not to involve the foreign concessions in the fighting. Neither Chinese faction wanted to see the foreigners become involved, as they well remembered the aftermath of the Boxer Uprising and feared another occupation, or worse, the division of the chaotic China among the powers. The solution was that the foreign powers opted temporarily for neutrality.

Fear gripped Peking when elements of the Peiyang Army demanded the abdication of the Manchu emperor and declared for the republic. The foreign diplomats wisely remained behind the walls of their well-guarded Legation Quarter. Soon thereafter Yuan Shih-kai, who in January had narrowly escaped assassination from a bomb thrower, obtained an agreement for Pu Yi to abdicate. The end of the Manchu or Ching, the Dynasty of Great Purity, came on February 12, 1912, the twenty-fifth day of the twelfth moon of the third year of Hsuan Tung, for the boy Pu Yi retained his reign name.

The abdication agreement did not recognize the provisional republican government in Nanking but referred to the revolutionaries as the Army of the People and instructed Yuan to organize a republican government. Yuan interpreted this to mean that it was he, rather than the republic in Nanking, who inherited the Mandate of Heaven. On the day of the abdication of the six-year-old Pu Yi, the Articles of Favorable Treatment were also signed. By those articles the emperor kept his title and was to be treated as a foreign sovereign; he would receive a liberal annual annuity, continue to reside in the Forbidden City, and retain his personal bodyguard and servants. Only three large halls in the Forbidden City were turned over to the new government for ceremonial purposes, and the emperor was stripped of his power to appoint any additional eunuchs. The 3,000 then located in the imperial palaces were apparently enough.

Two days after the emperor's abdication, the members of the Nanking government, short of money and desiring a unified central government, voted to go to Peking. A delegation went to Peking, headed by the revolutionary Sung Chao-jen, to negotiate the location of the capital and other matters. Within a few days of the delegates' arrival in Peking, military mutinies broke out there. Although the mutinies soon ended, the Nanking delegation was convinced that Yuan would not leave Peking and, hence, the capital must be located there. On March 10, 1912, Yuan was inaugurated provisional president, and the entire Nanking government soon after moved to Peking or returned home. After Yuan had selected a cabinet, half of whose members were revolutionaries, Sun Yat-sen formally resigned. As of April 1, China had but one provisional president and one government.

Once Yuan Shih-kai had assumed the presidency, and incidentally had his pigtail cut off to demonstrate that he was a republican, he had to deal primarily with two problems: arranging a foreign loan and negotiating with the revolutionary parties for control of the government and the provinces. Above all else, Yuan knew that the revenue income of the new government was barely enough to keep it going and that the army, to be kept in the field and loyal to himself, required that he obtain money by taxing or borrowing. New taxes were out of the question, and so the solution was to borrow. While still premier of the Manchu government, Yuan had tired unsuccessfully to borrow from Chinese banks. The only solution was to turn once again to the foreign banks, just as the throne had done for the railway loan. Again a four-power consortium, consisting of British, French, German, and American banking interests, was established to negotiate with Yuan's government. By June 1912, the Japanese and Russians, those rivals for the control of Manchuria, had joined in the consortium, though neither had much money to loan. The terms required by the foreign bankers for the so-called Reorganization Loan were not easy for any Chinese nationalist, including Yuan, to accept. The consortium asked to supervise the use of the money loaned and to appoint their agents to collect the revenue of China's salt tax as loan security. These two requirements proved too much for Yuan, and negotiations temporarily broke off, even though China's government was virtually bankrupt.

President Yuan and the National Assembly, mostly referred to after August 1912, when new members were added from the provincial assemblies, as the Senate, represented opposite political views. Yuan's military and bureaucratic followers held executive power and believed in an all-powerful president. The revolutionary parties in the Senate firmly believed in the paramountcy of the legislature. Yuan wanted a strong authoritarian central government with a rubber-stamp legislature that would approve his proposals. Not being a political theorist, he did not wish to engage in political-party bargaining and compromise. The revolutionary parties, who were dominated by the Kuomintang (Nationalist) party after its organization on August 25, wanted the executive, i.e., Yuan, to be subservient, or no more than coequal, to the legislature. Unfortunately, compromise in the political process had not yet taken hold in the Chinese revolution. Although Sun Yat-sen had come to Peking to participate in the founding of the Kuomintang, and at the same time to be appointed by Yuan to a meaningless sinecure, he was not in the Senate, nor was he inclined to participate in its activities. Dr. Sun, for all his fund raising and revolution-promoting talents, was not called upon to lead the Kuomintang. That role was taken over by the relatively young Sung Chao-jen. It was he who, it was hoped, would lead the party to victory in the December 1912–January 1913 elections.

By the end of 1912, most provinces were in the hands of military governors who shared power with gentry and administrators. However in the south, particularly Kwangtung, the Kuomintang had a strong political following and still controlled a substantial military force. As long as Yuan kept the allegiance of his former Peiyang Army colleagues, who were scattered throughout China as military governors or commanders of substantial military units, he could probably expect to stay in power.

The Senate elections that concluded in January 1913 proved that China could conduct elections in a responsible way. It also demonstrated that the student revolutionaries and intellectuals could rally enough gentry voters to carry a large majority for the Kuomintang and other revolutionary parties. Many gentry voters had turned away from Yuan because of his policies over centralization and use of military force. One modern historian has written about the election: "Though the electorate had been restricted to the small minority who had property or educational qualifications, a Chinese election would never come any closer to meeting democratic standards."[3] President Yuan, however, made it abundantly clear that he did not consider the elections very important and would pay little attention to an elected Senate.

[3]Harold Z. Schiffrin, *Sun Yat-sen, Reluctant Revolutionary* (Boston: Little, Brown, 1980), 173.

Two incidents in 1913 brought the contending factions into armed conflict. The first occurred on March 20 in the Shanghai railway station where the Peking Express was about to depart. The leader of the Kuomintang in the Senate, Sung Chao-jen, was shot and mortally wounded as he was about to depart for Peking, where he hoped to talk with President Yuan about the Senate's relations with the government. He died two days later at the age of thirty-one. It was widely believed that President Yuan was involved in the assassination, and the result was a rupture in the Yuan-Kuomintang relations.

The second incident was not so dramatic as the shooting of Sung, but it also had a profound impact. On April 26, the Yuan government and the foreign banking consortium signed the long-awaited Reorganization Loan agreement. From the point of view of the Kuomintang and other parties supportive of the parliamentary process, it was a slap in the face: Yuan had not discussed the loan with their leaders, nor had the Senate approved it. Sun Yat-sen had appealed to the consortium not to grant the loan, as he considered the terms insulting and feared that the money would be used by Yuan against his political opponents. The loan was for 25 million pounds sterling, with 21 million of that going to China. The United States had withdrawn from the consortium when the recently elected American president, Woodrow Wilson, learned of the loan conditions and rejected them on the grounds that they curtailed China's independence as a nation. The other five consortium members were not so sensitive and quickly financed the loan.

With the murder of Sung and the approval of the Reorganization Loan, Yuan was ready to confront his opposition. The test came in June when he dismissed three military governors who were members of the Kuomintang. Early the following month, troops loyal to the president were shifted so as to threaten those provinces where Yuan's men were not in control. Sun Yat-sen called for war and began organizing to resist any military efforts made by the president. Fighting broke out between the two sides on July 13, and the second Chinese revolution was under way.

The fight by the revolutionary parties against the government of President Yuan was ill-planned and almost totally uncoordinated. Fighting erupted in Kiangsi, Kiangsu, and Nanking. By early September 1913, the insurgent bases at Nanking and Nanchang had fallen to Yuan's army, and the revolt had collapsed. Although the insurgency was over, a number of provinces, particularly those in the south, were not yet under the control of Yuan. But the Senate capitulated, lured by money and a display of military power. On October 6, its members met and elected Yuan Shih-kai to a five-year term as president of China.

By the end of 1913, Yuan had permanently adjourned the Senate and dissolved the Kuomintang. Also by that time Dr. Sun was in exile in Japan, and other opponents of the president had fled to Hong Kong, Singapore, and Japan.[4]

[4]Yuan Shih-kai was to remain in office in Peking until his death in June 1916. His attempt to have himself made emperor proved foolhardy nonetheless, as it caused a number of provincial governors to declare against his rule. By the time of his death China was well into that time known historically as the "warlord period." Sun Yat-sen would return to China in 1921 and become president of the republic, with Canton as his capital city. There he would struggle, until his death in 1925, to see China unified. The ex-emperor, Pu Yi, would remain in the confines of the Forbidden City until November 1924, when at the age of eighteen he would leave his palatial imprisonment and find sanctuary in the Japanese concession in Tientsin. He remained in Tientsin until 1931, when the Japanese placed him on the throne of their puppet state of Manchukuo. Pu Yi died in 1968 in Peking, a private citizen of the People's Republic of China.

Ewing Papers,
February 1909 to April 1913

Charles to Edward and Ellen Ewing, February 16, 1909, Hsien Hsien, Chihli

Dear Father and Mother:

Before you read this letter we shall have a new U.S. president, W. H. Taft. You, mother, wrote about things you would like different in him, one being his attitude toward Sunday ball-playing. We have had to meet a similar question with reference to playing games on Sunday at the Waverly Club, the club that was started by the Temperance Society. Most members of the Society want no Sunday games, but we are unwilling to insist, for fear of killing or seriously hurting the club or sending its members to other places (bad places) for Sunday games. In the serious discussion that we had on the subject (which threatened to disrupt the Temperance Society) attention was drawn to the fact that even the Old Testament law forbids, not playing, but working on the Sabbath. This may be because playing was not in vogue in those ancient times, but on the other hand, the Puritan attitude towards games in general was extreme, was it not?

To return to Mr. Taft,[1] he seems to me on the whole the best-balanced statesman that we have had in the United States for a long time. Everyone can pick some flaws, I suppose, mine is this: Taft voiced the most serious criticism that can be made on him, when he admitted his inability to answer the question what a poor man out of work was to do. His reply was, "God knows." Yes, of course, but Taft ought to know. That question may not be the most important, but it expresses one aspect of the most urgent problem before the American people at the present time, and no one ought to be a leader in political affairs who has not some reply to make, even tho all may not agree as to the wisest course. It may be that Taft is ready to meet the main problem, if so, it was unfortunate that he should give the impression of not being ready.

---

[1]As previously indicated in the pages of this book, but not mentioned in this letter, William Howard Taft, as secretary of war and president, had encouraged American investment in China.

Charles to Myra Smith, February 27, 1909, Hsiku, Tientsin

Dear Aunt Myra:

You have been kind enough to send me on three successive Christmas days three popular novels of the day. The latest one was "M. Crew's Career" by Winston Churchill[1]. . . . [It]is an interesting story and a forceful presentation of political conditions that prevail, I suppose, both in New Hampshire and in some other states. How far the "Consolidated" owns Connecticut it might be difficult to say, but it is almost impossible for any bill to pass the legislature if it is prejudicial to the interests of the railroad. In other states, the controlling factor is not a railroad, but some great combination of financial concerns—what [Thomas William] Lawson[2] called "the Interests." Of course, our books, periodicals, and daily papers are so full of this general subject that one wonders if the indignation is not overdrawn in an excessive endeavor to pander to the popular taste. But there can be no doubt that they voice a real warning against a real danger. It is outrageous to have a state controlled by an interest except the interest of the whole people. And when the same predatory powers are seeking to control the national government, and too often succeeding, it is time to call a halt at once. Someone has said that Winston Churchill has done immense injury to New Hampshire, but that is like Ahab calling Elijah the "troubler of Israel"[I Kings 18:17].

I have just been writing today to Will Ament.[3] You must know of the death of his father Dr. [William] Ament, on January 6. I wanted to give Will a new view of the largeness and strength of his father. He is the best evangelistic worker and the most successful organizer that we have ever had in the Mission. His loss will be felt seriously, both by the work and by the workers personally. But he had done his work so thoroly and well that no other station could lose its leading worker and still be left so strong as Peking. After many years of most faithful, earnest, painstaking labor, he had just succeeded in getting everything into such shape that, as he faced death, it was not with the sense of duties left undone, but in the calm assurance that now at last he could be spared.

[1]The Winston Churchill here referred to by Charles was the American novelist, not the British statesman.
[2]The writer Thomas William Lawson was generally critical of American business.
[3]William (Will) Ament, Jr., was at this time a student in the United States.

Charles to Enoch Bell, April 15, 1909, Hsiku, Tientsin

Dear Mr. Bell:

Here is a story about the little Emperor of China, which the Chinese people themselves appreciate. When the day for the coronation came—or, to be more exact, the day when the little boy was to ascend the dragon throne— he was not yet four years old. The Manchu and Chinese officials were gathered in the palace, with their fine garments and brilliant decorations. The little boy looked all around, as if trying to find somebody. Then he turned to his father, the Prince Regent, and asked, "Where is Mow?"[1] His father did not know who Mow was, but the new emperor was bound to have him present. So word was sent out to his mother, "Who is Mow?" She said that Mow was a five year old boy who had been a neighbor and constant playmate. So Mow was sent for. But according to the rules of the court, he could not be admitted unless he had some official rank. That was easily managed, as he was made a military officer, was given a cap with a button on it, and was admitted to the throne room to see his little playmate ascend the dragon throne.

[1]Also spelled Mao.

Charles to the Ewing Family, May 9, 1909, Hsien Hsien, Chihli

Dear Ewing Family:

During the last three months I have spent 52 days in touring. This constant travel is not luxury, and I suppose it comes harder on Bessie than it does on me, but it seems to be demanded by the work in the country field. Of course, it is pleasant to have one's work appreciated, and you will pardon me if I quote, just in our family circle, a sentence from Secretary Barton's last letter to me. "There is no missionary that is covering the ground better than you are, in my judgment, and keeping his hand more fully upon the outstation work." I have no doubt that I spend more time in country touring than any other man in our own Mission, for conditions are such that no one can devote himself to touring without neglect to other parts of his work. But while my present responsibility is for the outstations, my heart is in the work in the city, and I believe it can be made to succeed if conducted vigorously. Another quotation from Dr. Barton is in order. I wrote to him of the remark [i.e., "Mrs. Ewing is incomparable"] of the Chinese husband concerning the impression that Bessie had made during the women's station class. He replied to me in these words: "I was very glad of the quotation which you gave me at the close of your letter . . . although I am not the least bit surprised at his judgment. We have always looked upon Mrs. Ewing as one of the most able and foremost workers among the women of China, and we appreciate it, and wish her continued health and strength for the important work she is doing." You will be glad to know that Bessie's health and strength are continuing.

Charles to the Ewing Family, June 23, 1909, Tungchow

Dear Ewing Family:

Our whole family has been here for the annual Mission Meeting, Bessie and the children for ten days [and then] returning home. . . . My longer stay was necessitated by several other meetings. These included examination and graduation in the Theological College in Peking, an English sermon, a talk to the Medical College students . . . and attending the first graduation of a class from the full course in the North China Union Women's College. This is the only institution in China which gives a real college course to young women. The occasion was unique, the exercises good, and the four young women who graduated appeared as attractive and promising as any similar class in America. We hope to secure one of them as teacher for our girls' school in Tientsin.

[T]omorrow Mr. Chang Po Ling is to speak to the students [at their conference] and later will address a specially invited group of Tungchow officials and gentry. . . . Chang Po Ling has joined our Mission Church in Tientsin. At his request, Dr. Stanley baptized him on April 18, at the dedication of our new church building at Hsiku. On that day there were over three hundred in attendance.

Charles to Enoch Bell, September 3, 1909, Hsiku, Tientsen

Dear Mr. Bell:

The [Provincial] University is six miles from the [Tientsin] foreign business and residence center, and a mile beyond our own compound [at Hsiku]. It occupies the ground formerly used for a military arsenal—the place to which Admiral [Sir Edward] Seymour's party retired when forced back from its attempt to relieve Peking in the early summer of 1900. Seymour captured the arsenal, and turned its guns against the Chinese in the city, remaining until the city was taken by foreign troops.[1] The University grounds are beautifully supplied with groves and avenues of trees, athletic fields, private tennis courts for the faculty families, etc. There is [*sic*] good equipment and buildings including a modest-sized gymnasium with running track gallery, a library with very few books, dormitories for the students, an assembly hall with Confucian tablet (Dr. Barton saw this), and a fine new science and engineering building erected last year (the architect, Prof. Myron Peck, being the same who prepared the plans for our new church building [at Hsiku]). There are fairly comfortable houses for the American professors, stretching along from the main building on the west to the river (Peiho) on the east. . . . [There are] four double houses. There are now ten American men on the faculty, five of them married. So far as I know the only Christians[2] among them are two who have married missionary ladies, Profs. Drake and Peck. But they all are fine men and, as far as I can judge, are doing good work, and some of them, at any rate, have the welfare of China at heart.

[1]Seymour's exploits were heroic but not quite as Charles has described them.

²Charles's notion of who was or was not a Christian must be viewed from his background and also from a point of view that encompasses the year in which this letter was written.

Charles to the Ewing Family, September 4, 1909, Hsiku, Tientsin

Dear Ewing Family:

During July and August while I was home alone [Bessie and the children were at Peitaiho] I wrote 100 letters and made four country trips. My vacation was the last two weeks in August at the shore. But it was hardly a restful time [as] among the meetings scheduled . . . were the North China Educational Union, the Board of Managers of the Tract [Bible] Society, . . . the Rocky Point Association, . . . conferences concerning [a proposed] Union business agency, . . . and an evangelistic conference.

An event of special interest to me was the arrival of guests whom I knew in Amherst College. . . . Storrs, a fraternity brother of Amherst '96, who came to China in 1904, and is in our Foochow Mission. . . . and his aunt, a missionary from India. . . . We all spent a day at East Cliff where Hawley of Amherst '01, with Storrs and myself had an Amherst confab. I saw them again in Tientsin on September first, when I took them to the University, to the Settlement and escorted them to their steamer for Shanghai.

Charles to Edward and Ellen Ewing, September 13, 1909, Hsiku, Tientsin

Dear Father and Mother:

Miss [Marian] MacGowan has reopened our boarding school for girls, even tho the new buildings for Women's work must be used, thus making another station-class impossible. There is accommodation for only fourteen boarders, but there are eight or ten day pupils. The teacher is Miss Li, the [recent] college graduate of the first class from Peking.

The boys' school is expected to begin its new term tomorrow. We have a college graduate there also as principal. Dr. [Charles] Stanley [Sr.] wants to limit the number of boarders to sixteen as they do not pay much toward their board, and every additional pupil means added expense. We ought to bring our schools, not indeed to full support, but to the point where the board will not be paid by the Mission. . . .

Charles to Edward C. Ewing, October 7, 1909, Hsiku, Tientsin

Dear Father:

Some of the problems in reopening the [girls'] school have been the securing of the full teaching force, the last one only arrived this week. This was the teacher for the Confucian Classics, a man who has the second literary degree and who will help to give prestige to the school. He will also teach Miss MacGowan the [Chinese] language.

Then there has been the problem of how to accommodate a school of 25 in a school room 12 by 30 [feet], and the necessity of refusing several [students] because there were dormitories for only 14. These students and the matron . . . [are] crowded into three rooms, five in each, and rooms are only 10 by 12. (They are not like our rooms as the Chinese brick platform, which is the bed for all, occupies most of the space.) Minor problems (?) were fumigation for itch and special head baths. . . . with the new pupils it took a good deal of persuasion to achieve the weekly baths, tho even the mothers of the day pupils sometimes gave permission when no bad effects were found. . . . Fortunately the Chinese young woman [Miss Li] knows just what to do and is a most delightful and efficient person. Another help in the situation is that several of the older girls spent last year in a well-managed school at Tungchow and one of them in Peking, the best school in North China.

We have had special meetings conducted by a team of [American] evangelists, not the old blood and thunder type, but men with a vital sane message which has helped both foreigners and Chinese. For some of the Chinese meetings I have been the interpreter and I enjoyed it immensely. . . . For myself, I enjoy preaching, either in English or Chinese. I try to give in Chinese the same type of sermon that I would to an English [speaking] audience and few preachers seem to do that. Bessie says I am the only preacher in Chinese to whom she cares to listen. . . .

Marion [aged fourteen] has started something new, not exactly missionary work, but a form of sharing only possible here. She has a new teacher, Miss Steele, whom she likes very much. To Marion's delight, Miss Steele has offered to help her with music twice a week if Marion will teach her Chinese, principally how to say the special sentences she wants to learn. If Miss Steele asks something that is beyond Marion's vocabulary, she asks us.

Charles to J. L. Barton, October 11, 1909, Hsiku, Tientsin

Dear Dr. Barton:

In my last letter to you I neglected to thank you for your book, "Daybreak in Turkey." I am quite sure that before reading it, I wrote in appreciation of the gift, but now that I have had the privilege of reading the book itself, I want to thank you again. After all the good things that have been said about it, I can hardly add anything along that line. I felt that I was reading a book that was authoritative, informing and delightfully clear. It always seems to me that to make clear an intricate or profound subject is not only a great service rendered, but a notable testimony to the ability and effectiveness of the expounder and to his mastery of his subject. This is what you have done for Turkey, so far as a situation actually so complex, and combined of so many and diverse elements, can be conceived as being in any

The Ewing children in a 1909 photograph taken in China. Marion (at right) was fourteen years old; Ellen (left), eleven; Edward (standing) was nine; and Andrew, seven.

sense simple. Your book is not only timely, but impresses me as being of permanent value, one that may be kept on hand for reference. It is not surprising that another edition has been issued very recently. If Turkey keeps up the present process, will you not be compelled to add a new chapter each year—something like an annual cyclopedia of the Ottoman Empire?

In China, affairs move quietly. There is, to be sure, the Chinese hatred for Japan, and the anti-Japanese boycott that has resulted from the exasperating conduct of Japan with regard to Manchuria. Officially, China opposes the boycott, but practically, the government can not make the people buy Japanese goods unless they choose, and I understand that, on top of the lull in trade that has continued now for a year and a half or more, this boycott is spoiling the business of Japanese firms here in Tientsin. How long this condition will continue, or what will be the remedy, it is hard to tell.

The new viceroy of this province, Tuan Tang, cares so little for the etiquette of official position that his subordinates feel that he is lowering the dignity of his office, and of theirs. These niceties of bearing are appreciated by Orientals, and it would hardly seem desirable that they should be discarded as new ideas come in. Tuan Tang is sincerely and keenly interested in education, and is much more ready to do all that is needed for the University and other schools than was his predecessor. . . .

The educational institutions of Tientsin have been developed very largely since the time of your visit here. Still, I have never ceased to regret that, at that time, neither Dr. Stanley nor I knew the city well enough to enable you to spend to the best advantage your days in Tientsin. Since then I have tried to remedy this deficit, and now when visitors come from abroad we keep them on the go. . . .

You will have heard of the death, a few days ago, of Chang Chih-tung. Apparently, this means a real loss to China. It is quite true that he was a man of the old order, a thorough Confucianist, but it is equally true that he was looking forward and moving forward. It would be of great value to China to have a number of such leaders to smooth the way of transition— men who welcome the new while yet retaining full reverence for the old.

Yuan Shih-kai, it seems likely, is to return to public life, and to be in charge of affairs in Manchuria. The situation there is delicate, and demands masterly yet tactful administration. It certainly seems a wise movement to put Yuan in charge—if indeed this is to be done.[1]

[1]It was not done. Yuan Shih-kai did not return to public life until after the revolution began in October 1911.

Charles to the Ewing Family, November 30, 1909, Hsiku, Tientsin

Dear Ewing Family:

The new railway is a topic of great interest to us, the line will connect Tientsin with a point on the Yangtze opposite Nanking. The section nearest us gives promise of being open next year. When trains are running there will be three advantages to us. First, we can reach our other Shantung Stations easier; second, we can reach our country field by train inside of four hours, instead of the present cart-ride of eight hours or a twenty-four hour trip by boat; and thirdly, the new station will be only a few minutes walk from us at Hsiku, thus increasing the importance of this location. . . .

The last week in October Bessie and I took a trip in the country. We went most of the way by boat, spending the nights at our chapels. Bessie was able to see in their homes most of the women who were in the station-class here last winter. It was a great pleasure to her to find that nearly all of them had continued their study of the Christian books and had made better progress than she had anticipated.

Charles to J. L. Barton, December 17, 1909, Hsiku, Tientsin

Dear Dr. Barton:

Speaking of the Y.M.C.A., I am reminded to write you concerning Mr. Hugh Hubbard, who was born in Sivas,[1] where his father was a missionary of our Board, graduated at Amherst in 1908, and came out here last year as athletic instructor in Chinese schools in Tientsin under the supervision of the Y.M.C.A. His agreement was for only two years, and his time will be up next June. He has practically decided to go into missionary work for life. . . . If he decides to do this . . . you may be keeping him in sight. He has made a good impression on all members of our Mission who have seen him . . . and there is every probability that the Mission, if he becomes available for our work, will ask for his appointment to North China.

Our Tientsin station will need reinforcement before that time: indeed, it is high time for me to let it be known that Mrs. Ewing is hoping to take all of our children to the United States in the early spring of 1911, and that propriety will demand that there be some family here by that time. I hold myself quite ready to remain on the field until 1914, as has been my intention, unless it seems wise to the Mission to permit me an earlier furlo [*sic*]. The departure of my family, however, at the earlier date appears to be necessary, and we shall plan to carry it out unless considerations affecting the work forbid it. . . .

At one village, the preacher has formed a Pipe Society, the members being Christians who have been in the habit of smoking, but have decided to give it up. They have handed their pipes to the preacher, and he keeps them tied up in a bunch, to show to visitors. He was planning, when I saw him last, to form a similar society among the Christians in another village in his jurisdiction. The Chinese pipes are not very injurious, as the Chinese tobacco is not strong, and the great and growing vice at the present time is cigarette smoking which is largely the result, I have to admit, of American enterprise in business. This particular preacher is anti-tobacco in any form. . . .

At Hsien Hsien inquirers have come to the chapel from a village bearing the interesting name of Wang-three-filial-sons Village. The reason for the name is quite as interesting as the name itself. When the Ming Dynasty was dethroned,[2] the plain of North China was largely depopulated by the disturbances attendant on the change of dynasty, and the new government drafted from the province of Shansi families to repeople the villages, taking (as I understand it) from each family in which there was more than one son, one of the sons, his wife and children, but allowing the brothers to decide which of them should go. In the Wang family, there were three brothers, each of whom offered to be the one to leave the ancestral home, but if the eldest went the father would be in distress. There was some equally cogent reason against the departure of the second, and the youngest could not be permitted to go alone. Accordingly, the three decided that they would all go and take their parents also, and as this was a great sacrifice for the sake of the parents and the unity of the family, the people who knew of it called the village by the name given above—Wang-three-filial-sons Village. . . .

The new railway will be a great benefit to us, as the Ching Hai chapel will be only a little more than a mile from the railway station, and the Yang Cheng chapel less than eight miles. The rails are laid already on a large part of the line, with construction trains running to the river bank below Tientsin. But the layout for the main line has only recently been finally decided for the last twenty miles at this Tientsin end. This line is to be very near to us here at Hsiku, even nearer than we supposed at first. It is to cross the highway half way between our place and the University (which, as you will remember, is a mile further from the city than our Mission premises), then cross the river [Pei Ho] to connect with the Peking railway near the city station. At that point, there will probably be a union station, but there is to be a station on our side of the river also, probably within three quarters of a mile of our place. This new railway, which is likely to be in running order early next year, must prove of great benefit, not only to our Tientsin station, but to both of the Shantung stations. Tientsin is sure to grow on the north and all around us here. This is one more justification of Dr. Stanley's wisdom in securing the property at Hsiku, for this will be a magnificent center for missionary work.

[1]Sivas is located in central Turkey.
[2]The Ming Dynasty lasted from 1368 to 1644 and was followed by the Manchu, or Ching, Dynasty.

Bessie to Myra Smith, January 21, 1910, Hsiku, Tientsin

My Dear Aunt Myra:

Since the girls' school opened Miss MacGowan and I have gained experience in Chinese ways. Our latest trial included the dismissal of two students, and because we could not understand the enormity of the offence as Chinese see it there has been a month of more or less misunderstanding between the head teacher [Miss Li] on one side and we [sic] two foreigners on the other. The offence was a matter of the girls taking a hand in their own matrimonial arrangements. This is so contrary to the old customs that the criticism made the young teacher feel that her reputation was seriously affected. From our point of view the new custom was very well guarded, as you will agree. During vacation, these two girls invited boys to their homes for a meal and visit, with the parents present. That was all we could learn, but when it developed to the point where we must lose the teacher or the pupils, we had to submit to Chinese pressure. The Chinese pastor's wife has been a great comfort to us, as she is very sympathetic for both sides and was wise and loving in all she said. The young teacher is most conscientious also, but because she is young and without experience, had less patience with our point of view. Not until last week did she speak out frankly and tell how she felt that the matter would reflect on her own character, as though she stood for flouting established custom. Now that she has talked frankly, she and Miss MacGowan are much better friends.

Charles to Myra Smith, January 29, 1910, Hsiku, Tientsin

Dear Aunt Myra:

I now for the first time have a typewriter, an Underwood, bought from Mr. [William P.] Sprague as he leaves for America. I have managed very well without one when all I had was private correspondence, but now I am secretary for two or three important societies that require many letters besides the minutes.

I suppose that Bessie has written to you of the good news we have had from Boston, authorizing us to go ahead with the building of the [permanent] girls' school plant. I already had the plans drawn and after corrections by our Mission Building Committee, we can soon make the contracts. As these buildings will be quite simple and in Chinese style, we decided against architects fees, especially as we have near us at the Government University, Mr. [Myron] Peck, an architect, . . . who is willing to give advice when needed.

As you know we are doing considerable thinking as to what course it will be best for us to pursue when Marion and perhaps Ellen, must go to America. On my brother's suggestion of some years ago, I have written asking him if his present plans are such that he could take Marion into his own home and let her go into the Boston Public schools. For myself, I have been thinking it decidedly probable that Bessie would need to go with all the children next year, and with that as a possibility I know that Bessie has written to you about finding a rent in New Haven. Even tho the Board has shortened their term of service from ten to seven years, I do not see how I can get away that soon, as there must be a family here before I can leave.

As to China in general, since Viceroy Yuan [Shih-kai] retired,[1] there is no one masterly man to take his place. To us in the West, rich in its individual leaders developed by a civilization that sets a premium on honesty and integrity in public life, this appears to be the greatest lack of China at the present time. Whether she can ever hope to have a similar wealth of her own until Christianity gives her the same high ideals and swings her into line with the new civilization is doubtful.

Whatever our work as missionaries, in all its variety, complexity and detail, we mean to make it all tend in this direction—real help to China in her struggle to "find herself" in the new conditions into which she is ushered perforce by the world with which she has come in touch. Sometimes we do the wrong thing instead of the right, but the fact remains that we (and doubtless also missionaries mother-countries similarly) are actually striving, in the best way we know, in what we see as God's way, to lead the way to personal and national salvation.

¹See chapter 4.

Charles to Edward and Ellen Ewing, March 1910, Hsiku, Tientsin

Dear Father and Mother:

Since moving out here on the river several of my country trips have been made on ice-sleds, and sometimes the family have taken pleasure outings in that way. The ice-sled has parallel runners a foot and a half apart and six feet long, with a flat covering of closely tied reeds about six feet by four and a half, on which the passengers sit. This sled is propelled by a man standing on the rear end of the runners and using a pole about five feet long and tipped with sharp iron, which he prods into the ice between his legs with strokes so vigorous that, when the ice is in good condition, progress is rapid, at least six miles an hour. On one of these trips I had a novel experience. We came to a place where a ferry kept the water free from ice for a rod or two, but instead of having to leave the sled and go on to the bank, as on former occasions, I retained my place, the sled was drawn onto a special ice-ferry, a cake of ice some twenty feet square, and ferried over to the other side, there to be drawn off again.

You speak of our "far away self-denying life." Far away from where? If we are far away from you, at least you are just as far away from us. And I fear that "self-indulgent" would be a more appropriate word that "self-denying" so far as I personally am concerned. We have many privileges here in a port city, privileges that are denied to the missionaries in the interior, but of course the same port life brings responsibilities that would be denied elsewhere also.

This month I am to have a paper before the Tientsin Missionary Association on "Self Government in the Chinese Church." . . .

We have come to be well acquainted with Mr. and Mrs. Seavey. Mr. Seavey is a professor in the law department at the University, is a thoughtful man, and, altho calling himself an agnostic, is a man of deeply religious sentiments, saying that he is more interested in religion than in anything else. Mrs. Seavey is a professionally trained elocutionist and has been in great demand as a reader, both here in Tientsin and last summer at Peitaiho. She has also been giving our girls' school some training in gymnastics and has introduced them to the delights of basketball.

On March 24th at Mr. Seavey's invitation I had the unique opportunity of speaking to the law students at the University on the work of Christian Missions. Mr. Seavey has an informal get-together every Thursday evening with any students who care to come. Of course nothing in the nature of appeal could be done nor any attempt to influence them in favor of Christianity, and yet, the very presentation of the subject afforded the opportunity to show what Christianity is, why it is a missionary religion, what is has accomplished in its work in the various countries of the world, and what it is trying to do here [in China].

Later on that same evening I went to the house of the bachelor member of their faculty, where I met for the first time our new American Consul General, Mr. [Samuel S.] Knabenshue.[1] I found that he is very much interested in family names and that he has a book that is coming out in sections in Great Britain giving the derivation and meaning of surnames. He took down my name (somewhat easier than writing his own, eh?) and the next day sent me the following information: Ewing has two derivations, one Irish and one Anglo-Saxon. (1) From the Gaelic Eaghan (pronounced Owen or Ewan). Eaghan means "noble birth" and so is generally translated Eugene. The similarity of the two words in orthography, however, is merely accidental. The name Evans is from the same word, Evan being the Welsh form and the final "s" meaning "son." (2) From the Anglo-Saxon Eawa-ing. The suffix "ing" means son or "descendant." Eawa was an Anglo-Saxon personal name. One Eawa was brother to Penda, king of Marcia. It might be that Ewing, in some cases, was a variant of Ewin.

Dr. Stanley's son [Charles Stanley, Jr.] came from Shantung last week by train. The tickets for this new line are not yet on sale, but as a train runs for the accommodation of railway men, and Stanley is acquainted with some of them, they let him on.

Last Sunday being Easter and Dr. Stanley's[2] last Sunday before leaving for America, the church was beautifully decorated with flowers from Dr. Stanley's conservatory, and five banners and a pair of scrolls, gifts from the people. The school girls gave a square of white silk with black velvet [Chinese] characters sewed on and the women gave the scrolls of light blue silk, with black characters.

After vacation Marion and Ellen will live at the Settlement with Mrs. Gordon. The boarding department of the English school is being given up, as the older boarders are leaving China. The girls will be happier for the change to an American home, especially Marion, who is very sensitive to things that are not homelike and attractive.

[1]Samuel S. Knabenshue, a native of Ohio, was a former journalist and teacher. He owed his politically appointed consular position to his work in the Republican party in his native state.

[2]Dr. Charles Stanley, Sr., an American Board missionary with more than forty years of service in China, died in the United States on November 10, 1910.

Charles to Enoch Bell, March 5, 1910, Hsiku, Tientsin

My Dear Mr. Bell:

I herewith submit the report of actual expenditures for the calendar year 1909.

Evangelistic		
(1) Preachers and student helpers	$310.76	
(2) Chapel keeping—janitor, lights, etc.	91.86	
(3) Touring	90.84	$493.46
Educational		
(1) Boarding school	280.05	
(2) Day school	49.22	329.27
Miscellaneous		
(1) Repairs on chapel property	20.94	
(2) Gate-keepers	62.31	
(3) Attending annual meeting	6.63	
(4) Incidentals	8.42	98.30
		$921.03

We have neither medical nor industrial work at the Tientsin station. I hope that these replies will help you to interest some societies to take special hold of the Tientsin field.

P.S. It should be noted that special conditions last year, including the retirement of two of the [Chinese] preachers with no one secured to take up their work brought the expenditure considerably lower on the item "Preachers" than it is ever likely to be again. From $70.00 to $100.00 should be allowed on this account.

Bessie to Myra Smith, April 1910, Hsiku, Tientsin

Dear Aunt Myra:

For two months we have had a very serious time with scarlet fever. The Chinese pastor, Mr. Chen, with his wife and little girl went out into the country by train. Riding in a hired cart from the station to the church, the driver casually remarked that his last fare had died of a bad disease. As the Chinese in general do not have any idea about contagion, he could not understand why such a remark should disturb the Chens. Very soon the little girl became ill and they hurried home, to find on the doctors' call that she had scarlet fever. We immediately moved Mr. Chen and the other three children to another room and set up a strict quarantine over Mrs. Chen and the girl. The church women said that I sat at my back window and if anyone started towards Mrs. Chen's house I would call out and send them away. That was an exaggeration but I did feel very responsible. The Chens themselves cooperated but the ignorant outside neighbors were hard to control. After the usual time for the run of the disease, with the doctor coming frequently, the day came for the farewell to Dr. Stanley and the doctor gave permission for the Chens to attend the meeting at the church. With quarantine broken, the family went back to their own home, the doctor and our foreign doctor not coming for a last visit. When Miss MacGowan saw the little sick girl she was astounded as her face was full of scabs. The result of that careless lifting of the quarantine too soon was that the other three children took the fever, the two smaller children died and a neighbor baby also. His mother had been the worst one to insist that quarantine was unnecessary. You can imagine what a sad time we have had. Of course the doctor was wrong but I cannot feel at all free from blame, for even tho I have never had scarlet fever in the home, I should have known that when the scabs are present that is the most contagious time. . . . When the first little boy died I had my first experience of Chinese wailing. I was with Mrs. Chen at the time and none of my words of comfort had any effect. After a time her husband said "that's enough," and then suddenly she was quiet. I knew it was an act to show the neighbors she was affected, because . . . she was only a step-mother.

Charles to Enoch Bell, April 7, 1910, Hsiku, Tientsin

Dear Mr. Bell:

As we anticipated, the departure of Dr. Stanley reemphasizes our need of another preaching missionary here at Tientsin, and all the more since it seems probable that after his return he will be with his son in Shantung instead of here. The need is still further emphasized by the possibility, not to say the likelihood, that Mrs. Ewing must take our children to America next year—in which case it will be imperative that we have another family in this station.

I think that I have written to you or to Dr. Barton of the advisability of Mrs. Ewing's going to the United States with all of the children next year, but I ought to write more definitely than I have done, in order that I may have advice from you as well as from the Mission. Let me state the case.

My eldest daughter [Marion] will be 15 in May of this year, will have completed the regular course in the Tientsin School, where she has been studying, probably next December, and must certainly go home for further study early next year. As the boarding department of the Tientsin School has now been discontinued, we are obliged to find board for both of our girls outside of the school, since the distance from home is too great for them to go back and forth every day, and of course we can not tell whether we can make satisfactory arrangements permanently. Furthermore it would be better for both girls to get into American school life as soon as possible, and it looks now as if we may be forced to send both home next year. If so, it is hardly likely that we can make any such arrangements for them there that they can be away from their mother. This might be possible for the elder, but hardly for the younger [Ellen, age 11], unless something unexpected turns up. Furthermore, we have two boys younger than the girls, one of whom is now 9 [Edward] and the other nearly 8 [Andrew]. They have been studying with their mother until now, but they need the discipline of regular school life, and yet are too young—the younger one, at any rate—to be away from home. I write all this, not because our problem is different from that faced by many missionaries at one time or another, but in order to indicate the reasons, the combination of reasons, why it looks as if we must make some radical change next year, not for the sake of one only of the children, but on account of all four, and in order that I may ask if you have any advice to give from the experience of the past. We are informed of the good provision made for missionaries and their children at Auburndale [Massachusetts], and are bearing that in mind as a possible aid, but it does not seem that, even with such provision, we ought to send all four of the children away from home at once without one of the parents. If Mrs. Ewing and the children do go home, they are likely to settle in New Haven, but it may be well for me to ask now whether, in case it should be desired, arrangement can be made for a whole family at Auburndale, and at what rates. According to the newly announced rule of the Board, my furlo would naturally come next year, so that we might all go home together, but the Mission is so short-handed that I see no way in which I can be spared for several years yet. If I remain at Tientsin, I must stay until some one is ready to relieve me, and even if we get a new man this year, he must not have the work thrust upon him earlier that the spring of 1913.

While I am quite aware that the Board follows the policy of spending extra money for the education of missionaries' children, if it is possible thereby for the parents to remain on the field, it is only fair that I should call attention to the considerable expense that is likely to be incurred if our four children are away at school with an extra school allowance of $100 for the eldest and $150 for each of the other three, $550 annually. We are calling for $250 now for the two girls. If Mrs. Ewing takes all the children to America, while it may be necessary for me to apply to the Board for some aid beyond my salary on account of renting a house, the financial saving would certainly be considerable. We are taking all of these things into account, shall counsel with the Mission and hope for your advice.

Charles to Edward C. Ewing, June 19, 1910, Hsiku, Tientsin

Dear Father:

On May 19th I was asked to address the Thursday evening audience at the Y.M.C.A. on the subject of Halley's Comet.[1] As I am nothing of an astronomer, this seemed to me rather a peculiar idea, and I had to laugh at myself for setting up as an authority to give "authentic information," as the advertisement of the lecture announced. However, I set myself to studying up the subject, with the result that it became very interesting to me, and I think also to the people who heard the address. I repeated it twice, once to the boys' school and again to the girls. Up to that time none of us here had seen the comet, but at the last speech I described what I was quite sure was it, and each day made it clearer that my suspicion was correct as to the location of the distant visitor. It has been disappointingly faint, but I judge that those who were fortunate enough to see it before it passed the line of earth and sun, saw it more clearly. . . .

After careful consideration some new steps were taken [at the annual Mission Conference] which will mean great advance for the church in China. This involved the relations between the missionaries and the Chinese leaders. In the first place we wish to transpose the idea of helper and helped: the Chinese are not helpers of the missionary, they are to be in charge of the churches, schools, hospitals, [while] the missionary holds himself as their assistant where assistance is needed. It follows that the Church members are not to look to the missionary for aid and advice but to the Chinese preacher and that the missionary must be careful not to infringe on such authority. . . . the missionary will entertain no direct appeals, which will mean a large gain for the self-respect of the Chinese Church and its leaders. This will also aid towards self-support, but since that cannot come all at once, the foreign funds will be available in areas that the Chinese designate as most worthy. The missionary will be left to devote himself largely to general oversight: his position will be no sinecure, but he will be relieved from many details that can be better managed by the Chinese. This new understanding is part of our hope.

[1]Halley's Comet approaches the earth every seventy-six years, and just as in 1910, it was again visible to the naked eye in 1986.

Bessie to Myra Smith, July 4, 1910, Peitaiho

Dear Aunt Myra:

The two hundred Americans who are here this summer celebrated this day by a baseball game, aquatic athletics and tea at the American Legation summer house. . . .

In June the Mission voted to ask the Board [in Boston] to allow me to take the children home in the Spring and they never refuse such a request. We have not seen our way clear to decide in any other way. If you think our coming to New Haven is not feasible, there is another way. In Auburndale, Massachusetts [there] is a Missionary Home for children and also furnished houses to rent to families at $25.00 a month. I suppose that is quite reasonable. If you can find a New Haven rent for that, and I can have my sister's old furniture, I think I could manage, even though my full income from the Board for the five of us will be only $100.00 a month. I know you all dread my settling at home without Charles, but he cannot leave for two or perhaps three years yet, and we don't see how we can delay the boys' better education so long. I am sure you would not advise our sending them to the English school in Chefoo, when they could come home [to Tientsin] only twice a year. I am very well and though the new life will be hard for me at first, I shall have to learn.

I inclose the program given by our two glee clubs, without having practised together, the first time in China when boys and girls appeared together.[1] [The program notes were entirely in Chinese, but the songs included "Carry Me Back to Old Virginny," "Sweet and Low," "Schneider's Band," "Union College Hymn," "Drink to Me Only with Thine Eyes," "Gloria," and "China Thy Land I Love."]

[1]There is no explanation as to how Bessie made this determination.

Charles to the Ewing Family, August 11, 1910, Peitaiho

Dear Ewing Family:

On July 24, at our Tientsin City Church, we held a special meeting for business. I explained to the members the meaning of Congregationalism, that the authority for all actions is with the whole membership not with the pastor, that up to the present the practise had been different because the missionaries had been treating them as a parent treats his small children, deciding things for them, but that the time had come to be on their own and to take over the responsibility of self-management. There were enough who had this point of view to lead the others to accept this task. The first new responsibility was the appointment of two committees who would investigate charges against some of the teachers and preachers, now retired from active work, and try to make peace. I had become convinced that these personal difficulties were such that the foreigner could not well unravel.

The greatest change was in the matter of self-support. For a year we have had no settled pastor in that church. We knew that there was a movement on foot to start an independent Chinese church in Tientsin and that Mr. Chang Po Ling was the chairman to make plans. I asked our members whether they would prefer to go into this new effort ENMASSE instead of trying a separate self-supporting unit, and whether or not they would like to include the members at Hsiku. That would mean that hereafter there would be no American Board church in Tientsin. That day the members voted unanimously in the affirmative. Then I said that the Board on our recommendation would offer to the new organization the free use of the city premises for five years, for both church meetings and for the school.

As if this were not enough good for one day, I had a request from Mr. Chang to call on him that evening. We sat in his beautiful garden beside the lotus pool and talked for an hour. When Mr. Chang felt sure that our offer had no strings attached but that the new church would be really independent, he said very decidedly that he would go into the movement and assure its success. He also said that he was ready to give not less that $100 a year, more if necessary, tho he did not think it well for any one man to give too large a share. . . . After the many difficult problems that we have been facing for many months you can perhaps form some idea of the joy in my heart that evening. It seemed too good to be true.

Charles to the Ewing Family, September 7, 1910, Hsiku Tientsin

Dear Ewing Family:

The new church is perfecting its plans and a fine pastor has been invited. After much discussion and the study of various forms of church polity and of requirements for membership the decision was stated in one sentence, as follows: "Any one may join this church who proposes to live his life according to the principles of Jesus Christ."

The members have subscribed $1200 for the first year and are paying their pastor a larger salary than has as yet been paid to any of the Chinese preachers in this part of the country. All of this is being done with the utmost good feeling between the Chinese Church and the Mission, and I hope without any friction with other Mission churches. Our church in Peking is also assuming self-support and self-management. In these two cities this is possible because here are Christian Chinese with larger incomes than elsewhere, who are glad to support such a church but would not give largely to a "foreign church."

Charles to the Ewing Family, September 25, 1910, Shanghai

Dear Ewing Family:

I was sent here as a delegate from the North to consult with others on the advisability of opening an undenominational [*sic*] Bible Teachers' Training School. Dr. White[1] was at Peitaiho [this summer] representing such a school from New York, and he agreed to provide expenses for this, so that is why I get the trip gratis. . . . Another pleasure of my being a delegate to Shanghai was a [chance to] visit Nanking. There were three of us who were guests of the Corys. Mrs. Cory met us at the [train] station which is three miles from their house, at the Disciples Mission. The road was well macadamized, and led past bamboo groves, some of them lighted by electric lights shining thru from beyond and producing a most beautiful effect. . . .

The next morning, by arising at five o'clock, we went to see the Ming Tombs before breakfast, going by carriage and donkey and returning in time for a late breakfast. Then we visited various Mission schools. Our plans in Shanghai hope to unite some of these [schools], thus wiping out denominational lines in education.

[1]Wilbert Webster White was a Presbyterian minister from Ashland, Ohio, who had established a Bible teachers training school in New York.

Marion Ewing's account of a trip into the interior of China, at age fifteen, Autumn 1910

I went with Dr. Edith Tallman from Tientsin to Lintsing Chow [Shantung], about as far as from New Haven to Philadelphia. . . . Dr. Tallman and I took rickshaws to the river where we boarded a little launch. After going several miles in the launch we made connections with Teh Chow [Shantung]. We were very much interested in the new stations that were being built all along the [rail] road. No two were alike, they were of red and gray brick, but all had the most graceful curves to their roofs, somewhat resembling Mohammedan mosques.

When we arrived in Teh Chow in the late P.M. we found a cart waiting for us, sent by a friend of our Mission, a wealthy Mohammedan, the owner of the bank and of several fine restaurants. We spent that night in our Mission compound. I might as well stop here and tell what a nice Chinese place is like. The big front gate, the cart entrance, was right on the street, and the first court which we entered was the stable. The court immediately back of that was the men's court, in this case having a side court for the boys' school, and the last court was the women's. Of course we stayed there, and it was one of the most homelike I have ever been in. . . . outside the walls was a pretty little pond, which we could see from the back window of our room.

We had scarcely settled ourselves when a servant from the restaurant came in with a steaming hot meal all ready for us. I never tasted anything so delicious as that feast, whether in America or in China. Later we received a message from our host inviting us to visit his wife the next day. When we made the call we were received by two or three of his wives, I'm sure I don't know how many he had.

[The next day] we were up bright and early again, leaving behind anything as progressive as trains, and now proceeded in a buckboard. This was built on special order for the missionaries with two seats and springs, and the wheels set to fit the same ruts as those of the Chinese cart, for all the country roads are simply two deep ruts. This [buckboard] was drawn by four mules.

All the morning we passed thru fields where the farmers were engaged in pulling peanuts and sifting them to remove the sandy soil, or in picking cotton. The Chinese do not live in farm houses several miles apart, but in little villages of fifty or a few hundred families, and go out to their fields every day. It was just the season for ripe dates so we gathered a great many, but altho they are excellent eating, they are very hard to digest. . . . we were obliged to stay over . . . to tell the truth, because I had eaten too many dates.

[A few days later] we went to an inn where foreigners were in the habit of going, but all the carter's coaxing and scolding were in vain—the innkeeper would not open his gate. . . . We made our way to another inn, where the innkeeper was afraid of foreigners. He received us for fear of what would happen if he didn't. This inn was very poor. We were led to a small mud room,[1] about 10 by 10, half of which was a raised platform, which the Chinese use as a bed. We set up on this our cot beds and spread on our bedding, as no one wants to use anothers. . . . I am mighty glad I had this opportunity as otherwise I would never know that there were such places.

[1] A mud room is built of sun-hardened mud and straw bricks.

Charles to the Ewing Family, December 1, 1910, Hsiku, Tientsin

Dear Ewing Family:

On the steamer up from Shanghai, one of my fellow passengers was a Chinese who was just returning to his home in Tientsin after spending five years in the United States. I had some very delightful talks with him, and found him very favorably disposed towards Christianity. He said that not more than one in fifty of the Chinese students in America is a Christian, that the majority of them are opposed to such an extent that they will not really give it a fair hearing, that a few take no interest whatever in it, and that a very considerable number have become persuaded that Christianity is the great hope for China, altho they themselves are not Christians. He said definitely that he himself was of this class, but that he thought it very likely that he should become a Christian.

I must tell you of three very different events connected with our students. In October some half dozen went to Nanking to take part in the FIRST national athletic meet. One of them won two second prizes. In November at our Tungchow College the student body revolted over poor food and other irritations and refused to attend classes. All who did not apologize and return promptly were suspended for a week, some for two weeks, while the leaders were expelled, as it was found that a few such had coerced the others. . . . I hope that nothing [further] will alienate them in any way, for students are very easily offended if they feel that they are not fully and sympathetically appreciated.

. . . I was in Peking just in time for the opening of a new form of work, which Miss Russell and Mrs. Ament [the widow of Dr. William Ament] have planned to conserve the influence they have already gained over ladies of official and literary families. They have fitted out a building in the best Chinese style, offering class work which is likely to appeal to the modern Chinese women of culture.

. . . I have not any excess of sentiment, family or other, but the conserving of the natural relationships [in a family] appears to me to be one of the not-too-many things that we retain in the twentieth century and in the American atmosphere . . . [and] there is good in family pride that perhaps in some countries is carried to an extreme. We who are younger possibly value this less than our parents, but I am sure that it is one of the things that is to be an abiding element of healthfulness in our memories. . . . China has that large "family" sense and it may be that we in the West have too much lost that idea.

Charles to Edward and Ellen Ewing, February 12, 1911, Hsiku, Tientsin

Dear Father and Mother:

I must write particularly about the plague. It would not be strange if you were to feel some apprehension as it is in an unusually virulent form right here where we live. The plague is the result of the work of a microbe which may attack the human organism in three different ways. The usual kind, which I suppose has been rife in India for years, affects the glands and is usually fatal. A second form strikes the blood, and the third affects the lungs. The first form has been in Manchuria in recent years, but by vigorous control by the Chinese government conducted under the guidance of the missionary doctors, with armed escorts, it was checked. This year it began in the third form, the pneumonic. This is transmitted by the breath and has therefore quickly become epidemic wherever the most stringent measures have not been taken to segregate even the "contact cases."

As the same microbe produces all three kinds, all forms may result from this one. The microbe is easily carried by rats, and fleas carry it from rats to people. At present the flea season has not begun, and will not for some three weeks yet. But the pneumonic plague can be readily carried, in some way, into the blood. The poison is extremely virulent and death ensues in a day or two. So far as I have heard, no cure is known for the disease in any of its forms. The surest preventive measures are to keep away from contact with plague cases and from rats and fleas, and to keep clean and to be inoculated with a vaccine that has been in use in India and elsewhere. Even tho it is not absolutely sure how effective this vaccine is, we are using all these measures, not only for ourselves but also for the Chinese who are in our service or connected with us in anyway. At the present time we are living, not exactly in a state of siege, but with our compound gates locked and orders that ingress and egress be only under strict oversight. We and our servants use medicated masks when we go out, and all have been inoculated. The infection in Tientsin is the worst just close to us, with eleven deaths in the last ten days. In view of these conditions it is decided that Bessie and the children are to start for America in March, instead of waiting until June as we had planned. . . .

As for myself I am not much susceptible to flea bites, and can easily protect myself from danger. Bessie and some of the children are susceptible, and I shall feel relieved to have them not here. Probably they will leave here on March 5, going first to Japan, then from there via Honolulu and San Francisco, reaching home before Easter. . . .

Our schools are not being opened for the new semester, tho some pupils are here. Several Christian families have moved on to the place including those of the men employed by us all. Taken all together we have so much of a colony, and are so segregated that we are planning to avail ourselves of the unusual opportunity for study, and have classes for men, women, kindergartners, school boys, and school girls. Thus we may be able to profit by our "scare," if it can be so called.

Charles to J. L. Barton, February 14, 1911, Hsiku, Tientsin

Dear Dr. Barton:

[E]ver since last summer when I must have overdone without being aware of it at the time, I have not been in condition to do anything more than was absolutely demanded by the conditions here. . . . Altho I am even yet very easily tired, and am obliged to content myself with a minimum of work that brings me into nervous touch with people, I feel that I am on the up grade; however, I shall not expect to be quite my vigorous self again until after a summer free from much responsibility, which I expect to get by being in some quiet place.

. . . You know already of the turning over of our city work to the Chinese Church. This was followed by the meeting of our local Congregational Association, when we all came to a clearer understanding than ever before that the missionary would not retain any claim of authority over Church affairs except where his loyalty to the givers of funds bound him. . . .

Some of the members wished to decide the location of preachers by rotation, to which I objected, but there was not real disagreement, only a temporary question as to meaning. This and the whole trend of affairs gives promise that, tho we may not always agree in opinions, the Chinese are ready to take over very much of the burden and responsibility of the work. . . .

The word concerning Dr. Stanley's death came as a great blow to the Church here and of course, to me as a surprise also, altho I find that many others had thought of him as so feeble that they did not expect to see him here again. We have more than ever before our need of reinforcement, and of course we are looking forward with eagerness to the coming of Mr. and Mrs. Chandler, who are so far as it is possible to say beforehand, to be located here.

You will have heard thru the newspapers of the ravages of the plague, not only in Manchuria, but also this side of the Great Wall. Dr. Young is the only member of our Mission who has been able to volunteer for service in the midst of the stricken region. Here in Tientsin, so far, the worst of the plague has been in the village of Hsiku, close to our back gate. Eleven deaths have been in this village in ten days, but the last three days have shown so great an improvement that no new cases whatever have been reported. The people in our compound, together with a few Christians who are near neighbors, have been inoculated, as have we foreigners, and in two or three days more, when the period demanding special care after inoculation is past, we shall feel more free to move about. For the present we are keeping ourselves in moderate quarantine, with the back gate locked and the front gate under careful supervision.

. . . In the present time of epidemic, we realize again the importance of having a doctor here. We feel no particular anxiety for ourselves, for the present at any rate, but if we had a doctor, we might be able to open our schools, which we do not feel like taking the responsibility of doing without a doctor on the place or within easy call. . . . We distinctly desire to start this [medical] work as a part of our general scheme of putting things into the hands of the Chinese, and with no intention of asking any further financial support than we now ask for our own medical allowance from year to year.

Ellen Ewing's account of leaving Tientsin, at age eleven, March 1911

[T]he last of February and the first of March were days of excitement. Papa packed while the rest of us turned the house topsy-turvy to lay things out for him to pack. There were so many things that we would have to leave behind. Marion gave away her big doll. I gave away my doll house. We gave away a whole lot of books to the children of the British army officers in Tientsin. At last March 5, the day for the starting came. It was Sunday, but never have I experienced one more unlike the Sabbath. The trunks were all packed and we were ready to go. The house was crowded with the Chinese Christians who had come to bid us goodbye and load us with parting gifts [at] the last minute.

At last we got into our rikshaws and rode to the gate. There we stopped, while the school boys and girls sang "God Be With You Till We Meet Again." Many of the women were crying and some of the men could hardly keep their tears back. Then we rode out of our gate, perhaps NEVER to enter it again.

Charles to Bessie, March 5, 1911, 4:45 P.M., Hsiku, Tientsin

My Dearest Bessie:

In spite of the loneliness—for it was lonely to come back to the house and find it empty and know that it never can be as it has been, still I am glad that you all can go, and glad that I could see you off with so promising a start. I am sending this hoping to catch you at Yokohama.

Bessie to the Ewing Family, March 1911, On Board the S.S. *Persia*

Dear Ewing Family:

As we sat on the deck of the river launch, knowing that there were only a few minutes before separation [from Charles and China] my courage almost gave out. . . .

The ice in the river was broken up but our steamer had to push hard against the huge blocks. . . .

On the Japanese steamer [S.S. *Yeiko Maru*] we were almost the only first class passengers and the captain gave us extra favors during the five days to Yokohama. Boarding the Pacific Mail liner the "Persia," the great surprise was when a jolly man almost ran into our boys and said "Boys, what do you think of that says Hooley Ann?" This was Captain [Thomas S.] Baldwin of flying fame. He had been in Japan for eight months for government conferences and for [flying] exhibitions. . . . As there was only one other family of children on the "Persia" our four had almost undivided attention [from Captain Baldwin].

Charles to Bessie, March 11, 1911, Hsiku, Tientsin

My Dear Bessie:

Since you left things have been happening enough to keep me from brooding much on my loneliness, which otherwise might be quite oppressive. . . . It is evident that the plague is under control, but I do not regret that you have left. A society has been formed by Chinese here in Tientsin to fight recurrence and a conference of experts has been called to meet in Mukden in April, to make an exhaustive study of the recent epidemic, with the hope that not only may preventive measures be taken, but possibly that a cure may be found. The Chinese are awake to the seriousness of this plague and are doing all that the most hopeful could have expected . . . would have been possible even so recently as five years ago. I hope these efforts will be widely publicized so that the world will be convinced of China's sincerity in the matter.

Charles to Bessie, August 1911, Shansi Province

My Dear Bessie:

My summer here in Shansi[1] is proving delightful, not only because of the place and because I like the people but still more because they have let me alone and allowed me to do as I chose—which sometimes meant doing nothing and sometimes quietly reading. There is a good tennis court, surrounded by trees . . . so that it is quite well shaded for playing in the latter part of the afternoon.

We are among the hills of loess, but with no high mountains in sight. There is a range, not very high, along the west side of the plain, and it is among the foothills . . . [where] I am. We are surrounded by lower hills that shut out the view except in the direction to the southeast. There down the valley and across the plain we can see the real mountains.

[A]fter a month at our station in Fenchow [Shansi] I came to the summer resort here. The houses we use are all Chinese buildings, formerly used as mills. The valley is full of such mills, only a few hundred yards apart, and the bed of the stream is used as a road for carts bringing wheat to be ground. As this is the only water-power in all this region, the mills are kept quite busily at work. The Mission bought two of these mills in the days when more opium was raised than wheat. Now that the raising of opium is absolutely stamped out over the entire province of Shansi, the mills are busy again. These two houses are on opposite sides of the stream, a stream that is generally not more than five feet across. However the bed of the stream is some fifteen yards across, with a dam opposite us on which we can walk across. But when the rains come this dam is washed away. This dam was carried away the day before I arrived, was rebuilt two days later of stones and sand—but was washed out again this week. . . .

I must tell you about the trees in this place. There are no forests, but beside each house there are clumps of tall sentinel poplars (50 to 70 feet)— quite unlike anything in Chihli province, tho they go by the same Chinese name as the mysterious aspen with the whispering leaves that we have there. At one of the houses, the trees afford such shade that hammocks are hung, while studying is done at tables set amidst the trees, and Sunday meetings are held out of doors. . . .

I have often spoken of the repression of growing opium in this province. It is really 100% effective because the penalties are severe. One wealthy man thought he was safe to grow a little in a remote mountain solitude, but his plot was found and as a result the crop was destroyed, all his land and property was confiscated and he had to flee the province, if found he might be beheaded. The explanation for this severity is that the new government has decided that the opium grower is to be treated as an enemy to the community, on the par with a murderer, and not merely an ordinary murderer, but as one who would introduce murder on the wholesale, since it is now recognized that opium is indeed a murderous weapon to use.

One day a few of us went on a picnic to the head of the valley, four miles from here. We had a donkey for the things. . . . It is a beautiful walk, sometimes in the bed of the brook, sometimes on the sides of the hills that border the brook, sometimes passing thru clumps of trees. At the end, we reached a temple, where there is the spring that gives rise to this brook and which has never failed. This spring is said to have been opened by a horse which in its extreme thirst, pawed in the stone until the water burst out, and the print of the hoof, deep in the stone around the well-like apertures above the spring are to be seen. We spent the day here, in hammocks, or reclining against trees.

[1]This was Charles's first trip to Shansi, scene of the worst Boxer excesses against foreigners, after twelve years in China.

Charles to Bessie, September 1911, Hsiku, Tientsin

Dearest Bessie:

I had a terrible time getting away from our mountain resort [in Shansi] to the city of Taiyuan.[1] The roads after the rains were worse than I had anticipated. The first day we were stuck in the mud for two hours. The second day we were stuck for over an hour and to make up the time I decided to travel in the evening. But when we were within a mile of the inn, at about ten o'clock, we stuck in the mud a third time. The carter suggested that he stay by the stuff while I went for help. This I tried but no one answered me at the inn. Then the carter went to a farm house, found and swiped a shovel, but still could not dislodge the cart. After all these failures, the carter acceded to my first plan which was that he take the animals and go to the inn while I stayed by the cart. Finally at one o'clock in the morning he went off, I set up my army cot on the raised path beside the road, the only dry place at hand—and I slept, looking up at the stars overhead. I was awakened by two small showers, but stayed out. . . .

¹Taiyuan was the scene of fighting and a massacre of Manchus in October 1911.

Charles to Bessie, October 1911, Hsiku, Tientsin

My Dear Bessie:

The national revolution is gaining tho no open break yet in the North. Most of the people seem to be waiting to see which way to jump in order to be on the winning side. Quite Chinese isn't it? How can you blame them? They are peaceful and naturally inclined to back up whatever may be the dominant power at the time. I do not even feel certain what is the sympathy of most foreigners, but it is noteworthy that the foreign consuls and other officials have been strictly neutral, when they would not be unjustifiable if they were to help the existing government.

Charles to the Ewing Family, October 29, 1911, Hsiku, Tientsin

Dear Ewing Family:

Again China is in the midst of stirring times. You will know so much more and later news before you receive this that the only value of my report will be the throwing into the light my individual point of view as it is at the present time. Affairs are developing rapidly from day to day, and we never know what a day may bring forth.

The revolutionists have been quietly busy for some years. Their first noticeable appearance, so as to attract much attention, was something like four years ago. At that time, there was quite a stir in this part of the empire, and it was reported that the revolutionists were organizing everywhere. At the time when the educational commission was about to start for America, bomb-throwing at the Peking railway station was attributed to them. On that account, care has since been taken to guard against any similar outbreak in this section of China, and very little has been heard of the organization. There can be no doubt, however, that it has been secretly organizing and disseminating its anti-Manchu doctrine, waiting only for a favorable time to put its campaign into effect. Aside from that continual propaganda, there is little evidence of any special preparation for an outbreak at the present time. This has been brought about rather by the concurrence of several causes that have served to irritate the people, especially in Central China, where as a matter of fact you know that the disturbance has begun.

It may be that you are already quite well aware of the genesis of the present movement, as I find that the home papers were devoting much attention to the matter even before we here thought that it might amount to as much as now seems likely. One of these causes was evident especially in the province of Szechwan, the largest in area and also in population of any of the provinces of China, but as this had much to do with the railway policy of the central government, it affected also the people in the province of Hupeh, from which the proposed railway to Szechwan was to run. To begin with, the people did not like the idea of the immense foreign loan that was negotiated a few months ago, as there is a great and widespread unwillingness to become more deeply indebted to other nations. Then, in the middle of the summer, the government issued a statement as to its policy for nationalizing the railways of the whole country, so that all trunk lines should be government enterprises from which even Chinese private capital would be excluded. As plans were already well under way for the construction of some such trunk lines with private capital, this announcement raised a storm of criticism. The brunt of this criticism fell, from the first, on one man, Mr. Sheng.[1] He is a man who was formerly the Customs Taotai at Tientsin, and he was well liked by the foreigners, but he certainly has succeeded in making himself thoroly unpopular with the mass of the Chinese. What the facts of the case are I do not know, but I suspect that he was too good a servant of the Manchu rulers to win approval from the Chinese. During the early summer also, and indeed even earlier than that, the unusual excess of floods in the Yangtze valley threw multitudes out of work, out of their homes, and left them with insufficient food and no prospect of any improvement in conditions. They felt, as the people in the south of France felt a year or two ago, that the government ought to come to their aid, and when the viceroy, who in most provinces is somewhat of an autocrat, failed to do this, the people began to take a threatening attitude.

All the time, seething underneath thru all southern and much of central China, is the hatred towards the Manchus—of which I may write further after a little. When affairs in the province of Hupeh came to such a pass that the imperial soldiers showed signs of definite insubordination, the viceroy acted strongly, if not wisely, in ordering the execution of several of the soldiers, for this act he was highly commended by imperial edict, but within a few days the government was obliged, as a direct result of this commended act, to dismiss him from office with severe blame for not controlling affairs in his province. This attitude of the government is nothing new, in 1900, several men at different times had to occupy the position of scapegoat for the folly of the imperial government itself. Just now, within the last few days, Commissioner Sheng [Hsuan-huai], of whom I have already written, has been dismissed as being the cause of all the present turmoil, when probably he was only too efficient a servant of the government. It was the action of the Hupeh viceroy in executing the rebellious soldiers that finally led to the immediate outbreak at Wuchang, the capital of the province, and in this outbreak the leaders were of the revolutionary party, while much of their strength came from the readiness of the army to follow their lead. Accordingly, while there had not been such special preparation for this outbreak as there would have been had it not been precipitated by circumstances as they arose, and while there is not evidence of any particularly strong leadership, the revolutionists find everything going their way.

That feature which makes such a condition possible is the attitude of the people toward the Manchu rulers. It must be understood that the Chinese are subjects of an alien race, not citizens under a government of their own. For the Manchus, while sprung from the same original stock, were as much a different race as would be two different peoples of Europe from each other. Moreover, the Chinese people, as is now better known than before recent authoritative utterances[2] of men who have known them well, are essentially of a democratic spirit and temper. They are not averse to having other people do the actual work of running the government, but they are quite insistent that affairs that concern them shall be done in a way that commends itself to them. So long as the Manchus conducted the government to the pleasing of the intelligent among the people, there was less objection. But as the people have come to be better and more widely informed on governmental affairs, and as they have begun to have some hope of self-government, and as they have come to realize more and more how the officials were unjustly enriching themselves at the expense of the people, while the imperial government is never strong in anything better than the machinations of political scheming, the anti-Manchu sentiment has grown apace. The Chinese can never have loved the Manchus as their rulers, because from the first introduction of this Manchu dynasty the entire race of Manchus has drawn its support from the government, being all pensioners (tho like most pensioners under the necessity of eking out existence in a desultory way by some trade or occupation) and thus appearing to the Chinese themselves to be battening at their expense, who paid the taxes. In Peking, the Manchus form so large a part of the population that they are taken as part of the status quo and are not only tolerated as they are not in other parts of the empire, but do not appear to offend the Chinese who live alongside of them. Elsewhere in this part of China, where the Manchu government is nearer at hand and its power more in evidence than further from Peking, while the whole idea of a favored race supported by the taxes of the

Chinese as a subject race is always highly distasteful to the people, there are no particular signs of hatred. But in the southern part of the country, and I judge also in the western and central parts, the anti-Manchu feeling is and probably always has been one that rose to the height of cordial hatred. It is this fact that has made the populace of most of the empire ready at any favorable time to fall in with any movement that gave promise of putting an end to the present dynasty. Heretofore, the government has always been able to put down every rebellion that has arisen, and the history of these centuries gives many precedents to lead to the prediction that this uprising will meet a similar fate. But on the other hand, this is definitely and openly intended to be against the Manchus. It is evident that, even here in North China, the almost unanimous sentiment of the people is with the revolutionists and against the government. I have been surprised to find how ready the Chinese are, in private conversation when they do not suspect that any one will make trouble for them, to admit where their sympathies are. As one prominent man said: I have wondered at the favor shown by the people to the revolution, until I questioned myself and discovered that my heart was with the people rather than with the rulers. And why not?

So far as I can learn, while it is not the part of foreigners to take sides in such a struggle, and while the official representatives of foreign governments are scrupulously careful, for the most part, to hold an entirely neutral position, it is not difficult for one to form the opinion that the sympathies of foreigners resident in China are also with the people and so against the government. In the struggle, both sides are using every precaution to avoid any conflict whatever with foreigners or foreign governments. For if there is one thing that China desires above another, it is that there shall not be another opportunity for any other nation to step in and dictate to them. For this reason, neither the foreigners resident in China nor the Chinese members of Christian Churches have anything to fear as such. It is hoped that only combatants may be in any way involved, and the only fear is that the roughs may take advantage of disturbed conditions to attempt to inaugurate mob rule. In Tientsin, some of the most representative public minded citizens are taking steps to guard against exactly this contingency. They evidently fear that, if conditions become troubled here, the police force of the city will become demoralized, so that, if they do not join the revolutionary army, they may at least decamp and leave the whole city without adequate protection, and with this in mind, they are forming a society with the object of standing ready to assure safety to the city in case of an emergency. You may think me an enthusiast for Tientsin, but I do not know of any other city in China where the leading citizens have enough public sentiment and enough wisdom in initiative to undertake such wise prevision. It promises to relieve us here of all fear as to safety in Tientsin. In other parts of China, the military authorities on both sides will without doubt do all in their power to protect foreigners, so great is the contrast between the present movement to that of 1900. But there are certain places where fighting is very likely to take place. Evidently the Chinese think that Peking is such a place, as the express trains from there to Tientsin are crowded with people, many of them of the highest class, who are deeming it wise to get away. Some of these will go on beyond Tientsin, but so many of them are planning to remain at Tientsin that even now all houses that are for rent are taken and all inns crowded, while many are left behind at Peking, unable to get a place on each train as it leaves. About two weeks ago, it was reported in one of the Tientsin daily papers that the little emperor had taken refuge in Tientsin, this was generally regarded as a fake, but I am told now that it is very generally believed by people in the foreign concessions that the emperor is actually living in one of the finest houses in the British concession, a house that was fitted up several years ago for official use for parties . . . which some thought meant the imperial family in case they might wish to use it.

Already it is rumored that the revolutionaries are busy in Tientsin and if it is not true now, it is easy to suppose that it will be true before long. One reason why one feels somewhat hesitant about forming either an opinion or a wish with regard to the outcome of the outbreak is that it is not yet clear that the revolutionists have either the power to succeed unitedly in their endeavor or the ability to set up any government that would be better than the present one. To this, however, some reply that no government could well be more inefficient and weak and unwise. We shall know more by the time that you read what I am writing now.

[1]Sheng Hsuan-huai was minister of posts and communications in 1911. He was responsible for negotiating a railway loan with a foreign consortium and also with nationalizing the Chinese trunk railroads.

[2]Charles does not cite the authoritative sources he refers to. However, he may be referring to the numerous books and periodicals that were written by persons with considerable experience with the Chinese in China during the decade following the Boxer Uprising.

Charles to Bessie, November 1911, Hsiku, Tientsin

My Dear Bessie:

I suppose your newspapers are overdoing the matter of reporting on the activities of the revolutionists, and probably making out that there is grave danger for the lives of foreign residents in China. We ourselves see no reason for such apprehension. So great and marked is the contrast to 1900 that, instead of the legations refusing to believe the reports of serious conditions that come in thru the foreigners resident in the interior, it is the legations and consulates (at least the American) that have the scare, while the rest of us are without fear. Everywhere in the North, the Chinese officials are taking extra precautions, to assure the missionaries of their cordial protection. The only thing to fear is the uprising of the roughs in the interim of a change of power.

In Paoting a guard of three soldiers was sent to our place and the head of the bank asked Mr. [James] McCann to allow him to store silver at our place. He knows that a banker is in more danger than the missionaries.

Charles to Bessie, November 5, 1911, Hsiku, Tientsin

My Dear Bessie:

At the urgent request of our American consul our ladies went to the Settlement, and we dismissed our girls' school and gave permission for the boys to go home if they wished. The reason for this sudden flitting was that the consul had received formal notice from the revolutionary leaders that they would take over the government at Tientsin within two days at the latest. Three days later it was learned that the revolutionaries decided not to fight for Tientsin, but to try to negotiate for a peaceful turnover, so the consul authorized the return of our [missionary] ladies. If there does prove to be fighting here, I have offered our church building to the Red Cross Society. This is a most intensely interesting time, evidently the grandest yet in Chinese history. The future is big with blessing and every friend of China must recognize the present as the best opening and promise there has yet been for the complete emergence of the new China. All missionaries must be praying for the welfare of the nation. Indeed, I hope that you have not felt so concerned for my safety that you have prayed for that more than for China.

Charles to J. L. Barton, November 6, 1911, Hsiku, Tientsin

Dear Dr. Barton:

It is so very long since I have written to you or to any one at the Board rooms that I might perhaps as well start in without any apology, but I do want to give you a word or two of explanation. Since August of 1910, my health has been such as to make it imperative that I do as little work as possible; this will serve to explain, I hope, both why I have written no letters to the Board for many months and why I have done very little active missionary work. Not long ago I was speaking with one of the senior missionaries of the M.E. [Methodist Episcopal] Mission, and saying that I felt rather ashamed to call myself a missionary and still do so little work, but he replied, Don't ruin your health to save your face. I am glad to report that a complete rest in Shansi during the summer has put me in better condition for work than at any previous time for more than a year. I am still moving carefully, as is likely to be wise for some time to come, but the things that need to be done find me usually with sufficient strength for the need as it arises.

. . . In Shansi I found much building under way—and more needed. My own opinion would be that perhaps the most urgent need there now is for a medical plant at Fenchow, but one item that is even more urgent is the securing of the narrow piece of property that cuts our Mission compound almost in two. The building already in progress at both of the stations was giving promise of being most satisfactory, and was certainly being done very cheaply. The young missionaries are of the right spirit, and are undertaking a large work in a wise way. It was pleasing to find that even now they are able to depend in larger measure than I had supposed on the efficient co-operation of earnest and devout Chinese workers, both those in Mission employ and volunteers.

The marvelous record of the provincial authorities in ridding Shansi of the curse of opium, and doing it with incredible thoroness, was a feature of the situation that must arouse remark from every visitor who has any idea of the hold that opium had on the province heretofore. The provincial officials seem to have been men of strong character and with a determination to succeed, both in this and in other efforts for the prosperity of the province. They are evidently quite ready to avail themselves of the sympathy, and sometimes the active help, of the missionaries. This was to be noted in our own stations, and also at Taiyuan, the capital of the province, where it was largely by an appeal to one of the senior missionaries of the English Baptist Mission and to one of the professors in the University that the oppressive features claimed by the Peking Syndicate[1] in its contract with the government were cleared away so as to leave the Chinese free to work their own mines. This is particularly interesting, because one has felt that the settlement made by the missionaries with the officials after the Boxer atrocities must have been more or less under compulsion—at least that the Chinese must have felt that this was the case, no matter how wisely and sympathetically it may have been done. If that was so, the attitude of the people now shows no signs of consequent ill-feeling.

Another surprise in Shansi was the totally different type of character in the people there, as compared with the people of the Chihli province, where my life in China has been mostly spent. I had known that the language would be strange, and that much of the common talk of the people would be unintelligible, but their entire attitude in many ways is a great contrast to that in the more cosmopolitan coast province. It would be hard to describe accurately in just what this different consists. Its evidence is seen in many ways—one of the most noticeable being the manner in which the natural curiosity of the people concerning the foreigner manifests itself. In Chihli, staring or handling the clothing is done, but is evidently considered rude by the people themselves, while in Shansi the same things are done more freely and apparently with no sense that they are rude and certainly with no intention of rudeness. If one were to be transferred from one province to the other, one would need to take some time to study, not merely to familiarize oneself with the language, but to get to understand the people themselves. They are more like unsophisticated children, and some of the missionaries say that they are more timid and less aggressive.

The proposed affiliation of the two Missions, as suggested by the North China Mission, while it would not probably mean any considerable exchange of workers between the sections, and while it is intended to leave the distinctive methods of developing the work quite free as heretofore, promises to be of sufficient advantage to warrant the carrying out of the plan. If it were to disturb existing conditions too much, the Shansi Mission would be likely to object, and no part of the enlarged Mission would be in reality the gainer, but the idea is to leave freedom to the provincial sections—Chihli, Shantung, and Shansi,—so that those features of Chinese Church life and activity which would normally work themselves out along provincial lines can do so without interfering with the unity of the Mission as a whole. This applies in particular to the fact that the Church federations, so far as they are being organized, are along provincial lines, and also to the probability that not only our Shansi missionaries, but even those in Shantung, will increasingly feel that the higher education for their pupils should be carried on nearer to their own homes than would be necessitated by the long journey to Tungchow. This does not mean that the college at Tungchow is likely to cease to grow. Already it has begun to be evident that, under present conditions, it is likely to grow beyond the ability of the Mission to conduct it there, and the division will mean a larger cooperation with those in other Missions who are doing similar work, both in the province where our college is located and in the neighboring provinces.

. . . As to the political conditions, . . . I will do little more than send you a letter which I sent in copy to the several sections of the Ewing family in America. . . . The revolution has been rapid, but we can not tell what may be the outcome.[2]

[1]The Peking Syndicate, an Anglo-Italian consortium that was organized in 1898, was permitted to develop coal and iron mines, together with a railway built in 1902, in Shansi province.

[2]This is the only known instance in the correspondence between Charles and the American Board secretariat in Boston where he has sent a copy of his correspondence with the Ewing family.

Charles to Bessie, December 1911, Hsiku, Tientsin

My Dear Bessie:

We have many of our Mission families here from other stations. All my rooms are full. . . . Some of the ladies are living at the girls' school. But

things are so quiet with us . . . that country trips [have been made]. . . .
This is a great help to relieve the scare among the Chinese as rumors are
frequent and there has been looting elsewhere.

On December 14th we had quite an exciting time. The Red Cross Society had a practice day. A sham battle was organized, and the sham
wounded were brought to our church for treatment. First aid was given on
the battle field and then the wounded were brought in on stretchers—in
one case a man was taken in a riksha. The whole corps of nurses and pupils
from the government nurses' school were on hand. So far from being rattled
by the rapid inflow of cases, or even by the crowd of people watching their
work, they went ahead in the most regular way, with care and speed, dis-
patching a great amount of work in a brief time. The whole occasion was
altogether worth while. One of the University Chinese graduates who has
studied law at Harvard for five years was present, and he was astounded to
see the self-possession of young Chinese women conducting themselves
with entire propriety, but also with entire freedom in public. Evidently
he had not at all realized the development of the new woman in the last
five years.

Charles to Bessie, January 19, 1912, Hsiku, Tientsin

My Dear Bessie:

The political situation is so uncertain that the college at Tungchow has
been dismissed. It seems quite likely that the Manchu dynasty may abdicate at anytime. Yuan Shih-kai appears to have given up hope of any other
peaceful solution of the situation. While I am inclined to think that the
abdication would mean more settled conditions, we can not feel at all sure.
It is very likely, at any rate, that things will be worse before they are better,
and they may become very much worse.

Charles's Article "Weakness and Strength of Chinese Christians," in the Chinese
Recorder, January 1912

The missionary is an optimist. Like his Master, he sees the best that is
in man; seeks opportunity to improve that best so that it shall become still
better; notes clearly the potentialities of each and of all. . . .

There are many elements not yet sufficiently developed in Chinese
Christians, notable lacks in character, needs that they themselves recognize
and into which the missionary who loves them may enter with sympathy.

Chinese Christians need the ability to work together. So long as they are
under the hand of a strong leader—a missionary who by force of character
or by virtue of his official position in the church can and does serve as a
final court of appeal and is able to carry his point almost as a dictator—the

preachers and teachers, together with the rank and file of the church membership, fall in line and may be welded together as a harmonious working force. It has been felt by some that in China the episcopal form of church government is most in line with the genius of the people, but even so there is still needed harmony of spirit among the workers, an esprit de corps that shall lead each to subordinate his own will and way to the welfare of the church as a whole. With less strongly centralized forms of polity, the same need is felt yet more emphatically, and the more the management of church affairs is turned over to the Chinese,—as it must and should be,—the more is it found that perhaps the greatest need is for this spirit of harmony, this ability to work together. . . .

[I]t may be said that here, as in other points, the need of the church is the same as the need of the nation—strong and wise leadership. The Chinese may be willing to submit to the dictatorship of a strong man of another race, but they will not submit to weak leadership, whether from abroad or from among themselves.

[T]hose who love the Chinese and have the deepest faith in them must admit that they exhibit much less eagerness in passing on the Gospel message with power to their friends and fellows. Like many of our own Western Christians, they need to be made into ardent workers for Christ and the Church.

Chinese Christians as a whole lack spirituality. The excess of this element among some races is indeed largely a matter of race temperament, and as it prevails especially among some of the races of the Orient, the comparative absence of such spirituality among the Chinese is perhaps the more remarkable. It is easy to explain, of course, that the Chinese are practical rather than ideal by nature. In logic, they are pragmatists, in life inclined to be materialists. But wherever Christianity has gone, it has developed in every other race a strong appreciation of spiritual things, transforming what was formerly superstition, with a mythological tradition behind it, into faith founded on well attested history, and the missionary is right in desiring that the same process shall be manifest in China.

As Chinese Christians need the ability to work together harmoniously, so they are threatened—as in their national, so also in their religious lives— with the danger of individualism. . . . This individualism has heretofore been largely held in leash by the sense of family authority, but as that is beginning to grow less marked than formerly, the individualistic spirit is given greater liberty. The Church inculcates filial piety that is more real than the formal observances of the Confucian code, but the very fact that in most Protestant churches, each Christian is received on his own profession so emphasizes the importance of the individual that, in church affairs perhaps even more than elsewhere, there is real danger. Suspicion fosters cliques, leaders who are mutually jealous gathering around them separate parties which may shake the local, and sometimes even the wider, Church fellowship to its very depths. This is perhaps the first and foremost of all the perils that beset Chinese Christians. . . .

Paralleling the need for efficient leadership, there is the danger of dependence. . . . The danger is that they shall depend on the foreigner—for oversight, for assistance in personal affairs of all sorts, for advice that only a fellow Chinese is competent to give, sometimes even for spiritual and moral dictatorship. . . . As anxiously as a parent trains his child to become self-dependent so that he may be released from the constant watchfulness of infancy, so must the Chinese Christians be taught, from his first coming into Church fellowship, that he is not to depend on the foreign missionary.

[There] is the danger that the Church [will] be considered merely as one more of the many sects of China. . . . [The Christians] will think that their children are born Christians and need no peculiar nurture, that there is no responsibility of the Christian for the salvation of others' souls; thus will be cut the nerve not only of propagandism, but even of evangelism. This danger is insidious.

[T]here is the . . . danger, that the external forms of religion shall take the place of the spirit of faith, that form shall be accepted in place of substance, that the Church and its observances will lull the spirit that should be stirred by the presence of Christ within. It is an easy peril in any land, this satisfying oneself with the husk of religion; comforting the soul with the assurance that careful observance of ecclesiastical requirements is good insurance for happiness here and hereafter; how much more among a people whose entire conception of religion has been in these observances, with scarcely a thought—except on the part of the few who have not been influential with the many—for the deeper things of the spirit. . . .

If Chinese Christians are lacking in depth of earnestness, and thus are in danger of satisfying themselves with their own salvation, without reaching out in evangelistic efforts for their fellow men, there is at least great hope in their peculiar fitness for presenting the Gospel. . . . among the Chinese, . . . there is to be found the natural capacity for transmitting to others what has been received. One sign of this, evident in most Oriental countries, is the presence of the story-teller wherever people congregate. Another is the honor in which the teacher is held, even though he be not a trained trainer of youth. The great sages of China have been teachers, who by word of mouth have passed on the torch to their successors. In the body of Christians, it is early evident that they possess preaching ability, and also teaching ability. Even the illiterate are often effective public speakers, listeners hanging on their words, they themselves enjoying the thrill of holding and touching an audience. . . .

Charles to Bessie, February 15, 1912, Hsiku, Tientsin

My Dear Bessie:

Just think: China is no longer a Monarchy. You know it already, but I heard it first thru telephone messages from Mrs. [Celia] Peck and Mr. [Howard] Evans at the Settlement on Monday evening, and I suspect that you read it in Monday morning's paper. Some think there will be anarchy until another monarchy is established, but I am too great a believer in the *People,* even tho they are Chinese, who have had no experience of democratic institutions, to admit the probability of that. The people in general will accept the status quo, whatever it is, and as it is to be a republic, they will accept that.

Yesterday was the first day that the new Chinese flag has been freely displayed along the streets. When I went into the city I was totally unprepared for what met my eyes. First I saw one, then another, then several close together, then crossed flags over shop doors, and so unexpected and overwhelming was the effect that, the dust storm being still on, I was afraid that my face would be like a mud puddle before I reached the Settlement. Talk about tears of joy, why I had no idea how happy I should be on account of the final decision in favor of a Government of the people. But when I saw that flag, when I thought how the people had never had a flag that they felt at liberty to fly, nor one that they could think of as their own, and of which they could be proud, and when I saw how gladly they seized this new privilege, it gave me new confidence that the republic will prove successful, even tho not easy of introduction.

It is a good flag of which to be proud, and for two reasons. First, it is beautiful and again it has so good a meaning. Like the American and British flags it means union.[1] There are five stripes, standing for the five races [*sic*].[2] The colors as they appear to the eye, are the standard shades, red for the Chinese, yellow for the Manchus, blue for the Mongolians, white for the Mohammedans (for they are a separate race as well as a religious sect), and black for Tibetans.

I suppose that everyone in America appreciates the marvelous success of Yuan Shih-Kai. He has won out with so little fighting and such wonderful diplomacy that it must have taken the whole world by surprise. The Chinese way of doing things, their way of conducting such political changes as this, reminds me of a game of chess. An experienced player, when pitted against another of equal experience, will often surrender a game when the onlooker sees no reason for such action, but both of the players know that, after a given number of moves, a checkmate will be declared, and the time and energy to be spent might as well be saved. Incidentally, in the present instance, many lives and much property have doubtless been saved also, and the Manchus can retire feeling that they have succeeded in saving their faces, not to mention their heads. Yuan may be unpopular with both North and South, but no one now, Chinese or foreign can fail to acknowledge his supremacy in statecraft and that he is the man needed for the crisis. He is not a Christian but the Lord has girded him even if he himself does not know it.

[1]Charles here displays a particular American trait for relating the display of the flag to nationalism.
[2]*Ethnic or religious groups* might have been more accurate, but in 1912 the term *races* was commonly used.

Charles to Bessie, March 1912, Hsiku, Tientsin

My Dear Bessie:

During the Chinese New Year's festivities there were enthusiastic cele-brations, but the holiday season was not past when the soldiers broke from restraint and began looting and burning in Peking and later in other places. I asked to have cables sent to relieve your mind.

American Board of Commissioners for Foreign Missions to Bessie, March 9, 1912, Boston

The American Board . . . received on . . . March 4 and 5, the following cable dispatches from China:

March 3. From Tientsin, "The disturbances are at an end. Missionaries are well and safe."

March 4. From Peking, "All Peking Missionaries and Mission Buildings safe."

March 5. From Tungchow, "There have been serious disturbances in Peking, Paoting and Tientsin. Telegraph line broken or interrupted. Cannot commu-nicate with Shansi. It is reported here and generally believed all Mission buildings and Missionaries safe."

March 5. From Peking, "Everything is now quiet in Peking. The Mission is under protection of American soldiers. Paoting and Tientsin are safe."

These despatches have been given to the press but we fear they have not been widely printed. They are sent to you for your information.

Charles to Bessie, March 1912, Hsiku, Tientsin

My Dearest Bessie:

The city of Tientsin had its holocaust on a Saturday night when I was away from home, at our nearest outstation five miles distant. From there we could see the fires and hear the rifle firing. Most of the shops from our place [at Hsiku] to the city were looted and many burned. The soldiers did the first looting, then the police, and last the people. Then the next day when orders went out for looters to be beheaded, the police turned around and arrested and executed the poor people found with loot. The places that suffered most were pawn shops and large and wealthy institutions where much valuable clothing is stored. One of these was very near us. Foreign property has not been touched. About a third of the stores were burned, the pawn shop nearest us burned from Saturday night thru Monday. This is the sort of thing that has always been a part of war in the past. This time there had been introduced into Tientsin a thousand extra police and it was these less disciplined ones that joined the soldiers in the looting. The very few large stores that escaped were those that probably handed out enough money to satisfy the soldiers.

I returned Sunday afternoon and found a squad of mounted American soldiers on hand to escort our ladies to the Settlement. They remained there for the nights for three weeks. Many of our Chinese neighbors sent their women and children to the girls' school, tho we could guarantee no protection.

Mr. Evans brought some rifles from the British Municipal Council [in the British Concession] and he and Mr. Morrill have stayed with us nights. There has been no further disturbance, largely due to the vigilance of the police in our immediate center, who tho numbering only thirteen, are an orderly lot. During the looting there were very few deaths as the rifle shots were directed into the air. The one death of a foreigner was a doctor who was with a rescuing party and was shot thru a gate without being seen. With visitors who are here we have four men and these with Chinese students keep a careful watch, patrolling all the time, four at each watch. The Chinese authorities have requested the foreign military to patrol the native city. You may be sure that I am glad that you and the children are not here.

Charles to Edward C. Ewing, April 1912, Hsiku, Tientsin

Dear Father:

Immediately after the outbreak of March 2 and 3, we made application for a guard of American soldiers, applying thru the Tientsin Consul to our Minister at Peking, who is the authority over the military commander of the American troops.[1] On Easter Sunday a guard of 25 men arrived, under command of a second lieutenant. They are quartered in my house most of which I have given up to their use. I keep my study and I sleep in the attic. The head men of Hsiku call for the purpose of expressing their appreciation for the soldiers. On the whole the American soldiers have a reputation for lax discipline and easy drinking habits, and we can not be entirely proud of them, but we find this set quiet and orderly. Their presence makes me feel much more free to leave home to visit the country churches. Our U.S. flag is a fine sight.

[1]Under the peace treaty following the Boxer Uprising, foreign military units could be stationed in Tientsin. The United States usually kept an army regiment, such as the Fifteenth Infantry, at Tientsin until 1938.

Charles to J. L. Barton, April 19, 1912, Hsiku, Tientsin

Dear Dr. Barton:

Of the political situation, you might like to hear at length, but definite prediction is so unwarranted and the general situation must be so well known to you already that I shall venture very little. The Republic is a fact, and while many of us were quite uncertain beforehand whether this was desirable, we have rejoiced in the new arousing of national sentiment that has come, and are hoping that the new form of government may prove to be stable—the more especially as there is no manifest way in which any monarchy could be established with the approval and support of the entire nation.

You already know that, almost immediately following on the rejoicing over the new regime, there came outbreaks in these northern cities, which included looting and burning and led to many executions by the old method of decapitation. One of the places of execution was across the river from our compound, and in plain sight from our windows, and heads were hung in various places along the streets for some days after they had been cut off. Tientsin is recovering slowly. In some places, rebuilding is going on vigorously, but in other places the owners are waiting to see what is to be the future before they make any definite plans. For the present, the foreign troops in Tientsin assure peace, but there is a general feeling that, if these troops were to be withdrawn from patrolling the Chinese city, there would be further lawlessness. The foreign officers themselves are evidently expecting to remain here for a considerable time, that is to be reckoned in years rather than months.[1]

When conditions were the most disturbed, our station made a request for a guard of American soldiers, following the plan of the several Mission stations in Peking. We received no reply to our request for so long that we thought very likely it was going by default, but then, when conditions were so much quieter that we began to question whether we cared for the guard, the officers came and saw the place, and sent the guard. We are glad that they are here. Their presence gives a renewed sense of security, not only to our own station [at Hsiku]—foreigners and Chinese alike,—but to our immediate neighbors and to the entire population on the northern side of the city, and also helps at the University, a mile beyond us, so that the American ladies of the University families are returning. The ladies of our station returned, with the permission of the Consul, even before the guard arrived, having only waited until the telephone (which had been out of commission for more than three weeks, on account of the injury to the lines by fire) was in working order. . . . The return of Miss [Grace] Wyckoff meant the reopening of the girls' boarding school, which had been dismissed last November on the occasion of the first scare.

. . . With the reopening of the [boys'] school [on March 4], there was a change in the assistant teacher. The young man who had been teaching for a year and a half went to Tungchow to be married, and hoped to enter the Theological College at Peking. His plans were changed, however, and he is now teaching in connection with our Tungchow station. The new teacher in our own school has just graduated from North China Union College at Tungchow, where he sang on the Glee Club, was a member of the football team, and excelled in pole vaulting and high jumping. He teaches half of each day in our school, and also is my writer. He has volunteered to teach singing to the school-boys in the evenings, having noted that our boys who go to Tungchow are lacking on the musical side of their preparation.

Six of our Tientsin boys graduated from college at the end of the last term. We were able to retain the services of only this one. Another has gone, on my recommendation, to teach in a Chinese school in Java. Three are teaching Chinese to foreigners in Tientsin and taking time to go on with their study of English. One has entered Tientsin University. In this connection, I should mention that our one graduate of last year has now (on my recommendation) taken a position as teacher in the Anglo-Chinese College, which is connected with the London Mission in the French Concession. There is sure to be, in the new conditions, when the Chinese schools reopen, a call for teachers who are graduates of our Christian schools and colleges. After that, we shall be so far from needing to find work for the graduates that we may have difficulty in keeping as many as we shall require for our own work. . . .

[Recently] in the city of Ching Hai, we distributed unground corn to nearly two hundred families, some of whom were in extreme destitution, and if there had been more time at our disposal, there were 71 other families which we should have been glad to examine. In two adjoining villages, we distributed small sums of money to needy families. . . . Money was given to more than forty families. The worst distress is now relieved, and I told the people that when I go again it will be for missionary work instead of relief. The failure of last year's crops has pushed the people who are always poor over the line of destitution, and even some of those who manage fairly well in ordinary years have been in trouble this time. However, while the spirit of helpfulness prompts to beneficence in such cases, I think that it is very bad indeed for the people to come to have the idea that they can appeal to the foreigner when they get into trouble. (It may be that I carry too far my principle of refusing help—sometimes I must appear to be refusing even sympathy,—but how can we ever expect to develop a strong race, or a strong Church, so long as we do for them even what they cannot do for themselves? And should we not thus train them to expect self-reliance of themselves? That this works well when we have a body of educated men, I think that the experience here in our Tientsin Church is proving, but it cannot work so well where there is not this preparation by previous training.)

You know that ex-President Eliot is traveling on the Carnegie Peace Foundation?[2] You will be interested to know that he has just been in Tientsin. He was in my congregation when I preached at the Anglo-Chinese Church last Sunday (one of the general exchange Sundays). On Monday afternoon, he spoke to the students at the University, very interestingly, and after the address, I had the pleasure of going with him to see the Chinese Church in the city, in which he seemed to have considerable interest. Wednesday evening he addressed a large meeting of Chinese and foreigners, in the Viceroy Yuan Hall at the Anglo-Chinese College, the meeting having been arranged by the Missionary Association Committee, and there he presented the plans and ideas of the Carnegie Foundation and answered questions that brought out many interesting points. Yesterday I persuaded him to go with me to see some of the government educational plants (the schools themselves are not, most of them, yet in session since the stoppage in the winter). On Saturday evening, he is to address a meeting of the American College Association at Peking.

[1]The foreign military officers were indeed correct. The last American military unit, a detachment of marines, finally departed Tientsin in November 1941. Only in the autumn of 1945, with the departure of Japanese and French units, did the last foreign troops operating under the Boxer peace treaty leave Tientsin.

[2]Charles William Eliot taught at both Harvard University and the Massachusetts Institute of Technology before becoming president of Harvard in 1869. His forty-year presidency changed Harvard, turning it from a small college into a major university. During 1911 and 1912 he traveled extensively as an emissary for the Carnegie Endowment for International Peace.

Charles to Bessie, May 1912, Hsiku, Tientsin

Dearest Bessie:

[One of] my special activities this month has been the distribution of relief funds in our country area [of Chihli province]. . . . Considerable relief has been needed because of loss of crops due to the extra heavy rains. We had some relief funds left over from last year and I met officials and

Church leaders to decide their use. This kind of work is very discouraging to me. In the first place it is very difficult to be able to decide who are the most needy ones, and in the second place it is bad for the morale of the people in the way of cultivating a spirit of dependence. The relief that was distributed three years ago has still left an attitude of always hoping for what they could get. It leaves the distributor "on the spot" . . . being either too severe or too indulgent. I shall be thankful when all such matters can be handled by the Chinese themselves. . . .

At the close of college the students organized a scheme which provides for someone to go during the summer to give addresses in a large number of places, explaining the new [political] situation and the meaning of republicanism. Their intention is evidently to reach the people all over the province. I am told that President Yuan and Premier Tang [Shao-i] have been consulted and that they heartily approve—which probably means that they will also provide some of the funds needed to carry out the program. I think that this is a real service to the Nation and to the Church, showing the appreciation of the students for the privilege that has been theirs in getting the information and the inspiration which they thus hope to pass on to others.

[A]t a meeting of Chinese . . . the pastor of the Chinese independent church made suggestions along the same line [of denominational cooperation]. He and I had talked over such steps but I had no idea that he was going to propose them now. The result is that all nine Chinese pastors of the several chapels and five missionaries representing the denominations have met and made some plans. These include a quarterly conference for planning, with no new places opened except in consultation, frequent union meetings, and a quarterly exchange of preachers. I have been appointed general chairman. Probably because of natural tendencies in my own character, this matter of organization and administration has been the most important part of my missionary work. With our Chinese leaders so ready to assume responsibility in Tientsin it is very likely that I will not be needed here after my furlough, and will be assigned to some other station where conditions call for closer organization. All this may seem slow progress but when you remember that all Mission work for over this first hundred years has been almost entirely managed and financially supported by the foreign missionary, you can see how I rejoice in Chinese initiative just as a parent likes to see his child grow up.

Charles's Article "The Chinese Christian Church in Tientsin," in the Chinese Recorder, May 1912.

. . . Another element that entered into the situation [in Tientsin] was the efficient work of the Y.M.C.A. This organization had undertaken to get into touch with a class of men who could seldom be reached by the more direct evangelism of the other Missions. The result was that a considerable number of men from scholarly and official circles had become interested, first in Bible study and then in personal Christianity, and that as time went on some of these became genuine Christians and were ready for Church membership. They were recommended by the Y.M.C.A. secretaries, who knew them, to the missionaries in charge of church work, and thus were received into Church membership, not in any one Church, but in the various Mission churches of the city. But as they had become Christians through no denominational agency, so they proved to have no denominational loyalty, nor indeed much apparent loyalty to the particular churches of which they were members. . . . It was evident that men of this type were ready for an undenominational church, without special affiliation with any particular Mission.

Charles to Ellen Ewing, June 1912, Hsiku, Tientsin

My Dear Mother:

The American guard, which came on April 7, was reduced on May 12 to a corporal's guard of eight men, with a hospital sergeant. On June 14 these men were withdrawn. I had been boarding with them for four weeks. It cost me a little less than boarding with the Chandlers and got me in closer touch with the soldiers. The meal hours were rather peculiar—7:00, 11:45, 4:45, but that suited me as I did not have to hurry back from the city or the Settlement for an evening dinner and also I could go to the University for tennis after supper. All my life I have lived in select company, and this company, while also select, is selected on an entirely different basis and enlarged my acquaintance and sympathy.

Charles to J. L. Barton, August 27, 1912, Hsiku, Tientsin

Dear Dr. Barton:

For [Chinese] Church life specifically, I believe that the missionaries should (so far as possible) keep their hands off, and that now, with our educated and capable Chinese graduates coming forward as leaders, all such responsibility may be turned over to them. It is not right, however, to lay down any too strict a rule; conditions are so different in different places, and the supply of these trained and efficient men so unequal, that I do not permit myself to say that in other places even so much would be possible as has been achieved at our own (Tientsin) station, and I am sure that, if I were to be located at any other station, I should need first to study the local situation before venturing to urge exactly the same forward steps.

I fear that I must have given you an incorrect impression as to President Eliot's visit, if I wrote anything to justify your conclusion that he had been seeing something of missionary work. The educational institutions which I had the privilege of showing to him were not connected with any Mission, but were government schools and colleges. He did indeed show marked interest in the Anglo-Chinese College, which is connected with the London Mission, and spoke there, but that was not at all my doing. He was also present and spoke at a public anniversary meeting of the Y.M.C.A., but this was not because it was a Christian organization. The fact is that while in Tientsin, he seemed to resist going to missionary supported institutions.

Charles to Edward and Ellen Ewing, October 6, 1912, Hsiku, Tientsin

Dear Father and Mother:

You raise the question, Father, whether the conditions of graft and crime now being uncovered in New York can be equaled or surpassed in China. I often think of your teaching years ago that only a well-developed and well-trained community or person can excel in either the best or the worst things, and that one may not be surprised to find that the worst crimes and criminals are those in Christian lands. However, except for the systematic and secret organization of crime in New York, I should say that probably the only reason why the Chinese have not a lower record is because there are not, here, the same opportunities. One reason why there are not these same opportunities here is that such things have never had to keep themselves secret here, being expected and not meeting with serious criticism. Of course we are hoping that the new regime in China will mean reformation in this, as in many other ways. It will be a mighty struggle to reanimate all public affairs with a new spirit of loyalty to humanity, when such a spirit has been practically out of court for a long time. . . . Both here and there [America] I believe heartily that the people will speak, and when they do it will be for the things that are best. That hope is almost idealism, I admit, but then I am an idealist and not ashamed to admit it, and indeed it is idealism that has always led the people on and up.

Charles to Bessie, December 1912, Hsiku, Tientsin

My Dearest Bessie:

The Ad Interim Committee of the [North China] Mission has met and this is their decision. (1) I am to take my furlough in 1913–1914. (2) After my return [to China], I am to teach for a year in the Union Theological College, as a substitute for Mr. [George D.] Wilder while he is on furlough. This means that (a) I will take special preparatory studies at Yale; (b) that I shall have the coveted privilege of inspiring the men who are to inspire the Church which is to regenerate at least part of this great nation; (c) that I may at last take up teaching at the only point where I feel that I can do it, namely with the men who are already trained sufficiently to study with me, rather than be instructed by me; (d) that I may hope to gain from this teaching the training that I need for the systematic instruction of the Christian constituency when I go back into regular work.

Charles to Bessie, January 1913, Hsiku, Tientsin

My Dear Bessie:

In looking up timetables for my homeward trip I have succeeded in discovering a route of which I had formerly not even had a suspicion, a route that is likely to prove the best combination of economy in time and money. I am planning to go by way of Russia and this is the approximate program: Tientsin to Mukden, Harbin, Irkutsk—May 23 to May 29. On to Moscow for a short time on June 4. In Berlin on June 6. Reach London Saturday evening or Sunday, June 7 or 8. To Liverpool on June 9, sailing on the Laconia. Arrive in Boston on the afternoon of June 17 or morning of June 18. Reach New Haven June 18.

Charles to J. L. Barton, February 6, 1913, Hsiku, Tientsin

Dear Dr. Barton:

You will probably have learned that famine has been threatening in a large section of the field of the Peking, Tungchow, Paoting, and Tientsin stations, as a result of the heavy rains and floods of last summer. I am not one of those who feel that famine relief is an important part of the work of the missionary—tho I am quite ready to admit that I may be wrong. But I have occasionally done a little to assist those who are undertaking this relief. Most of what I have done this winter has been to pass on information and appeals to those who are in charge of the relief. During this week, I have distributed corn in one village where the distress appeared to be excessive and where we have some Christians. The entire surrounding region is covered with water—or rather, with ice, so that I made almost all of my return trip of fifteen miles or more on a sled poled by a man.

. . . In spite of the fact that your political attention, since it has been allowed to wander from America, has been especially directed to Turkey and the neighboring states, you doubtless want political forecasts from your China correspondents. I am quite prepared to acknowledge that we all ought to be able to give what you want, but for myself I am obliged to confess that I have no wisdom on the subject. I do not keep myself sufficiently well informed to permit me to inform others, but it appears to me that at the present time there would be great difficulty in speaking with assurance at any rate. Being an optimist, believing in China and the Chinese, and being encouraged by the progress of the past year, I am still thoroly hopeful that quiet will increase as time goes on, that the republican government will approve itself at home and abroad, and that China will soon win and receive recognition from the other nations of the world— America first.

Charles to Bessie, April 1913, Hsiku, Tientsin

Dearest Bessie:

The Chinese Government has done something remarkable and unprece- dented in the history of the world. A non-Christian nation has asked the prayers of all Christians, and has the last Sunday in this month (April) as a special day for such prayer. Our Union Committee plans a general meeting in the afternoon in some large hall, perhaps at the Li Hung Chang Memo- rial Temple, to be attended by all who shall have received tickets, and also by officials, who (so I am told) have been directed by the government to attend such meetings and themselves to pray.

The board of Managers of the Tientsin Chinese Christian Church gather for a farewell to Charles Ewing on May 11, 1913. Charles is in the back row, and Chang Po Ling is the second to his right.

Members of the Tientsin Christian Church bid farewell to Charles Ewing in May 1913. The central banner, in orchid satin, reads "Sowing the Seed without Weariness." The small black banner proclaims "The WAY has Come to the East." Charles is in the center near the back.

Epilogue

CHARLES Ewing returned to Bessie and their children in New Haven, Connecticut on June 18, 1913. For the next two years, Charles, representing the American Board of Commissioners for Foreign Missions, made numerous speeches throughout the United States. Although Bessie made many appearances at local churches and other organizations, her main concerns were with their home in New Haven and the education of the four Ewing children. In 1915 Charles accepted the invitation to be pastor of the First Congregational Church in Janesville, Wisconsin. He remained there until 1918 when he left for France, where as a Y.M.C.A. chaplain he counseled the Chinese laborers who were digging trenches and working on public works projects during and after World War I.

Charles returned once more to China as a missionary in 1920. Following the completion of their children's educations in Wisconsin, Bessie joined Charles in China. They remained there until 1927. Shortly after their return to America, Bessie and Charles were involved in a tragic automobile accident in New Haven. Bessie survived unhurt, while Charles, aged fifty-eight, died of his injuries. After Charles's death Bessie moved to Cleveland to be close to her children. There she was active in her local church, supporting missionary work as well. Although a longtime member of the East Cleveland Congregational Church, she never lost her deep interest in China and the Chinese. Bessie Smith Ewing died in 1966 just a few days short of her ninety-sixth birthday.

Conversion

Wade-Giles to Pinyin

In both the chapter introductions and the Ewing papers a modified Wade-Giles system of Chinese words is used, from which, for the sake of simplicity, all diacritical marks have been omitted. Since the Pinyin system was adopted in 1958 by the People's Republic of China and is now in common use, the following list of Chinese names and places used in the text is shown here for both Wade-Giles and the Pinyin systems.

Wade-Giles (Modified)	*Pinyin*
Amur River	Heilongjiang
Anhwei	Anhui
Canton	Canton
Chang Chih-tung	Zhang Zhidong
Chefoo	Zhifu
Chihli (province)	Zhili
Ching (dynasty)	Qing
Chinwangtao	Qin Huangdao
Chun (prince)	Chun
Dairen	Dalian
Fenchow	Fenzhou
Foochow	Fuzhou
Fukien (province)	Fujian
Hankow	Hankou
Harbin	Ha-er-bin
Honan (province)	Henan
Hsiku	Xi Gu
Hwang Ho River	Huanghe
I Ho Chuan	Yihequan
I Ho Tuan	Yihetuan
Jung Lu	Rung Lu
Kaifeng	Kaifeng
Kaiping	Kaiping
Kalgan	Zhang Jiakou
Kang Yu-wei	Kang Youwei

Wade-Giles (Modified)	Pinyin
Kansu (province)	Gansu
Kiangsi (province)	Jiangxi
Kiangsu (province)	Jiangau
Kiaochow (bay)	Jiaozhou
Kuang Hsu (emperor)	Guangxu
Kuomintang (party)	Guomindang
Kwangchowan	Quangzhouwan
Kwangtung	Quangdong
Liang Chi-chao	Liang Qichao
Liaotung (peninsula)	Liaodong
Li Hung-chang	Li Hongzhang
Li Ping-heng	Li Bing-heng
Li Yuan-kung	Li Yuanhong
Lin Ching	Linqing
Machiapu	Makiapu
Manchuria	Manchuria
Ming (dynasty)	Ming
Mukden	Mukden
Nanchang	Nanchang
Nanking	Nanking
Newchang	Niuzhuang
Pang Chuan	Pangzhuang
Paoting	Baoding
Pechihli (Gulf)	Beizhili
Pei Ho River	Beihe
Peitaiho	Bei Daihe
Peitang (cathedral)	Beitang
Peiyang Army	Beiyang
Peking	Beijing
Port Arthur	Lushan
Pu Chun	Pu Chun
Pu Yi	Pui
Shanghai	Shanghai
Shanhaikwan	Shanhaiquan
Shansi (province)	Shanxi
Shantung (province)	Shandong
Shensi (province)	Shaanxi
Sian	Xian
Sung Chao-jen	Song Jaioren
Sun Yat-sen	Sun Yat-sen
Szechwan (province)	Sichuan
Taku Bar	Dagu
Tientsin	Tianjin
Tsinan	Jinan

Wade-Giles (Modified)	Pinyin
Tsingtao	Qingdao
Tsungli Yamen	Zongli Yamen
Tuan (prince)	Duan
Tung Chih (emperor)	Tongzhi
Tungchow	Tongzhou
Tung Fu-hsiang	Dong Fuxiang
Tung Meng Hui	Tongmeng Hui
Tzu Hsi (empress dowager) (Yehenola in Manchu)	Ci Xi
Wang Ching-wei	Wang Jingwei
Wuchang	Wuchang
Wuhan	Wuhan
Yangtze River	Yangzejiang
Yuan Shih-kai	Yuan Shikai
Yu Hsien	Yu Xian
Yu Lu	Yu Lu

Index

Africa, 43 n.3
Alliance Society (Tung Meng Hui), 134
Alvord, Christopher Columbus, 21
Ament, Dr. William S., Sr., 18, 19 n.3, 25, 26, 27, 115, 152, 162, 208; as minister, 27, 58; at Shun I Hsien, 123–24; division of labor, 59, 66; in Peking, 121–22, 126; siege of Peking Legation Quarter, 73–74, 78, 102, 103; tool of imperialism, 54 n.1, 112
Ament, Mrs. William S., Sr., 121, 147, 152, 228
Ament, William S., Jr., 208
American Bible Society, 30, 39
American Board of Commissioners for Foreign Missions, 15, 115, 117, 222, 224; deputation to China, 31, 181; financial problems, 12, 116, 140, 155; interest in China, 7, 17, 22 n.2, 24 n.1, 73 n.6; Japan mission, 106; Prudential Committee, 112, 113 n.1, 132 n.2, 149; Secretary Judson Smith, 1, 168 n.1, 171; speaking engagements, 114, 118, 259
American Board Mission Church (Tientsin), 145, 151; Chinese Church, 210, 224, 225, 230, 250. *See also* North China Mission of the American Board
American Board Mission Compound (Peking), 18, 20, 39, 74 n.8, 79, 119, 122, 225; Teng Shih Kourh, 21 n.1
American Board Mission Compound (Tientsin), 14 n.1, 105 n.60, 166 n.1, 169
American Board Press, 27
American Civil War, 1, 15, 143

American College Association (Peking), 250
American Congressional delegation, 155, 156 n.1
American Consulate (Tientsin), 15, 146, 151, 152, 239, 247, 248; Thanksgiving service, 126, 161, 175
American Legation (Peking), 15, 35, 147 n.3; Chinese Christians, 9, 92; Legation guards, 82, 238, 247; Legation Quarter, 47, 75, 122; Peitaiho Beach, 224; sanctuary, 73, 83, 103
American Presbyterian (North) Society, 7
American soldiers: army, 103, 247, 248 n.1
—marines, 64, 81, 83, 104; defense of Legation Quarter, 82, 90, 98, 111; in Tientsin, 48, 62, 250 n.1; Legation and mission guards, 43, 46, 59, 74, 79, 252; transfer from Peking, 61, 63
Amherst College, 3, 211, 215
Anglo-Chinese Church (Tientsin), 250
Anglo-Chinese College (Tientsin), 149 n.1, 244, 253
Anwhei province, 185
Anti-American boycott, 133, 151, 155, 159, 168, 169
Anti-Chinese attitude in America, 186
Anti-Japanese boycott, 213
Army of the People. *See* People's Republic of China
Articles of Favorable Treatment. *See* Manchu dynasty
Austria (and Austrians) in China, 45 n.4; concession in Tientsin, 189 n.1; guards, 43 n.3; marines, 74 n.9; Peking Legation Quarter, 75

Union Committee of China, 149
Union Medical College (Peking), 154, 164, 210
Union Theological Seminary (Peking), 154, 210, 249, 253
Unionville, Connecticut, 116, 117, 118, 119
United States of America (and Americans) in China, 41, 45 n.4, 167 n.1, 173, 181, 202, 245, 248 n.1; and Chinese students, 159, 193, 227; and the Open Door Policy, 41, 137; anti-American sentiment, 133, 136, 155, 159; as an international power, 14, 15, 203, 205; Boxer Indemnity, 138; Ewing return, 215, 221, 223, 259; immigration laws, 133–34; treaties with China, 16 n.3, 31 n.1. *See also* American soldiers; Protestants

Vancouver, British Columbia, Canada, 119, 120
Verde, Dr. Carl, 71 n.1
Viceroy Yuan Hall. *See* Anglo-Chinese College
Viceroy's Yamen (Tientsin), 186
Victoria, Queen, 10, 92
von Ketteler, Baron Klemens (German minister), 47, 48, 55, 82
von Rosthorn, Baron Arthure (Austrian diplomat), 38, 40 n.4
von Waldersee, Count Alfred (German army commander), 54

Wade-Giles System, ix, 261
Walker, W. F., and family, 104
"Wang-three-filial sons Village," 215, 216
Warlord period in China, 206 n.4
Washington, D.C., 64, 193
Water-gate (Peking), 122
Weihaiwei, 5, 10
Wen An Hsien (village in Chihli province), 24 n.1, 28, 69 n.1
Wesley Methodist Episcopal Church. *See* Methodist Mission (Tientsin)

Western Hills (Hsi Shan), 20 n.1, 31 n.1, 32, 66, 67, 68
White, Thaddeus (husband of Princess Der Ling), 148 n.2
White, Dr. Wilbert Webster, 226 n.1
Wilder, George D., 31, 112, 253
Wilhelm II (German emperor), 30
Wilson, President Woodrow, 205
Woman's Boards of Boston and Chicago, 179
Women's College Peking. *See* North China Union Women's College (Peking)
Wuhan (the cities of Hankow, Hanyang, and Wuchang), 199. *See also* Hupeh
Wyckoff, Grace, 102, 249

Yale University, 1, 3, 148, 159, 253
Yale Volunteer Band, 2
Yamaguchi, General Motoomi (Japanese), 52, 53
Yang Ti, Emperor, 126 n.1
Yangsun (village in Chihli province), 45, 50, 52, 148
Yangtze River, 126 n.1, 135, 182, 186 n.1, 199–202, 214, 235
Yellow River (Huang Ho), 126 n.1
Yenching University, 24 n.1
Yokohama, Japan, 17, 107, 231
Young, Dr., 230
Young Men's Christian Association (Y.M.C.A.), 2, 22, 24 n.6, 172, 193 n.1, 215, 223, 252, 253, 259; Bible Institute, 176, 188; success in Chinese mission work, 157, 166, 175, 251
Yuan dynasty, 127 n.2
Yuan Shih-kai, Viceroy, 56, 134, 159, 201, 202, 205, 206 n.4; conflict with National Assembly (1912), 204, 242; departs Tientsin for Peking, 187, 192; governor of Shantung (1900), 51, 69 n.1; president of republic, 203, 245, 251; retirement to province (1909), 197, 214, 217; viceroy in Tientsin, 137, 155, 169, 184, 191
Yu Hsien, Governor, 51, 55
Yu Iu, Governor, 45, 46, 50, 55